S0-ARY-905

CAROLYN COGGINS'
COMPANY COOKBOOK

BOOKS BY CAROLYN COGGINS

SUCCESSFUL ENTERTAINING AT HOME

Juveniles

LANCE AND HIS FIRST HORSE
LANCE AND COWBOY BILLY

CAROLYN COGGINS' COMPANY COOKBOOK

Hanover House, Garden City, New York

Library of Congress Catalog Card Number 54–11105

Printed in the United States of America
Designed by Alma Reese Cardi
First Edition

ACKNOWLEDGMENTS

Everyone has a lot of friends, but when the time comes to say "Thank You," I appear to have more than anybody. The only thing to do, without filling another book, is to say I appreciate the blessing each one of you provides. This includes all of you outside my own land whose hospitality I have enjoyed, as well as the friends in it, which covers half the world and literally a gold mine of wonderful people.

The engineers who designed the kitchen equipment which is part of my daily life are the unknown friends I must thank most of all. What a marvel is our modern American kitchen. Mine is rather old-fashioned, but the work savers in it are as brand new as space suits and many times more useful. Having them would make any woman alive glad to stay in her kitchen.

CAROLYN COGGINS

CONTENTS

THE QUANTITY YOU BUY . . . . . MEANS THIS:

Butter

1 pound	16 ounces	2 cups	4 sticks
½ pound	8 ounces	1 cup	2 sticks
¼ pound	4 ounces	½ cup	1 stick

Sugar or Flour

1 pound granulated sugar	2 cups
1 pound powdered sugar	2⅔ cups
1 pound brown sugar	2⅔ cups
1 pound flour	4 cups

THESE ARE THE TEMPERATURES YOU USE IN COOKING

Oven

Slow	300–325 F.
Moderate	350–375 F.
Hot	400–450 F.
Very Hot	475–550 F.

THESE ARE THE MEASUREMENTS—ALWAYS LEVEL

1 cup	16 tablespoons
4 tablespoons	¼ measuring cup
2 cups	1 pint
1 quart	2 pints
4 quarts	1 gallon (16 cups)
1 tablespoon	3 teaspoons
2 tablespoons	1 ounce butter, sugar ½ ounce flour
1 teaspoon	60 drops

part one

COFFEE TIME

CHAPTER 1
GRACE BEFORE MEALS

CATHOLIC *Bless us, O Lord, and these Thy gifts, which we are about to receive from Thy bounty. Through Christ our Lord. Amen.*

JEWISH *Lift up your hands toward the Sanctuary and bless the Lord. Blessed art Thou, O Lord our God, King of the universe, who bringest forth bread from the earth. Amen.*

PROTESTANT *Bless, O Lord, this food to our use, and us to Thy service, and make us ever mindful of the needs of others, in Jesus' Name. Amen.*

"The smell of baking bread," Sally sang out as she entered the kitchen, "is the mark of a happy home. It probably makes one," she continued, with her eye on the crusty loaves fresh from the oven.

When I was little my father's head bent over his plate before each meal and his Grace always included "Thanks for our daily bread." Since we had home-baked bread every day of our lives, both he and God knew what he was talking about, for believe me, it was bread to be thankful for.

The aroma of freshly baked bread is not so familiar now, and it had made my friend Sally, who had come to have dinner with us, ecstatic as she entered the front door. It would be difficult, I suppose, to make a person who entered a home fragrant with baking feel anything but welcome and content. It is the perfume that cannot be bought; but bread can be baked occasionally with more ease than you have been led to believe if you never baked any.

This was my day in the kitchen. Makings for a steak and kidney pie were in the pressure cooker, a chicken was gently simmering in a pot of its broth, several batches of cookie dough were ready to store in the refrigerator, mayonnaise was whirring into creamy thickness in the electric blender. Two loaves of French bread were on the cooling racks, and I was about to deep-fry Swiss cheese fritters for dinner. Two cakes had been baked, and I intended splitting and frosting them in a minute, to cool and freeze. One was a chiffon cake, which freezes so well. It would be frosted before it was put away. For on this full day spent in the kitchen, supplies for the week as well as for the next meal were on my mind. A few extra flourishes always went into the freezer, with company in mind. Like most women, I dearly love to cook, but the day comes when I am thoroughly sick of it. On such days the freezer supply saves me. I don't freeze for my descendants. I freeze things only for the convenience on busy days through the next two weeks.

Before Thanksgiving the long view is practical for each of us, of course. Then good things can be made and put away in early November to come out quickly on every occasion up to January. Freezing cookie dough is especially handy for this season. Then the work of mixing them is done; the baking when you want them takes only a few minutes, and no question about it—you have freshly made cookies in texture and flavor.

My kitchen is fairly modern, but long ago, as a bride, my equipment was the best that money could buy—from the ten-cent store. This was just as well, for at the time I had no opinions about the advantage of even heat when cooking with copper pans, nor the dreary work of polishing them. The value of thick aluminum, I did not know about. By the time the originals were being replaced, copper and aluminum and stainless steel meant something to me, and so did iron. By then I knew why I wanted bright and shining cookie sheets or cake pans and that dark pans for brown piecrusts were necessary. And I appreciated the wonders of a Dutch oven and a skillet each made of iron and glass-covered. I also wanted stainless steel with copper bottoms among my cooking utensils, and I hung on for dear life to the ancient copper saucepans that came from France. Shiny or not, they were my friends.

To me a copper saucepan is the most important pan of the lot. Whether it is shiny or dingy, I can cook a filet mignon to a turn in it or make a brown sauce or heat up the beans. We are friends. The others fool me occasionally.

There is an electric blender at each end of my kitchen—hardly a necessity—but if I also had a play room in the basement for grownups or for teen-agers to enjoy themselves, I'd have another electric blender down there. But in the kitchen an electric blender, a copper saucepan, a good sharp-pointed knife—what you can't do with these I sometimes think you don't need to do, except with your hands. An electric mixer is fine, too, when family requirements keep it in use. A portable one does me very well and hangs in front of me along with the colander. A freezer, large or small, is so convenient there is no point in talking about it. A freezing compartment is the "mink-coat touch" for the kitchen but far more useful.

It is on such a day as this one of baking and cooking, a day when you get an early start, that the mood comes over you to whip up an extra pan of biscuits or sweet rolls, an upside-down cake or some kind of *coffee companion* to share with "the girls." So—you call them up and say, "Be here in half an hour. Come as you are." And it's a party even if it is ten-thirty in the morning.

CHAPTER 2

TO SERVE WITH "COME-AS-YOU-ARE" COFFEES OR WITH COLA

COME AS YOU ARE . . . . FOR COFFEE

Women are so clever really. The young ones who weathered making a new home every few weeks all during World War II learned to solve any problem that came along. One was to have fun despite lunch to get for children home from school and no baby-sitters any time, anyhow. Too little time to do everything and too little money for big company meals simmered down into morning coffees or cola parties.

About half an hour before the biscuits or sweet rolls come out of the oven—or whatever is planned to go with coffee that day—the self-appointed hostess telephones half a dozen friends, more or less.

"Come as you are for coffee," she says. "Be here by ten."

And they come as they are, knowing that curlers or kitchen apron adds to the hilarity, that they can talk and laugh over coffee for an hour and be home in time to get the children's lunch.

"I'm all for face and hair being as tidy as for an evening dance," one woman told me, "but funny clothes are more amusing than curlers and unfinished faces."

And she's right.

Coffees offer the best food in the world—sweet rolls, berry blossoms, biscuit pies, broiler-frosted cakes. Let's see what can come out of the oven to add to the breads or cakes you have already served. And while we are about it, why not vary the coffee? Try Café au Lait —*cafay oh lay,* I suppose you would pronounce it in French. Make the coffee double strong, twice the amount of coffee ordinarily used, or make the coffee with a double-roast blend. The point is to have it strong. Then have a pitcher of warm milk—don't boil it and spoil it by having an ugly scum form on top—just heat it—and serve with the steaming coffee.

Half the fun is in the pouring. Hold the pitcher in one hand, the coffeepot in the other, and fill the cup by pouring them together. Sweeten if you like. Add honey if you like. Or drink it plain. A lovely taste. Milk made from non-fat powdered milk will do for this if you are weight watchers. But why did I mention that, with buns and cakes right in front of me ready to pop into the oven?

CAFÉ AU LAIT

Half strong black coffee and half hot (but not boiled) milk is the European way of enjoying morning coffee. Add sugar to please the taste. But whatever you do, fill each cup by pouring milk with one hand and coffee with the other, showing no favoritism until the cup is filled with half of each. Pouring together makes all the difference in the resulting flavor. Don't ask me why.

MOCHA JAVA

Make hot coffee and hot cocoa. Pour into cups as for Café au Lait, filling cups with half of each. Spoon whipped cream on top of each cup.

CAPPUCCINO

In Italy the dark strong coffee is served with ⅓ hot milk, favoring the coffee and sweetening to taste. It is pronounced Cap-poo-*chee*-no in Italy, and they use a double-roast coffee. You can too, or make it from regular coffee with twice the amount of coffee per cup.

SPICED VIENNESE COFFEE

Makes 8 servings:

7 tablespoons instant coffee
8 cups boiling water
16 cloves
5-inch stick cinnamon
½ cup sugar
heavy cream, whipped
ground cinnamon

Combine coffee, boiling water, and spices in a saucepan. Place over high heat and bring to a boil. Remove from heat, cover, and let stand 5 to 8 minutes. Strain through cheesecloth placed in a strainer. Add sugar and stir until it dissolves. Reheat but do not boil. Serve with bowl of cold whipped cream which has been sprinkled with cinnamon.

INSTANT COFFEE FOR THE CROWD

Makes 24 servings:

1 2-ounce jar instant coffee
6 quarts (24 cups) boiling water

Combine; stir only until blended. Serve.

COFFEE COOLER

Make that "double-roast" strong coffee; pour over ice cubes in a tall glass; fill with cold ginger ale. Add a little milk if you like, or drink it plain. Delicious.

ICED COFFEE TRINIDAD

Makes 12 servings:

8 cups very strong coffee
4 cups (1 quart) chocolate or vanilla ice cream
2 cups shaved ice
1½ tablespoons Angostura bitters

Beat until blended. Return to refrigerator to chill until ready to serve if this has not been prepared at the last minute.

COFFEE FLOAT

Makes 8 servings:

4 tablespoons sugar
4 tablespoons water
3 tablespoons instant coffee
8 cups chilled milk

Combine sugar and water in a small saucepan. Place over low heat and stir until blended, about 5 minutes. Remove from heat. Add coffee and stir. Add to chilled milk and whip with a rotary beater to blend thoroughly. Chill and serve in chilled glasses with blobs of whipped cream on top.

ICED COFFEE OR TEA

Makes 4 servings:

3 cups double-strength coffee or tea
warm water

Pour coffee or tea into ice tray with cube divider. Place in freezer compartment to freeze firm. For each serving place 2 tea or coffee ice cubes in tall glass. Fill ¾ full with warm water. Stir until cubes are almost dissolved. Add 2 more cubes.

LET'S BEGIN . . . . WITH REFRIGERATOR ROLLS

BASIC REFRIGERATOR ROLLS

Makes 4 dozen:

¼ cup sugar
3 teaspoons salt
6 tablespoons shortening
1 cup scalded milk
¾ cup water
1 egg, well beaten
2 cakes compressed yeast dissolved in ¼ cup lukewarm water
6 cups (approx.) sifted all-purpose flour

Combine sugar, salt, shortening, and milk in large bowl, stirring until shortening is melted. Add water to first mixture and cool to lukewarm.

Add egg and dissolved yeast and mix well. Add flour gradually, beating well after each addition, mixing to a soft dough. Knead on a lightly floured board 3 to 5 minutes until dough is smooth and satiny. Shape into ball; place in greased bowl; grease top of dough. Cover tightly and store in refrigerator.

When ready to use, remove from refrigerator and shape for Cloverleaf or for Parker House Rolls. Cover; let rise in warm place until double in bulk. Bake in hot oven (425 F.) 10 to 12 minutes.

CLOVERLEAF ROLLS

Use part of Basic Refrigerator Roll dough to form balls 1 inch in diameter. Place 3 balls in each section of greased muffin pans; brush with melted butter or margarine. Finish as directed above.

PARKER HOUSE ROLLS

Roll Basic Refrigerator Roll dough ¼ inch thick on lightly floured board. Cut with 2-inch biscuit cutter. Brush with melted butter or margarine. Make a crease with back of knife across each round, just off center. Fold so top slightly overlaps to keep rolls from springing open. Press edges together at end of crease. Place fairly close together on greased baking sheet. Finish and bake as for Basic Refrigerator Rolls.

NOTE: TO FREEZE: Cool baked rolls thoroughly at room temperature. Wrap in moisture-vaporproof material in convenient numbers for serving, using drugstore wrap. Insert in Stockinette, label, place on refrigerated shelf or floor of freezer compartment, and freeze.

TO THAW AND HEAT: Remove Stockinette and place wrapped rolls on baking sheet in hot oven (400 F.) 10 minutes. Serve immediately.

LET'S MAKE FRUIT . . . NUT . . . OR HONEY BUNS

RICH BUN DOUGH

Makes 16:

¾ cup dark corn syrup
¼ cup butter or margarine
¼ cup brown sugar
3 cups sifted all-purpose flour
4 teaspoons baking powder
1½ teaspoons salt
½ cup shortening
1 cup milk

Place first three ingredients in a saucepan; bring to a boil over medium heat and boil 1 minute. Pour into 9-inch square cake pan. Mix dry ingredients and sift once; cut in shortening with pastry blender or two knives. Add milk to make soft dough. Turn out on floured board. Roll into rectangle ¼ inch thick.

TO FILL:

Spread filling. Roll as for jelly roll. Cut into 1-inch slices and place cut side up in syrup. Bake in moderately hot oven (375 F.) 45 minutes. Let stand in pan 1 to 2 minutes. Then invert pan to remove buns.

CINNAMON BUNS: Combine ¼ cup dark corn syrup and 2 tablespoons melted butter or margarine; spread over surface of dough. Sprinkle with ¼ cup brown sugar, 2 teaspoons cinnamon, ½ cup raisins, and ¾ cup chopped nuts. Proceed as directed for Rich Buns.

FRUIT ROLLS: Add juice drained from No. 1 tall can fruit cocktail to first three ingredients; pour into pan. Then brush rolled-out dough with melted butter and spread with fruit cocktail. Sprinkle with mixture of ½ cup brown sugar, ½ teaspoon nutmeg, 1 teaspoon cinnamon, and 1 tablespoon grated lemon peel. Roll, brush tops of buns with butter, and bake.

PINEAPPLE ROLLS: Brush dough with melted butter; spread with 3 cups crushed pineapple; proceed as for Fruit Rolls.

DATE-NUT ROLLS: Brush dough with melted butter. Sprinkle with 1 cup seeded chopped dates and ¾ cup coarsely chopped pecans. Sprinkle with ½ cup brown sugar. Proceed as for other rolls.

ORANGE ROLLS: Use No. 2 can orange slices, chopped. Add juice drained from slices to first three ingredients, bring to a boil, and pour into square pan. Brush dough with butter; spread with orange slices; sprinkle with 1 teaspoon cinnamon. Roll, cut, brush with butter, and bake.

HONEY BUNS: Replace dark corn syrup in first mixture with same amount of honey. After honey syrup is poured into pan, sprinkle with ½ cup pecan halves. When ready to roll, brush with melted butter, sprinkle with ½ cup chopped pecans, spread with ½ cup honey. Proceed as directed for rolling, cutting, baking Rich Buns.

UPSIDE-DOWN ROLLS . . . FROM BROWN 'N' SERVE

CRANBERRY TAFFY TOPS

	TO SERVE 8	TO SERVE 50
chopped nuts	*2 tablespoons*	*¾ cup*
jellied cranberry sauce	*½ cup*	*3 cups*
brown sugar	*¼ cup*	*1½ cups*
brown 'n' serve rolls	*8*	*50*

Grease muffin cups. In each muffin cup sprinkle a few chopped nuts. Crush cranberry sauce with a fork and combine with brown sugar. Put 1 tablespoon cranberry mixture in each muffin cup. Then turn brown 'n' serve roll upside down and press into each muffin cup. Bake in hot oven (400 F.) 12 to 15 minutes. Invert pan and gently remove rolls.

PECAN HONEY TOPS

Replace cranberry sauce and brown sugar with honey. Double quantity of nuts, using broken pecans. Moisten nuts in honey. Spoon mixture into greased muffin tins, press rolls into place, and bake as directed for Cranberry Taffy Tops.

CRANBERRY GEMS

With cloverleaf brown 'n' serve rolls gently separate rolls just enough to insert a ¾-inch cube of jellied cranberry sauce. Paint top with melted butter and sprinkle with brown sugar. Bake in hot oven (400 F.) 12 to 15 minutes.

APRICOT GEMS

Proceed as for Cranberry Gems, placing 1 cooked apricot half into each cloverleaf roll.

MIXED FRUIT GEMS

When making rolls for a crowd, vary the fruit, jelly, jam, marmalade placed in the center of cloverleaf rolls. Proceed as for Cranberry Gems and have colorful variety with as many flavors as you choose.

LET'S BAKE BISCUITS . . . . . . WITH BUTTER

Good biscuits are the result of tenderness, of gentle handling. Liquids and fats used to make them should be very cold. Ingredients should be combined with a light quick hand.

For soft biscuits, place them close together with sides touching. For crusty ones, arrange biscuits well apart for baking so that they brown on all sides.

Fluffy, dropped, or plain, serve them hot . . . hot . . . hot.

Makes about 18 biscuits:

1¾ cups all-purpose flour
1 teaspoon salt
4 teaspoons tartrate of phosphate baking powder or 2½ teaspoons combination type
5 or 6 tablespoons butter
⅔ cup milk

Combine dry ingredients; sift once. Cut in butter with pastry blender. Make a well in the center of the mixture and pour the milk into it. Stir until well blended and the dough is slightly dry and leaves the sides of the bowl (stir hard and fast about 20 times). Place the dough on a board dusted with flour; knead it lightly. Roll it lightly until ¼ inch thick or the thickness needed for its use. Cut with a biscuit cutter which has been dipped in flour. Brush the tops of the biscuits with milk in which a little sugar has been dissolved, or with melted butter. Use a feathery pastry brush for this. Place on a greased baking sheet and chill in the refrigerator for several hours if you can, keeping them covered with waxed paper. Bake in hot oven (425 F.) until done, 12 to 15 minutes.

FLUFFY BISCUITS

Makes about 18 biscuits:

2 cups cake flour
4 teaspoons tartrate of phosphate baking powder or 2½ teaspoons combination type
1½ teaspoons salt
1½ tablespoons sugar
¼ cup (4 tablespoons) butter
¾ cup undiluted evaporated milk or rich milk or cream

Mix as for regular biscuits, or thin batter for Drop Biscuits.

LET'S BAKE BISCUITS . . . . . . WITH SALAD OIL

BISCUITS MADE WITH COOKING OIL

Makes 18 small biscuits:

2 cups flour
1 tablespoon baking powder
1 teaspoon salt
⅓ cup cooking oil
⅔ cup milk

Sift together dry ingredients. Pour oil and milk into a measuring cup. Do not stir. Pour all at once into the dry ingredients. Stir with a fork until the mixture rounds up into balls, kneading the dough about 10 times without additional flour. Roll between 2 pieces of waxed paper to ½-inch thickness. Cut with an unfloured 1½-inch biscuit cutter. Bake in hot oven (475 F.) 10 to 12 minutes.

DROP BISCUITS: For Drop Biscuits made with sweet milk, thin batter to drop consistency by adding 2 tablespoons milk to regular recipe. Drop by spoonfuls on greased baking sheet and bake as other biscuits.

BUTTERMILK BISCUITS

Makes 18 small biscuits:

2 cups sifted all-purpose flour
3 teaspoons baking powder
1 teaspoon salt
¼ teaspoon baking soda
¼ cup salad oil
¾ cup buttermilk
2 12-inch squares waxed paper

Mix and sift dry ingredients together. Combine salad oil and buttermilk. Pour all at once over entire surface of flour mixture. Mix with fork to make a soft dough. Shape lightly with hands to make a round ball. Place on 12-inch squares of waxed paper and knead lightly 10 times or until smooth. Use second waxed paper square to pat or roll out to ½-inch thickness between 2 pieces of waxed paper. Remove top sheet of paper; cut biscuits with unfloured 2-inch cutter. Place on ungreased baking sheet. Bake in hot oven (450 F.) 12 to 15 minutes.

BUTTERMILK DROP BISCUITS: Increase buttermilk to 1 cup. Mix dough and drop by spoonfuls on baking sheet.

20 BISCUIT BLOSSOMS . . . . FILLED

Serve these filled biscuits with coffee or cola. They will taste good at your ten o'clock morning gatherings . . . at an afternoon recess for Mother . . . or as hot-out-of-the-oven finales after watching TV.

FOR FILLED BISCUITS

Make any biscuit dough you like, or use a biscuit mix. Roll the dough very thin, ¼ inch or thinner. Cut into rounds and spoon a little mound of filling onto the center of half the rounds. Cover with the other rounds. Moisten the edges and seal by pressing all around with a fork. Prick the tops, place them on a greased baking sheet and bake until brown in a hot oven (450 F.).

Fill the biscuits with anything you have in the refrigerator, or with anything you like, for wonderful treats. Use the same filling for all of them, or use a little of a dozen things so that each biscuit is a surprise.

SWEET FILLINGS

Fillings can be fruit jams, mincemeat, chopped watermelon pickle, preserved black cherries, drained crushed pineapple, banana slices soaked in frozen orange juice (undiluted) drained and sprinkled with cinnamon, thawed frozen strawberries, raspberries, blueberries, or peaches crushed to nestle into the biscuit.

SAVORY FILLINGS

Any meat, fowl, or fish can be put through the food grinder, seasoned, and used for delicious biscuit fillings.

• Sprinkle a little dry mustard on the ground ham, a little curry powder on the chicken, a few chopped sweet pickles on minced salmon. Add a teaspoon of mayonnaise or cream to hold the meat together.

• Crush sardines, blend with mayonnaise, and fill biscuits.

• Chop smoked turkey, thin with spoonful of jelly, to fill biscuits.

• Grate Swiss cheese, sprinkle with dry mustard, fill biscuits, and sprinkle a little of the cheese on top of each one.

• Crush chile con carne and spread.

• Squeeze anchovy paste from a tube onto the biscuit, or make it mild by adding a little mayonnaise.

• Mix leftover corned beef hash or smoked tongue with horseradish for filling.

COME FOR BERRY BISCUITS AND COFFEE . . OR COLA

BERRY BISCUITS

Blueberries . . . Strawberries . . . Raspberries . . . Cranberries . . . Gooseberries . . . Loganberries . . . Almost any kind of berries that have been sweetened and drained of the juice make superb "biscuits with coffee."

Cook and sweeten the fruit, then drain. Add 1 cup of berries to any of the recipes for biscuits. They are particularly good added to Fluffy or Drop Biscuits, and so easy.

POLKA-DOT BISCUITS

Another way to add the berries is to make a little well in the center of the biscuit, dot with a little of the berries or of preserves, and bake.

Try a candy-mint pillow in the center of your biscuits, or a piece of chopped preserved ginger.

BISCUIT CRISPS

Make dough for Rolled Biscuits. Roll out ¼ inch thin. Spread with any filling, fruit or savory, making a very thin layer. Roll up as for a jelly roll. Slice into ½-inch lengths. Place cut side down on greased cookie sheet. Brush with melted butter or melted jelly, and bake until golden brown. Serve hot or cold.

• In addition to the fruit and savory fillings, try one with grated Swiss cheese: ½ cup grated cheese, ⅛ teaspoon cayenne, ½ cup finely chopped pecans.

FROSTED BISCUITS

Bake biscuits whenever you like. When about ready to serve, cut them in two, fry in hot fat until brown on each side, and dip immediately into a cake icing, any kind you prefer. Let them set a moment and consume on the spot.

QUICK BISCUIT PIES

Make your dough the consistency for Drop Biscuits. Spread or spoon into a greased pie pan, making a layer that is thick, rough, and a little higher at the rim. Spread with topping; bake in hot oven (400 F.) until done, 40 to 45 minutes. Cut into wedges and serve hot or cold.

TOPS FOR BISCUIT PIES

• Spread with peanut butter, dot with coarsely chopped dates.

• Make layer of chopped cooked prunes. Cover with uncooked apple slices. Sprinkle with brown sugar, dot with seedless raisins.

• Cover with tart apple slices. Spread apple layer with mixture of ⅓ cup soft butter or margarine, ½ cup brown sugar, ½ teaspoon cinnamon, ⅛ teaspoon nutmeg. Dot with sour cherries for decoration.

• Mix ⅔ cup honey with ⅓ cup butter. Stir until creamy. Spread on biscuit layer, garnish with pecan halves.

• Drain No. 2 can black bing cherries, pouring juice into measuring cup. Add water to make 1 cup. Stir in 1½ tablespoons cornstarch; stir until smooth. Add sugar. Place over low heat and stir until sauce is thickened and sugar dissolved. Add cherries and spread on "pie."

• Spread with cooked spiced prunes which have been drained and pitted. Make thick layer and scatter broken walnuts over top.

• Grate Swiss or Cheddar cheese; spread 1 cup over biscuit. Bake only about 20 minutes, or until biscuit is done and cheese crusty brown.

• Spread with any kind of preserves on hand, making a thin layer. Serve hot with icy-cold whipped cream.

• Bake biscuit pie as for other biscuits, remove from oven, and while hot spread with Banana Hard Sauce, or with Mint or Vanilla Butter Frosting.

MAKE IRISH BISCUIT PIE:

Make rich Drop Biscuits—2-cup recipe with biscuit mix—using

undiluted evaporated milk. Stir in 1 cup seedless raisins, 2 tablespoons sugar, and 1½ tablespoons caraway seeds. When biscuits are done, increase heat for 3 or 4 minutes if necessary to brown.

CELEBRATION BISCUITS . . AS GOOD AS THEY LOOK

BISCUIT CHRISTMAS TREE

Use a biscuit mix, using undiluted evaporated milk to make Drop Biscuit dough. Grease a cookie sheet and drop by spoonfuls onto the greased sheet, one at the top, two biscuits right under that, forming rows beneath into a wide base at the bottom. Put a green or red candied cherry on top of each biscuit and bake as directed on the package.

These can be iced or not as you like. Make a sweet coffee cake icing of 1 cup confectioners' sugar mixed with 2 tablespoons hot milk flavored with ¼ teaspoon vanilla extract. Combine and stir until blended.

BISCUIT WEDDING RING

Make batter as for the Christmas Tree. Spoon good-sized biscuits onto a greased cookie sheet, putting them close enough together so that they touch to make a complete circle. This can be done by dropping large spoonfuls in a single circle to make large biscuits, or making a double circle of small spoonfuls for tiny biscuits.

Bake as directed on the package and frost while hot with the confectioners' sugar frosting. Decorate with squares of rock candy or snowy-white mint pillows while the frosting is still warm to represent the diamonds.

CHRISTMAS WREATH

Make the Biscuit Wedding Ring, stirring into the batter ½ cup mixed preserved fruit (chopped citron and candied cherries and lemon and orange peel). Glaze as for the circle above and decorate with red cherries and green leaves made of angelica or slivers of green gumdrops.

SAVORY BISCUITS . . . . UNFORGETTABLE

MUSTARD BISCUITS

Makes 20 2-inch biscuits:

Preheat oven to 450 F.

Follow directions on package of biscuit mix. Instead of rolling out on board, pat or roll onto a baking sheet (which has been lightly floured) to ¼-inch thickness. Spread with a rich prepared mustard or with herb-flavored mustard, and from this cut circles with a 2-inch biscuit cutter, making the circles very close together.

Gather up the biscuit dough between circles or leave and bake it for nibbling. Fold the circles in half, leaving them on the baking sheet. Press down with one finger on the outside edge to form a "pocketbook" or Parker House type of biscuit. Allow them to stand 20 minutes to ½ hour. Bake 8 to 12 minutes, or until brown. Serve immediately.

For Mustard Biscuits more quickly made than these "pocketbooks" add 2 teaspoons rich prepared mustard to the milk when mixing the dough. Pat out on the baking sheet as above and cut into squares to make pillows of the desired size, and bake.

HERB BISCUITS

Add almost any herb that touches your fingertips when you reach your hand toward the herb shelf—1 teaspoon to any of the recipes given for fluffy, rolled or drop biscuits.

SAGE BISCUITS

Until you become daring enough to be inventive, try a teaspoon of sage in biscuits to be served over chicken pie. Add rosemary, thyme, or marjoram in a similar quantity.

GARDEN BISCUITS

Add chopped chives, parsley, or finely chopped tops of scallions or leeks in quantities of 1 tablespoon to the regular recipe for dough. Add these singly, not together.

GARDEN TOPPING

Make a topping for these Garden Biscuits by steaming ⅓ cup chopped onion in 1 tablespoon water. Combine in a small saucepan; cover tightly. Place over low heat; leave for 8 minutes. Remove from heat. Add 1 tablespoon watercress leaves. Stir in beaten yolk of 1 egg. Cover tops of biscuits and bake.

FRUIT AND NUT LOAVES . . . . ONE-LOAF RECIPES

PRUNE-NUT LOAF

1 cup prunes
3 cups sifted flour
4 teaspoons baking powder
½ teaspoon soda
1½ teaspoons salt
2 tablespoons sugar
¼ cup shortening
2 eggs, beaten
1 cup rich milk or diluted evaporated milk
½ cup chopped nutmeats

Rinse prunes. If prunes are very dry, boil them 5 minutes; drain on a paper towel until dry. Remove pits and chop very fine. Sift flour with baking powder, soda, salt, and sugar. Cut shortening into flour mixture. Combine beaten eggs and milk and stir into flour mixture. Add prunes and nuts. Pour into well-greased loaf pan about 9 x 5 x 3 inches. Place extra halves of prunes and whole nutmeats on top. Bake in moderate to moderately hot oven (350 to 375 F.) 1 hour, or until brown. Turn out on rack to cool.

PEANUT BUTTER DAISY LOAF

2 cups sifted flour
⅓ cup sugar
3 teaspoons baking powder
1 teaspoon salt
¾ cup peanut butter
1 egg, beaten slightly
1 cup rich milk or diluted evaporated milk
¼ cup peanuts
8 cherries

Sift together dry ingredients. Cut in peanut butter with pastry blender. Combine egg with milk and add to mixture. Blend well. Pour into well-greased loaf pan. Make "daisies" on top of the loaf with peanut petals around cherry centers. Bake in a moderately hot oven (375 F.) 1 hour, or until brown. Turn out on rack to cool.

APPLE-WALNUT LOAF

2 cups flour
¾ cup sugar
1 tablespoon baking powder
1 teaspoon salt
½ teaspoon soda
½ teaspoon nutmeg
1 egg, well beaten
1 cup medium-thick unsweetened applesauce
¼ cup cooking oil
1 cup coarsely chopped walnuts

Combine dry ingredients and sift together. Combine egg, applesauce which has been beaten until smooth, and the cooking oil. Add to the dry ingredients and stir just until blended. Add nuts and stir. Pour into a 5 x 9 greased loaf pan and bake in moderate oven (350 F.) 50 minutes, or until done.

DELICIOUS NUT BREAD

Makes one 9 x 5 loaf:

3 cups sifted flour
3 teaspoons double-acting baking powder
¼ teaspoon soda
1½ teaspoons salt
½ cup granulated sugar
¼ cup firmly packed brown sugar
1 egg, well beaten
1¼ cups milk
¼ cup melted shortening
1 cup finely chopped nutmeats

Sift flour once; measure; add baking powder, soda, salt, and granulated sugar and sift again. Add brown sugar. Combine egg and milk. Add to flour mixture; add shortening, then mix enough to dampen flour. Fold in nuts. Turn into 9 x 5 x 3-inch pan or into two 8 x 4 x 3-inch loaf pans lined on bottoms with paper. Bake in moderate oven (350 F.) 1 hour and 5 minutes for large loaf, or about 50 minutes for small loaves. Cool. Wrap in waxed paper and store overnight before slicing.

For one small loaf, use half of all ingredients in above recipe, using ⅔ cup milk. Bake in one 8 x 4 x 3-inch loaf pan, lined on bottom with paper, in moderate oven (350 F.) about 50 minutes.

APRICOT PUFF LOAF

56 apricot halves, dried or canned
1 egg, slightly beaten
milk
3 cups biscuit mix
¼ cup melted butter or margarine
½ cup sugar
1 teaspoon cinnamon
½ cup chopped nutmeats

Cook dried apricots or drain canned halves. Add to egg enough milk to make ¾ cup. Stir into biscuit mix. Knead slightly; roll out on lightly floured board to 12 x 21-inch oblong. Cut into 28 3-inch squares. Place 2 apricot halves in center of each; bring up corners over fruit; pinch together to form a ball. Dip each ball in melted butter, then in mixed sugar and cinnamon. Arrange 8 balls close together in 2 rows in greased 9 x 5 x 3-inch loaf pan; sprinkle with ⅓ of the nuts. Top with 12 balls in 3 rows, pressing lightly on others; sprinkle with ⅓ of the nuts. On top, press 8 balls in 2 rows and top with rest of nuts. Bake in moderately hot oven (375 F.) 45 to 55 minutes. Let stand in pan 10 minutes before removing. Slices best after 24 hours.

SERVE A GINGERBREAD RING . . . WITH FROSTING

Let every woman help herself to frosting as she helps herself to a slice of gingerbread and coffee. Follow the directions on the package of gingerbread mix. To make a ring—simply bake it in a 9-inch ring mold instead of the usual pan and take it out of the oven about 5 minutes sooner. It bakes more quickly when the heat can get at it in the center. Count on 8 servings to a ring. It is delicious served hot.

A confession . . . I sometimes use 2 tablespoons undiluted orange juice (frozen), omitting that much water when mixing gingerbread. And a teaspoon or two of grated orange peel can be added with no ill effects. Quite good, in fact.

TO FROST:

• Cream cheese, out of the refrigerator long enough to soften, can be thinned with heavy cream or with undiluted evaporated milk. Mash together, then whip with a rotary beater until consistency of whipped cream. Flavor with ¼ teaspoon ginger per cup, or that amount of cinnamon. Chill and serve in center.

• Another time, don't spice the cream cheese mixture. Just heap it in the center, sprinkle the top with grated orange peel . . . or fold ½ cup of whole cranberry sauce into the cream cheese.

• Whip heavy cream, sweeten very little, and flavor with few drops of peppermint and color with few drops of green vegetable coloring.

• Fill center of ring with marshmallow fluff as it comes from the jar. Sprinkle coarsely chopped nuts on top.

• Whip cream and fold in ½ cup of tart jam for each cup of whipped cream. Crushed pineapple or cranberry sauce, drained, is good this way too. Or spoon these on top of the cream in the center, as garnish to be eaten.

• Whip cream; sweeten slightly. Pile in the center. Sprinkle banana slices with lemon juice; pile on top of the cream. Sprinkle with freshly grated nutmeg. Or fold in the banana slices and sprinkle with nutmeg.

ONCE IN A WHILE . . MAKE A FANCY COFFEE CAKE

MAPLE-NUT COFFEE CAKE

BUTTER CRUNCH MIXTURE:

½ cup melted butter
½ cup maple (or brown) sugar
½ cup finely chopped pecans
½ cup fine dry bread crumbs

Combine all ingredients; mix thoroughly. Press on bottom and sides of 1-quart ring mold. Add batter:

1 egg, beaten
⅓ cup sugar
⅓ cup milk
3 tablespoons melted butter or margarine
1 cup pancake mix

Combine beaten egg and sugar; beat until fluffy. Add milk and pancake mix, stirring lightly until combined. Gently stir in the melted shortening. Pour into the crunch-lined mold. Bake in moderately hot oven (375 F.) 25 to 30 minutes. Let cool 5 minutes. Turn out crunch side up on a platter; serve warm.

BLUEBERRY COFFEE CAKE

BATTER:

1 egg, beaten
⅓ cup sugar
⅓ cup milk
1 tablespoon grated lemon rind
1 cup pancake mix
¼ cup melted butter or margarine
½ cup fresh or frozen blueberries, drained

Place all ingredients except blueberries in bowl; beat with rotary beater until fairly smooth. Do not overbeat. Stir in berries. Spread batter in greased 8-inch round pan. Add topping:

2 tablespoons brown sugar
1 tablespoon grated lemon rind
1 tablespoon pancake mix
¼ cup finely chopped nuts
2 tablespoons melted butter or margarine

Combine all ingredients, spread over batter, and bake in hot oven (400 F.) 15 to 20 minutes.

PLAIN CAKES . . . . FANCY TRIMMINGS

GINGERBREAD RING

Prepare as below, baking in a ring mold and piling the whip high in center and around the edge of the ring.

GINGERBREAD SNOWSTORM

Makes 8 servings:

2 cups undiluted evaporated milk
1 package gingerbread mix
1 cup chopped dates
1 cup chopped nuts
¼ cup undiluted frozen lemon juice
2 cups chopped marshmallows
¼ cup grated orange peel

Chill the evaporated milk in freezing tray or in a bowl of ice.

Make the gingerbread as directed on the package. Add dates and nuts just before pouring into the pan, and bake as directed.

When the milk is thoroughly cold (and no more than ½ hour before you want to serve it) pour into a cold mixing bowl and whip until it begins to thicken, about 1 minute. Add lemon juice and whip until very stiff, about 2 minutes. Fold in marshmallows and orange peel. Pile in a bank around the gingerbread, covering the sides with the "drifts" and piling the rest around the edge of the top, leaving only the brown center exposed.

EVERY MONTH . . . . IS MUFFIN MONTH

QUICK MUFFINS

Makes 12 big ones:

2 cups sifted all-purpose flour
3 teaspoons baking powder
1 teaspoon salt
2 tablespoons sugar
1 egg, beaten
1¼ cups milk
⅓ cup salad oil

Last: When you feel like it, here is the place to add fruit or nuts—See Muffin Calendar.

Combine dry ingredients in sifter and sift into a bowl. Make a well and add remaining ingredients. Stir only enough to dampen flour—you WANT a lumpy batter! Fill greased muffin pans only ⅔ full. Bake in hot oven (400 F.) about 30 minutes.

BRAN BANANA-NUT MUFFINS

Makes 16 large or 32 small muffins:

2 cups sifted flour
1½ teaspoons soda
1 teaspoon salt
½ cup sugar
2 cups bran
2 eggs, well beaten
¼ cup sour milk or buttermilk
¼ cup melted shortening
4 cups thinly sliced ripe bananas (6 to 8)

Sift together flour, soda, salt, and sugar. Add bran and mix well. Combine eggs, milk, shortening, and bananas. Add to dry ingredients, mixing only enough to dampen the flour. Turn into well-greased muffin pans. Bake in moderately hot oven (375 F.) 30 to 35 minutes, or until muffins are done.

OATMEAL MUFFINS

Makes 16 small muffins:

1 cup sifted all-purpose flour
¼ cup sugar
3 teaspoons baking powder
½ teaspoon salt
3 tablespoons shortening
1 cup rolled oats
1 egg, beaten
1 cup milk
½ cup raisins or chopped nuts

Sift together flour, sugar, baking powder, and salt. Cut in shortening until mixture resembles corn meal. Add rolled oats. Blend. Add beaten egg and milk, stirring them in lightly. Fill greased muffin pans ⅔ full. Sprinkle tops with raisins or nuts, and press them in lightly. Bake in hot oven (425 F.) until done, 15 minutes for small ones.

Try making nice cinnamon tops by combining ⅓ cup brown sugar, 1 tablespoon flour, 2 teaspoons cinnamon, 1 tablespoon melted butter. Mix; sprinkle over muffins before baking. When you use this you can forget about adding the raisins or nuts.

CORN MUFFINS

Oh, why not make these with a mix? It's been years since I made these from scratch. Add an extra tablespoon of melted butter, an extra egg. Perfection—mix or no mix? No one could guess.

YOUR MUFFIN CALENDAR . . . . .

JANUARY: *Swiss Cheese Muffins.* Mix 1 cup grated cheese with dry ingredients. Sprinkle tops with few shavings of coarsely grated cheese, few grains of cayenne.

FEBRUARY: *Bacon Muffins.* Add ⅓ cup crushed bacon bits (cooked bacon drained and crushed).

MARCH: *Pineapple Muffins,* another fruit here the year round (in cans). Wonderful in muffins. Add ¾ cup crushed, *drained* fruit when stirring in milk.

APRIL: *Dates,* another year-round accessory to fine-flavored food. Crowd some of those bananas out of Banana Muffins, make half chopped dates, mm . . . mmm.

MAY: *Cherries* are ripe. Pit 1 cup cherries, increase sugar by 2 tablespoons. Sprinkle fruit with a little of the flour and stir into batter at the end.

JUNE: *Blackberry Muffins.* Increase sugar by 2 tablespoons, sprinkle 1 cup berries with 3 tablespoons of the flour, stir in just before filling muffin tins.

JULY: *Blueberries* are plentiful. Make muffins sweet, increasing sugar to ½ cup. Sprinkle with flour as for other berries and stir in at the last.

AUGUST: *Bing cherries.* Seed, chop a little, halving the cherries. Sprinkle with flour, add last.

SEPTEMBER: *Peaches,* juicy and ripe. Peel, seed, and chop. Stir in with milk.

OCTOBER: *Cranberries*—lovely to look at, with wonderful taste. Double sugar. Add whole fresh berries.

NOVEMBER: *Pecans* with the sweet and buttery kernels are superb in sweet muffins, made with double the usual sugar. Sprinkle sugar and more nuts on top of the muffins when ready to bake. Sprinkle lightly with cinnamon when they come from the oven.

Black Walnuts are good too. Add as suggested for pecans.

DECEMBER: *Salami Muffins.* Tear 3 thin slices of salami into dime-sized bits. Add to muffin batter. Result? A pleasant surprise in a month when all surprises must be good ones.

HOLLY BERRY DOUGHNUTS

Makes 2 dozen:

3 cups pancake mix
⅔ cup sugar
1 tablespoon grated orange peel
⅓ cup chopped nutmeats
2 eggs, beaten
⅔ cup milk
2 tablespoons melted shortening

Mix pancake ready-mix, sugar, orange peel, and nutmeats. Combine beaten eggs and milk and add to dry ingredients; fold in melted shortening. (If dough seems too stiff, add a little more milk.) Roll dough to ⅜-inch thickness on lightly floured board; cut with floured doughnut cutter. Fry in deep hot fat (375 F.) until brown. Drain on absorbent paper; cool.

Dip each doughnut into thin confectioners' sugar frosting. Decorate with candied cherries.

DOUGHNUTS . NEW FASHIONS WITH THIS OLD ONE

Make your own in the deep-fat fryer, or buy them ready-made. Then when the girls come in for coffee . . . everyone for herself.

• Serve little bowls of frosting, two or three kinds, and tint them if you like. Let each person frost her own as if buttering bread, before enjoying with her coffee.

• Split doughnuts the night before and put in an airproof bag, plastic or aluminum wrap, to have ready for the ten o'clock coffee callers. Plug in the grill and toast the cut side of the doughnuts; butter and eat them as they come off steamy brown.

• Summertime arrives. So do more doughnuts. Serve a big bowl of berries, sweetened and mixed with heavy cream, whipped. Spoon this fruity fluff onto a doughnut and eat as if it were shortcake. Try peaches awash with whipped cream this way too.

• Combine ½ cup brown sugar, 1 teaspoon cinnamon, 2 tablespoons melted butter. Mix well. Brush tops of doughnuts with this about ½ hour before company arrives to consume them.

• Make honey butter with ½ honey and ½ butter, blended. Serve with doughnuts and coffee. It is even good in the coffee!

• Frost doughnuts with coffee-flavored butter frosting the night before serving.

• Pile vanilla ice cream on a plate, top with a doughnut, and let each person fork it up together.

CHAPTER 3
TO FILL YOUR COOKIE JAR

COOKIES FOR CUTOUTS . . . DECORATED OR FILLED

Here is a butter cookie recipe to be used whenever children are around who want to try their hand at decorating shapes. When the cookie jar is emptied at your house faster than you can fill it, substitutes for butter are in order. But cookies are show-offs when full of butter, and nothing else makes them quite the same.

BUTTER COOKIES

Makes 5 dozen:

3½ cups sifted enriched flour
1 teaspoon salt
1 cup butter or other shortening
1 cup sugar
2 eggs
1 teaspoon vanilla

Sift together flour and salt. Cream shortening and sugar until light and fluffy. Add eggs and vanilla extract. Beat well. Add flour mixture to creamed mixture, mixing only enough to combine ingredients. Chill. Roll out ⅛ inch thick on floured board or pastry cloth. Cut with fancy-shaped cutters. Bake on ungreased cookie sheets in moderately hot oven (375 F.) 10 minutes.

FILLED COOKIES

This is the cookie dough you want, too, when Filled Cookies are the order of the day. Double this recipe to make 5 dozen Filled Cookies, or use it in these quantities to make 2½ dozen filled beauties, using the Butter Cookie recipe.

Roll out the dough and cut with a round cutter. Put 1 teaspoon of filling on half the cookies; cover with the other half; press edges together with a fork. Bake on ungreased cookie sheets in hot oven (400 F.).

FRUIT-NUT FILLINGS . . . . . . FOR COOKIES

Each of these recipes make about 1¼ cups . . . enough to fill the Butter Cookie recipe. When making more cookies, use two or three different fillings, or increase these recipes to correspond with your increase in cookie dough.

RAISIN OR DATE FILLING

1 cup seedless raisins or finely chopped dates
¼ cup brown sugar
⅛ teaspon salt
1 tablespoon quick-cooking tapioca
½ cup water

Combine all ingredients, except water, in a saucepan and mix well. Place over low heat; add water gradually, stirring constantly until mixture thickens. Chill before using. Double recipe if cookie dough is doubled, or fill some with Raisin or Date Filling and try one of these for the others:

APRICOT FILLING

2 cans apricot purée baby food
sugar to taste
2 tablespoons melted butter or margarine

Combine; stir until blended. Chill.

ORANGE-NUT MINCEMEAT

¾ cup mincemeat
1 tablespoon undiluted frozen orange juice
1 teaspoon grated orange peel
1 tablespoon molasses
½ cup coarsely chopped nuts

Combine all ingredients. Stir until blended.

FIG-NUT FILLING

1 cup finely chopped figs
1 tablespoon chopped orange peel
2 tablespoons undiluted orange juice
¼ cup water
¼ cup sugar
⅛ teaspoon salt
¼ cup chopped nuts

Mix all ingredients except nuts. Cook until thickened, stirring constantly. Cool. Add nuts.

CHERRY FILLING

1 cup sour pie cherries, drained
¼ cup sugar
1 tablespoon quick-cooking tapioca
½ cup cherry juice

Combine all ingredients in saucepan over low heat. Cook until thickened, stirring constantly. Chill.

EVERYBODY LOVES BROWNIES . . . HERE ARE 7

BROWNIES

⅔ cup sifted all-purpose flour
½ teaspoon baking powder
¼ teaspoon salt
⅓ cup butter or other shortening
2 squares unsweetened chocolate
1 cup sugar
2 eggs, well beaten
½ cup broken walnut meats
1 teaspoon vanilla

Set oven for moderate heat (350 F.). Grease an 8 x 8 x 2-inch pan. Assemble ingredients and utensils needed. Sift flour once; measure; add baking powder and salt and sift again. Melt shortening and chocolate over hot water. Add sugar gradually to eggs, beating thoroughly. Add chocolate mixture and blend. Add flour and mix well; then mix in nuts and vanilla. Spread in greased pan. Bake in preheated oven 25 minutes, or until done. Cool in pan, then cut into squares or rectangles.

Beginning with this recipe, make:

CHOCOLATE-PEPPERMINT BROWNIES

Follow direction for Brownies; remove from oven and place about 20 chocolate-peppermint patties on top. Return to oven for 3 minutes. Remove from oven and spread patties with spatula to cover entire top.

MOCHA BROWNIES

Add 4 teaspoons instant coffee with sugar when mixing Brownies.

BROWNIE PIE

Mix as for Brownies; add top decoration of coarsely chopped nuts and bake as directed in a pie pan. Serve in wedges with or without whipped cream.

PEPPERMINT BROWNIES

Mix Brownies; omit vanilla and add ½ teaspoon oil of peppermint.

FILLED BROWNIES

Use recipe for Brownies. When cool, cut into squares and split each Brownie in half, spread with butter frosting in any flavor or color you like, and put the halves together again.

BOUQUET BROWNIES

Makes 6 dozen:

Bake Brownies in a greased 9 x 9 x 2-inch pan. Cool in pan, cut into small squares, and decorate with tinted butter frosting on each square. Gives the dainty squares a party look.

THREE KINDS OF COOKIES . . . . . ONE DOUGH

BANANA OATMEAL COOKIES

Makes 6 dozen:

4 cups sifted enriched flour
2 teaspoons cinnamon
½ teaspoon nutmeg
3 teaspoons salt
2 teaspoons baking powder
½ teaspoon soda
2 cups sugar
2 cups softened butter
2 cups mashed ripe bananas (4 to 6)
4 eggs
4 cups rolled oats

Combine flour, spices, salt, baking powder, soda, and sugar. Sift once. Add shortening, bananas, and eggs. Beat until smooth, about 2 minutes. Fold in rolled oats. Divide dough into three parts.

FRUIT BARS: Add ½ cup mixed chopped preserved peel and candied fruit to one portion of dough. Stir. Spread in a well-greased 8-inch square pan. Bake in moderately hot oven (375 F.) 15 or 20 minutes. Turn out of pan; cut into bars; roll in confectioners' sugar while warm.

DROP COOKIES: Drop second portion of cookie dough by teaspoons on a well-greased cookie sheet. Decorate with chocolate chips, nuts, or raisins. Bake in moderately hot oven (375 F.) 10 to 12 minutes.

SUGAR COOKIES: Chill third portion of dough in refrigerator overnight. Sprinkle board with confectioners' sugar. Roll dough to ¼-inch thickness, sprinkling with more sugar if needed to prevent sticking. Cut in fancy shapes. Bake on greased cookie sheet in moderate oven (350 F.) until brown, 8 to 10 minutes.

CRUMB MACAROONS

Makes 2½ dozen:

1 cup fine dry bread crumbs
1 cup sugar
¼ teaspoon salt
1 cup chopped nuts
2 eggs
1 teaspoon vanilla

Combine crumbs, sugar, salt, and nuts. Beat eggs well. Add vanilla. Combine eggs with dry ingredients, mixing well. Drop by teaspoonfuls on greased baking sheet. Bake in moderate oven (350 F.) 15 minutes, or until lightly browned. Remove from baking sheet at once.

QUICK CHOCOLATE COOKIES

Makes 3 dozen:

½ cup sifted all-purpose flour
½ cup sugar
¼ teaspoon salt
⅓ cup salad oil
1 unbeaten egg
2 tablespoons top milk or cream
1 square unsweetened chocolate, melted
½ teaspoon vanilla
½ cup chopped nutmeats

Mix and sift together first three ingredients. Make a well and add in order salad oil, egg, top milk or cream, chocolate, and vanilla. Beat with spoon until smooth. Turn into greased 15½ x 10 x 1-inch jelly-roll pan. Sprinkle with nutmeats. Bake in hot oven (400 F.) 10 to 12 minutes. Cut into squares while warm.

UNBAKED FRUIT BALLS

Makes about 28 balls:

2 cups vanilla wafers, crushed
⅔ cup apricots, drained
2 tablespoons apricot syrup
⅛ teaspoon salt
¼ cup chopped nuts
confectioners' sugar

Combine all ingredients except sugar. Work until just moist enough to form into balls about the size of an egg yolk. Roll in confectioners' sugar; store in a tin and chill a few hours before serving.

GINGER SCOTCH SHORTBREADS

These thick, melt-in-the-mouth cookies are about "the best I ever ate" in anybody's language. The Scotch make them without the ginger, and with or without it, cool and store them in a tightly covered tin for a few days to "mellow" them.

Makes about 50:

2 cups sweet butter
1 cup confectioners' sugar
¼ teaspoon salt
½ teaspoon ginger
4 cups sifted all-purpose flour

Cream butter until softened; add sugar gradually until blended. Combine salt and ginger with flour in sifter and add to butter mixture a little at a time. Chill about 30 minutes. Roll out to ¼-inch thickness and cut into rounds or crescents. Prick tops with fork and bake on an ungreased baking sheet in moderate oven (350 F.) about 20 minutes. Do not brown.

OATMEAL CRISPIES

Makes 6½ dozen cookies:

1½ cups sifted all-purpose flour
3 cups quick-cooking oatmeal
1 cup margarine
2 cups sugar
1 teaspoon soda
1 teaspoon salt
2 eggs
½ cup chopped nuts
1 cup seedless raisins
1 teaspoon grated lemon rind
1 tablespoon fresh lemon juice

Combine flour and oatmeal. Cream margarine and 1 cup of the sugar together until fluffy. Blend in soda and salt. Beat in 1 egg. Gradually add the remaining sugar, mixing until creamy after each addition. Beat in remaining egg. Stir in nuts, raisins, lemon rind, and lemon juice. Gradually add flour and oatmeal mixture. Chill 30 to 40 minutes, or until stiff enough to handle. Shape into 1-inch balls; place on greased cookie sheets. Bake 12 to 15 minutes in a preheated moderate oven (350 F.). You are going to like these.

MORE COOKIES . . . . DELICIOUS DROPS

BLACK WALNUT COOKIES

Makes about 20 cookies:

1 cup sifted flour
¼ cup non-fat dry milk
1 teaspoon baking powder
⅛ teaspoon salt
¼ cup butter
⅓ cup sugar
1 egg
½ teaspoon vanilla
2 tablespoons water
⅓ cup chopped black walnuts

Sift flour. Measure and sift again with powdered milk, baking powder, and salt. Cream butter. Gradually add sugar, creaming until light and fluffy. Beat in egg. Add vanilla. Add dry ingredients alternately with water, mixing well after each addition. Add black walnuts. Drop by teaspoonfuls on a greased baking sheet about 2½ inches apart. Bake in moderate oven (350 F.) 15 to 20 minutes, or until lightly browned.

FROSTED ORANGE DROPS

Makes 5 dozen:

2½ cups sifted all-purpose flour
¼ teaspoon salt
½ teaspoon baking soda
¾ cup shortening
½ cup sugar
½ cup light corn syrup
2 eggs
2 cups chopped, shredded coconut
3 tablespoons grated orange rind
½ cup orange juice

Sift together flour, salt, and baking soda. Cream shortening. Add sugar gradually and cream until light and fluffy. Add syrup; blend thoroughly. Add eggs one at a time, beating well after each addition.

Stir in coconut and grated orange rind. Add sifted dry ingredients alternately with orange juice. Drop by teaspoonfuls on lightly greased cookie sheet. Bake in moderate oven (350 F.) 15 minutes. Cool and frost with Butter Cream Frosting.

BUTTER CREAM FROSTING

Cream ⅓ cup butter or margarine and ¼ teaspoon salt. Gradually add 1 cup sifted confectioners' sugar, blending well. Add alternately 3 to 3½ tablespoons hot milk and 2½ cups sifted confectioners' sugar, beating until smooth and creamy. (Use only enough milk to make a good spreading consistency.) Add I teaspoon vanilla and 1 tablespoon grated orange rind; blend.

QUICK CHERRY DROPS

Makes about 4½ dozen:

2 cups sifted enriched flour
½ teaspoon soda
1 teaspoon salt
1 cup brown sugar
¾ cup butter
1 egg
1 teaspoon vanilla
2 tablespoons milk
½ cup chopped nuts
½ cup chopped candied or maraschino cherries
½ cup coconut

Sift together flour, soda, and salt. Add sugar, shortening, and egg. Mix vanilla with milk and add to flour mixture. Stir to combine ingredients, then beat 2 minutes. Stir in nuts, cherries, and coconut. Drop by teaspoonfuls on greased baking sheets. Bake in moderately hot oven (375 F.) 10 to 15 minutes.

RAINBOW COCONUT KISSES

Makes 3 dozen:

½ cup evaporated milk
½ cup sugar
2 cups shredded coconut
¼ teaspoon almond or vanilla extract
few drops vegetable coloring

Combine all ingredients except vegetable coloring. Divide in half and add pink coloring to one half and green to the other. Drop from a teaspoon onto a well-oiled (not buttered) baking sheet. Bake in a moderately slow oven (325 F.) 15 minutes. Remove from pan while hot.

SPICED COFFEE DROPS

Makes about 5 dozen:

1¾ cups sifted enriched flour
½ teaspoon baking powder
½ teaspoon soda
½ teaspoon cinnamon
½ teaspoon cloves
½ teaspoon nutmeg
1 teaspoon instant coffee
¼ teaspoon salt
1 cup brown sugar
½ cup butter
1 egg
½ cup water
½ cup chopped nuts
½ cup chopped dates

Combine flour, baking powder, soda, spices, coffee, and salt. Sift twice. Add sugar, shortening, egg. Stir to combine ingredients, then beat 2 minutes. Stir in nuts and dates. Drop by teaspoonfuls 2 inches apart on greased baking sheets. Bake in hot oven (400 F.) 10 minutes.

CHAPTER 4

THE LITTLE CAKES—
THE ONE-LAYER CAKES

9 UPSIDE-DOWN CAKES . . . . . WITH THIS RECIPE

BASIC UPSIDE-DOWN CAKE BATTER MADE WITH 1 EGG

Makes one 8-inch square:

1⅓ cups sifted cake flour
2 teaspoons double-acting baking powder
¼ teaspoon salt
¾ cup granulated sugar
¼ cup butter or other shortening
1 egg, unbeaten
½ cup milk
1 teaspoon vanilla

Sift flour once; measure; add baking powder, salt, and granulated sugar, and sift together three times. Cream shortening. Add sifted dry ingredients, egg, milk, and vanilla. Stir just until all flour is dampened, then beat vigorously 1 minute.

Pour batter over any of the following toppings in 8 x 8 x 2-inch pan. Bake in moderate oven (350 F.) 50 minutes, or until cake springs back when pressed lightly. Cool cake in pan 5 minutes. Then invert on serving plate and let stand 1 minute before removing pan. Serve warm with whipped cream.

Toppings

CHERRY UPSIDE-DOWN CAKE: Prepare Basic Upside-Down Cake Batter. For the topping, melt ¼ cup butter in 8 x 8 x 2-inch pan or 8-inch skillet. Add ½ cup granulated sugar and blend well. Remove from heat. Arrange 1¾ cups pitted and drained red cherries (fresh or canned) on sugar mixture.

COCONUT BUTTERSCOTCH UPSIDE-DOWN CAKE: Prepare Basic Upside-Down Cake Batter. For the topping, sauté 1 cup finely cut coconut in 1 tablespoon melted butter in an 8 x 8 x 2-inch pan until golden brown. Then add 3 tablespoons more butter, ½ cup firmly packed brown sugar, and ¼ cup water; heat until blended, stirring constantly.

CRANBERRY SAUCE UPSIDE-DOWN CAKE: Prepare Basic Upside-Down Cake Batter. For the topping, spread 2 cups (16-ounce can) cranberry sauce in bottom of greased 8 x 8 x 2-inch pan.

CRANBERRY UPSIDE-DOWN CAKE: Prepare Upside-Down Cake Batter. For the topping, melt 3 tablespoons butter in 8 x 8 x 2-inch pan. Add 6 tablespoons sugar and 1 tablespoon grated orange rind; mix well. Sprinkle 1½ cups fresh cranberries, cut in halves, over sugar mixture.

FRESH BLUEBERRY UPSIDE-DOWN CAKE: Prepare Basic Upside-Down Cake Batter. For the topping, melt 3 tablespoons butter in 8 x 8 x 2-inch pan. Add ⅓ cup firmly packed brown sugar; mix well. On this arrange 1¾ cups fresh blueberries; sprinkle with ½ teaspoon grated lemon rind and 2 teaspoons lemon juice.

LOG CABIN UPSIDE-DOWN CAKE: Prepare Basic Upside-Down Cake Batter. For the topping, melt 2 tablespoons butter in 8 x 8 x 2-inch pan. Remove from heat and add ⅓ cup corn syrup. On this arrange 4 slices pineapple cut in wedges or 1½ cups drained canned fruit combined with 1 teaspoon grated orange rind. If you like, sprinkle 1 cup broken pecan meats over the fruit.

NORMANDY UPSIDE-DOWN CAKE: Prepare Basic Upside-Down Cake Batter. For the topping, melt ¼ cup butter in 8 x 8 x 2-inch pan. Add ½ cup firmly packed brown sugar and ¼ teaspoon cinnamon and mix well. Pare and slice thin 2 large apples; arrange on sugar mixture, overlapping slices. Sprinkle with 1 teaspoon lemon juice.

PEACH UPSIDE-DOWN CAKE: Prepare Basic Upside-Down Cake Batter. For the topping, melt ¼ cup butter in 8 x 8 x 2-inch pan or 8-inch skillet. Add ½ cup firmly packed brown sugar and blend well. Arrange 1¼ cups well-drained sliced peaches over the sugar mixture.

PRUNE UPSIDE-DOWN CAKE: Prepare Basic Upside-Down Cake Batter. For the topping, melt ¼ cup butter in 8 x 8 x 2-inch pan or 8-inch skillet. Add ½ cup firmly packed brown sugar and blend well. Arrange 6 cooked prunes, halved, pitted, and stuffed with pecans, over the sugar mixture.

THE COLA PARTY TABLE . . QUICK BUT BEAUTIFUL

You want the table to look pretty, flowers or no flowers, even if it is early in the morning—at least before noon—when friends come in for cola.

• Make three cakes with mixes—chocolate, white, and Honey Spice. Bake single layers in oblong pans.

• Take a third of the cake needed for the cola party from each oblong. Use the rest of the cake for the family dinner or wrap and freeze. Your table will look like a flower garden if you serve these with three colors in the frostings for the three cakes.

• Frost white cake squares with Nesselrode, Orange, or Chocolate Frosting.

• Use Pink Mint, White Vanilla, or Deep Chocolate Frosting on the chocolate cake.

• Try Mocha, Maple, or Lemon Frosting on spice cake.

• Add a big spoonful of raspberry jam or apricot to whipped cream to frost cupcakes or a big cake.

• Ice cakes as the French do, with your favorite jelly, which appears to be a glaze after it has set a little, then with the pastry gun make a whipped cream decoration of a fancy edge or crisscross design.

• Add crushed pineapple to whipped cream when you are going to serve it on gingerbread squares. This is especially nice for children.

• Fill cake with chilled applesauce, frost with Nutmeg Butter Frosting, or 7-Minute Frosting Elégante flavored with ½ teaspoon ground nutmeg.

• Try strained cranberry sauce with cream cheese to make a cream cheese frosting on cupcakes or big cakes.

PEANUT BUTTER FROSTING

To frost 16 cupcakes:

1½ tablespoons butter
3 tablespoons peanut butter
½ teaspoon vanilla
½ teaspoon salt
1½ cups sifted confectioners' sugar
3 tablespoons milk, scalded

Combine and blend first four ingredients. Beat in sugar, alternately add scalded milk, beating constantly until blended. If necessary, add a little more milk for the correct spreading consistency.

CREAM CHEESE FROSTING

Covers two 9-inch layers:

3 tablespoons butter
6 ounces (2 packages) cream cheese
⅛ teaspoon salt
1¼ cups sifted confectioners' sugar
½ teaspoon vanilla

Combine softened butter, cheese, and salt; blend. Add the sugar a little at a time, continuing to stir vigorously. Add vanilla and chill until right consistency for spreading.

ORANGE-CREAM CHEESE FROSTING

Make Cream Cheese Frosting, adding 1 teaspoon grated orange peel to the butter when it is being softened, and food coloring to tint it.

MAPLE FLUFF TOPPING

Makes 2½ cups:

2 eggs, well beaten
½ cup maple-flavored syrup
2 tablespoons sugar
¼ teaspoon salt
3 tablespoons lemon juice
1 cup heavy cream, whipped

Combine eggs, syrup, sugar, salt, and lemon juice in top of double boiler. Mix well. Cook over boiling water, stirring constantly, until mixture is slightly thickened, about 3 minutes. Remove from heat. Cool; then chill. Just before serving, fold in whipped cream.

Delicious on gingerbread, chocolate cake squares (on fruit betty or steamed puddings too).

CAKE SQUARES . . . WORTHY OF ACQUAINTANCE

COCONUT-PINEAPPLE SQUARES

Makes 3 dozen:

½ cup soft butter
¼ cup sugar
1¼ cups sifted flour
1 cup canned crushed pineapple, well drained
½ cup sugar
1 egg, well beaten
1 tablespoon melted butter
1½ cups shredded, cut coconut

Mix ½ cup butter and ¼ cup sugar with pastry blender or fork. Add flour and mix until crumbs are formed. Then mix thoroughly with hands until soft dough is formed. Press evenly into bottom of 9 x 9 x 2-inch pan, extending dough about ½ inch up the sides. Prick bottom with fork. Bake in moderate oven (350 F.) 15 minutes, or until crust begins to brown. Remove from oven.

Spread pineapple evenly over crust. Add ½ cup sugar to well-beaten egg; beat until blended. Fold in 1 tablespoon melted butter and the coconut. Spread mixture evenly over the pineapple. Return to oven and bake 20 minutes longer, or until topping is browned. Cool. Cut in 1½-inch squares.

FUDGE SQUARES

Makes 16 squares:

⅔ cup sifted cake flour
½ teaspoon baking powder
¼ teaspoon salt
1 cup sugar
2 eggs, well beaten
2 squares melted chocolate
¼ cup salad oil
1 teaspoon vanilla
½ cup coarsely chopped nutmeats

Sift together flour, baking powder, and salt. Gradually add sugar to well-beaten eggs and beat well. Add melted chocolate and salad oil. Add vanilla, sifted dry ingredients, and nutmeats; blend well. Bake in oiled 8-inch-square pan in moderate oven (350 F.) 35 minutes. Cut into squares while warm.

BAKED-ON . . . . OVEN-FROSTED CAKES

COCONUT HONEY-TOPPED CAKE

Makes one 9-inch square:

1 package white cake mix
Coconut Honey Topping

Prepare white cake mix according to package directions. Pour batter into 9 x 9 x 2-inch pan. Bake in moderate oven (350 F.) 40 to 45 minutes. While still hot, spread Coconut Honey Topping over cake and bake as directed.

COCONUT HONEY TOPPING:

¼ cup sugar
1 cup shredded, coarsely cut coconut
dash of salt
⅓ cup melted butter
2 tablespoons light cream
½ cup honey
½ teaspoon vanilla

Combine all ingredients and mix thoroughly. Spread carefully over hot cake in pan. Place in moderate oven (350 F.) 15 to 20 minutes, or until topping is brown and bubbly.

COCOA MACAROON TOPPING BAKED ON CAKE BATTER

Makes one 9-inch square:

1 package white cake mix
3 egg whites, unbeaten
dash of salt
¾ cup sugar
¼ cup cocoa
¼ teaspoon vanilla
¾ cup cut coconut

Prepare cake mix according to package directions. Pour batter in 9 x 9 x 2-inch pan which has been lined on bottom with paper.

Beat egg whites and salt until foamy throughout. Add sugar, 2 tablespoons at a time, beating after each addition until sugar is blended. Continue beating until mixture will stand in stiff peaks. Fold in cocoa and vanilla. Then fold in coconut. Spread on cake batter in pan. Bake in moderately hot oven (375 F.) about 10 minutes longer than directed for cake. Cool 10 minutes, then remove cake from pan.

When you feel reckless, sprinkle an additional ¾ cup cut coconut on cake batter in pan before spreading with meringue mixture.

FROST YOUR CAKE . . . . . . THEN BROIL IT

BROILED BANANA-COCONUT TOPPING

To frost 9 x 13-inch cake:

3 to 4 bananas, sliced diagonally
¼ cup butter
¾ cup brown sugar, firmly packed
1½ tablespoons milk
¾ cup shredded, coarsely cut coconut

Arrange bananas in four rows lengthwise on cake, overlapping ends of slices.

Cream butter and sugar together. Add milk and beat until smooth. Add coconut. Spread over cake and bananas and place under broiler about 3 minutes, or until sugar is bubbly and coconut is slightly browned. Serve while slightly warm, cutting cake in pan.

COCOA-CARAMEL TOPPING

To frost 9-inch square:

2 tablespoons butter
⅓ cup brown sugar, firmly packed
4 teaspoons cocoa
2 tablespoons milk
¼ cup finely chopped nutmeats

Cream together butter, sugar, and cocoa. Add milk and mix well. Spread over hot cake in pan and sprinkle with nuts.

PINEAPPLE BROILED FROSTING

To frost 8- or 9-inch square cake:

3 tablespoons butter or margarine
⅓ cup drained crushed pineapple
½ cup shredded coconut
½ cup brown sugar, firmly packed
¼ cup chopped walnuts

Heat butter and pineapple; add other ingredients and blend well. Spread lightly on hot or cold loaf or layer of plain cake; place low under broiler and broil slowly until bubbly and lightly browned. Serve slightly warm.

part two

THE DESSERT "400"

DESSERTS ARE PHOTOGENIC . . . COLORFUL, DELICIOUS

This is a Dessert "400" for the reason that the cakes and pies, sweet-filled pancakes and fritters, the cookies and the refrigerator cakes and ice creams, and all the other desserts included are *selected.* They are here because each is something special in its class, or something long recognized as tops in flavor and for which a recipe must be included. A Christmas pudding is an example of this last. You can't snub an English pudding, even if you decide to freeze yours instead of steam it or settle for a Coffee Delight Parfait Pie for Christmas. Or for that great beauty of an Ice-Cream Cranberry Pie.

How I long for color . . . color . . . color. Each of this "400" should have its portrait painted, for you might like to see exactly how it looks. The cakes, too, the way they look filled with one creamy in-between layer, frosted with something different suggested by those "fashion separates" for cakes. All these I wish that you could see.

CHAPTER 5
CAKES, PUDDINGS, AND HOLIDAY DESSERTS

LET'S TALK ABOUT CAKE

BAKING IT . . . FILLING IT . . . FROSTING IT

Let's talk about fillings and frostings for fabulous layer cakes. We don't have to talk about eating them. That will happen fast enough. Most of you are cake bakers already. As for me, I am a cake *eater,* and you won't catch me missing my afternoon nap to bake one from start to finish when the mixes have done it pretty well for me. Anyway, my interest lies in the flourishes, in splitting the snowy-white or chocolaty layers and filling them (I make that part), and in frosting them.

A little row of those bottles of vegetable coloring are as necessary as the cake layer, in my opinion. With them you can make a lemony filling *look* as it is going to taste—full of lemon. And you can whip up a fashionable plate of cake squares with the one white cake batter baked in an oblong pan. Then divide frosting into four parts and sprinkle away with whatever colors strike your fancy, making four tinted frostings and goodness knows how many different squares by the time you shave a bit of chocolate on top of one or two and a bit of orange peel on another and drop bits of coconut on a few others or plant a banana circle in the middle of a few. Between colors and conniving, the Ritz itself couldn't outdo you. All because of those color bottles getting you started.

Aunt Minnie's banana cake and Mother's angel food are the ones I remember best. Thank heavens neither one of them ever heard of a mix. Aunt Minnie's white fluffy layers were baked in the days when "break sixteen eggs" might appear in a recipe for a big cake and she broke 'em without batting an eye. Somehow, when the budget was low, as it often was, she could bake a two-egg cake that would melt in your mouth. The layers were put together with creamy frosting in which banana slices were well immersed. The frosting was thick all over it and the cake was decorated modestly with a circle of the banana slices around the top. Two bananas would do it. But it "stood" awhile. By slicing time banana flavor was all through the cake, delicate as perfume and just as heady.

As for angel food at our house, it rarely got frosted. After tiptoeing for the duration of its baking so as "not to make it fall," it was a prima donna without being adorned by frosting. We permitted it to cool, but then we ate it. Usually with ice cream. And with ice cream, angel food does not need frosting. Besides, it is so nice and crumbly brown on the outside.

Whether or not you bake your cakes the whole way or halfway, emphasis here is on filling, frosting, and decorating them, and on combinations of colors and fillings and frostings you may not have tried.

A few recipes of each type of cake are given for convenience in case your own are not handy.

Baking is made easier, surer, when you have a few of the right measuring gadgets. Do you have a measuring cup that holds exactly 1 cup to the brim? If you do, and one of those little flour sifters that can sit on it, half the measuring battle is won. Sift the flour into the cup, level by swooping a spatula across the top, and there you are with 1 cup sifted flour, just like the recipe says.

Measuring liquids is easier in a measuring cup that extends above the 1-cup mark, and since it is a nuisance to have numerous gadgets when a few will do, why not have a 2-cup measuring cup for the liquids and for larger amounts?

And spoons. A set of four attached at the handle ends, measuring the ½ teaspoon and ¼ that worry you without them.

If you use shortening that must be cut in, one of the pastry blenders will make short, light work of the job.

And do you know why mixing bowls have round bottoms? It is so part of the contents will not get off in a corner and be neglected—unmixed and a troublemaker.

A scraper from the ten-cent store—or from anywhere. That you must have. Rubber paddle on a colored stick, but it scrapes your bowls clean, puts the batter you are mixing off the side and down into the beater traffic. That you need.

Pastry brushes are easy to come by. With them you paint on the oil or butter with evenness, quickly and thoroughly, whether it is brushing the top of a loaf with butter or greasing a cookie sheet or the bottom of muffin tins.

And if you have inherited a marble-topped chest, don't worry about a pastry board, you have the perfect one. Marble is cold as well as smooth and hard. On it pastry "handles" well, stays chilled yet workable. Just thought I'd mention it.

These are the pans you use for baking:

9-inch square, 2-inch deep cake pan
cookie sheet
muffin tins
9 x 5 x 3-inch loaf pan
15 x 10 x 1-inch jelly-roll pan
13 x 9 x 2-inch flat pan
8-inch spring-form pan, 3-inches deep
9-inch spring-form pan
melon mold with lid
two 9-inch pie pans
three 9-inch cake pans
8-cup ring mold
angel-cake tube pan

CAKE LORE . . . . REMINDERS

• Put cakes on a cake rack when they come out of the oven. Let them stay in the pan for 10 to 15 minutes. Then loosen the sides from the pan with a spatula, being careful not to break the edge. Put another cooling rack on top of the warm cake—turn it over and lift off the pan.

• Cakes should be thoroughly cooled before they are frosted, unless directions say otherwise.

• Brush loose crumbs from cake with a pastry brush before you begin to frost it.

• When joining two layers for a cake, join the bottom of each layer. Turn one bottom side up so that the rougher portion is covered with the filling or frosting. Place the second layer on top side up for the smooth surface that the slight crust of the cake provides.

• Frost the sides of your cake first, using up-and-down strokes. Bring the frosting up and just over the top of the cake. Then pile the rest of the frosting on top and spread it out to the rim in graceful swirls or peaks, depending upon the frosting.

• If you intend to add decorations, make a smooth top.

• There are two ways to frost cupcakes. One is to cover the tops in a circular motion, ending at the center and leaving a little peak where the spatula left it. The other way is to turn the cupcakes upside down and frost the sides and then the tops.

• If nuts are to be added, press them into the frosting while it is soft.

• For coconut-covered cake, press the moist shreds onto the cake while the frosting is soft.

• To toast coconut, spread a thin layer in a shallow pan and place in a moderate oven (350 F.) until it browns. Stir it occasionally for even toasting.

• Chocolate "curls" can be made by shaving sweetened or unsweetened chocolate with a vegetable peeler or a sharp knife.

• Nuts and fruits, chopped or halved, are convenient quick cake decorations. With them make designs or outline words.

• Stake your course with a wood pick when decorating, then follow those lines dotted into the frosting.

Does this bore you? I hope not, for we might as well carry on about the decorating part. Decorating isn't work. It is every bit as much fun as blowing soap bubbles was at an earlier age.

TO GET YOU STARTED . . . DECORATE YOUR CAKES

Nuts, fruit, coconut, chocolate, small candies, and of course vegetable coloring are the handiest decorations for making a picture out of your cake.

The most fascinating part of cake-making in France was when the chef got ready to put on the final coating of frosting. A cake made of thin layers of cake, put together with numerous layers of filling, awaited this moment on a cooling rack. When the frosting was exactly the right temperature, the chef perched the rack up on a tin mold, drenched the cake with the warm sweet, and let 'er drip. In a matter of minutes the cake was airily cooling, smooth as glass without a mark on it, and the extra frosting scooped up off the marble slab for later use.

Simple Dribble Decoration

The "dribble" décor on our cakes always brings a picture to my mind of this frosting bath given the cakes in France. Suppose your cake has a delicately colored or a white frosting. Put ½ ounce unsweetened chocolate and ½ teaspoon butter or margarine in a little pan. Melt over hot water. Stir until blended. Cool a little. Spoon it around the rim of the cake and let it dribble down in irregular fingers of chocolate. Double the amount of chocolate mixture and pour it on top of a smoothly frosted cake and spread to cover the top and dribble down the sides as it will.

Be Brave—Buy and Use a Gun

Aluminum decorating guns with a variety of tips are inexpensive and so easy to use with professional-appearing results. With them, try decorations each time you bake. In a few days pictures of wedding bells, children, a message on the top or side of a cake, bands resembling ribbons "tying up" the cake as if it were a hatbox will make cake-making more pleasure than eating it . . . Well, anyway, you can make your cake and eat it too.

ANGEL CAKE HATBOX

For a gorgeous cake decoration that can be done by a beginner, cover an angel food cake with white Butter Frosting. Tint ½ cup Butter Frosting a delicate pink and put it in the decorating gun. Using a tip that allows frosting to come out in about a ¼-inch strip, put "ribbons" straight up one side, across the top, and down the other.

Now do the same across the cake, making the ribbons divide the cake into quarters. Do two more times across, and don't worry how ragged it is at the center hole or at the base of the cake. This divides the cake into portions, but also looks very gay. Lift it onto a paper lace doily. Put a wiggle of "ribbon" around its base and a little bunch of fresh garden flowers in the middle of the cake. Absolutely dreamy, and your first try.

THE "BEST" LAYER CAKE . IS THE ONE YOU LIKE BEST

DEEP DARK CHOCOLATE CAKE MADE WITH 2 EGG YOLKS AND BUTTER OR MARGARINE

Makes two 9-inch layers:

2 cups sifted cake flour
¾ teaspoon salt
4 squares unsweetened chocolate
4 tablespoons butter or margarine
2 cups sugar
2 egg yolks, unbeaten
1¾ cups milk, room temperature
1 teaspoon vanilla
1 teaspoon soda

Sift flour once; measure into sifter; add salt. Set aside.

Melt chocolate and shortening over hot water. Turn into mixing bowl. Cool to room temperature. (This is important.) Then add sugar and mix well. Mix egg yolks and 1 cup of the milk; add to chocolate mixture and blend. Sift in flour and mix until all flour is dampened, then beat 1 minute at low speed of electric mixer or about 150 strokes by hand. Add vanilla and ½ cup more of the milk; stir until smooth. Dissolve soda in remaining ¼ cup milk. Stir into batter quickly and thoroughly. Turn the thin batter into 2 greased 9-inch layer pans. Bake in moderate oven (350 F.) 30 minutes, or until done.

You can mix this cake entirely in a 2-quart double boiler. Melt chocolate and shortening first. Cool. Then proceed. Easy?

• Look at this recipe and the next for Devil's Food, and you will know how much they differ when chocolate or cocoa is used. Never try to use one for the other. It won't work.

DEVIL'S FOOD CAKE MADE WITH 4 EGGS

Makes two 9-inch layers:

2 cups sifted cake flour
1½ cups sugar
1½ teaspoons salt
4 teaspoons baking powder
⅔ cup cocoa
⅔ cup salad oil
4 egg yolks
1 cup water
1 teaspoon vanilla
¼ teaspoon cream of tartar
4 egg whites

Mix and sift first five ingredients. Make a well and add in order salad oil, egg yolks, water, and flavoring. Beat until smooth. Add cream of tartar to egg whites. Beat until whites form very stiff peaks. Gently fold first mixture into egg whites until well blended. Turn batter into 2 ungreased deep 9-inch layer pans. Bake in moderate oven (350 F.) 35 to 40 minutes, or until cake springs back when touched lightly with finger. Invert pans on 2 custard cups so that cake hangs free. Let stand until cold.

Cake may also be baked in an ungreased 10-inch tube pan at 325 F. 75 to 80 minutes. Invert pan over funnel or bottle to cool. Let stand until cold.

WHITE CAKE MADE WITH 3 EGGS AND BUTTER

Makes two 9-inch layers:

2¼ cups sifted cake flour
1½ cups sugar
2½ teaspoons double-acting baking powder or 4 teaspoons tartrate baking powder
¾ cup butter or margarine
¾ cup milk
1 teaspoon vanilla
1½ teaspoons milk
3 eggs, unbeaten

Sift flour, sugar, baking powder, and salt into mixing bowl. Drop in shortening and ½ cup milk, vanilla, and 1 egg. Beat 200 strokes (2 minutes by hand or in mixer at low speed). Use rubber scraper to scrape bowl and spoon or beater. Add remaining milk and 2 eggs and beat 200 strokes as before. Bake in 2 well-greased cake pans in moderately hot oven (375 F.) about 30 minutes. Fine texture, moist and delicious, this buttery cake is good for coffee, and coffee good for it.

A LARGE WHITE CAKE MADE WITH 4 EGGS AND SALAD OIL, NO BUTTER

Makes two 9-inch layers:

2⅔ cups sifted cake flour
1½ cups sugar
1½ teaspoons salt
4 teaspoons baking powder
⅔ cup salad oil
4 egg yolks
¾ cup water
1 teaspoon vanilla
2 teaspoons orange extract
¼ teaspoon cream of tartar
4 egg whites

Mix and sift first four ingredients. Make a well and add in order salad oil, egg yolks, water, and flavorings. Beat until smooth. Add cream of tartar to egg whites. Beat until whites form very stiff peaks. Gently fold first mixture into egg whites until well blended. Turn batter into 2 ungreased deep 9-inch layer pans. Bake in moderate oven (350 F.) 35 to 40 minutes, or until cake springs back when touched lightly with finger. Invert pans on cooling rack or rest them on 2 custard cups so that cake hangs free until cool.

PARTY CAKES . . . WITH COCONUT IN THE BATTER

SENEGALESE CAKE MADE WITH 3½ EGGS

Makes three 9-inch layers:

2¾ cups sifted cake flour
1¾ cups sugar
2 teaspoons double-acting baking powder
1½ teaspoon salt
1 cup butter or margarine
¾ cup milk
1 teaspoon almond extract
1 teaspoon orange extract
3 eggs, unbeaten
1 egg yolk, unbeaten
1 cup finely cut coconut

Combine the cake flour, sugar, baking powder, and salt. Sift together. When blended, add the shortening, milk, flavorings, and 1 unbeaten egg. Beat 200 strokes (2 minutes by hand or in mixer at low speed). Use rubber spatula to scrape bowl and spoon or beater. Add the remaining 2 eggs and the 1 yolk. Beat 200 strokes as before. Stir in the coconut. When thoroughly mixed, pour into 3 round 9-inch well-greased pans. Bake in moderately hot oven (375 F.) 25 minutes, or until done.

CHOCOLATE SENEGALESE CAKE MADE WITH 2 EGGS

Makes two 9-inch layers:

1¾ cups sifted cake flour
1½ cups sugar
¾ teaspoon salt
½ teaspoon double-acting baking powder
¾ teaspoon soda
½ cup butter or homogenized shortening
3 ounces chocolate, melted
1 cup thick sour milk or buttermilk
1 teaspoon vanilla
2 eggs, unbeaten
1 cup finely cut coconut

Combine sifted cake flour, sugar, salt, baking powder, and soda and sift together to blend. Add shortening, melted chocolate, milk, and vanilla. Beat 200 strokes (2 minutes by hand or in mixer at low speed). Use rubber spatula to scrape bowl and spoon or beater. Add the unbeaten eggs and repeat beating as before. Stir in the coconut, and when blended pour into 2 round 9-inch well-greased pans. Bake in moderate oven (350 F.) until done, about 25 minutes.

SERVE A SPICE CAKE . . . . WHEN IT'S COLD OUT

Makes two 8-inch layers:

2 cups sifted cake flour
1⅓ cups sugar
2 teaspoons double-acting baking powder
¼ teaspoon soda
½ teaspoon each cinnamon, nutmeg, allspice
1 teaspoon salt
½ cup homogenized vegetable shortening
½ cup unsweetened prune juice
½ cup milk
1 teaspoon vanilla
2 eggs, unbeaten

Combine dry ingredients and sift together into a mixing bowl. Add vegetable shortening, prune juice, ¼ cup milk, and vanilla. Beat 200 strokes (2 minutes by hand, or in mixer at low speed). Use rubber spatula to scrape bowl and spoon or beater. Add remaining milk and the eggs. Beat as before. Pour into well-greased pans and bake in a moderate oven (350 F.) until done, about 30 minutes.

APPLESAUCE MERINGUE CAKE

Make a two-layer spice cake. Split layers in half; spread cut sides of layers with thin coating of melted currant jelly. Cool. Put the four thin layers together with Applesauce Filling, making the applesauce layers about ¼ inch thick, alternating so that with uncut cake layer forming smooth top and bottom, the cake and applesauce layers are almost the same thickness. Chill 30 minutes. Coat the outside of the cake with Meringue Frosting and brown lightly.

APPLESAUCE FILLING:

Chill sweetened applesauce and spread ¼ inch thick between layers. This is good with either white or chocolate cake, as well as with gingerbread or spice cake.

FEATHER-LIGHT . . LET'S BEGIN WITH ANGEL FOOD

ANGEL FOOD CAKE MADE WITH 10 TO 12 EGGS

For 9-inch angel food pan:

¾ cup sifted cake flour
1¼ cups sifted sugar
¼ teaspoon salt
1¼ cups egg whites
1 teaspoon cream of tartar
1 teaspoon vanilla

Sift flour once, measure, add ¼ cup sugar, and sift together four times. Add salt to egg whites and beat with rotary beater or flat wire whisk. When foamy, add cream of tartar and continue beating until eggs are stiff enough to hold moist peaks, but not dry. Add remaining cup of sugar, 2 tablespoons at a time, beating with rotary beater or whisk after each addition until sugar is just blended. Fold in vanilla. Then sift about ¼ cup flour over mixture and fold in lightly; repeat until all flour is used. Turn into ungreased 9-inch angel food pan. Cut gently through batter with knife to remove air bubbles. Bake in slow oven (325 F.) 50 minutes, or until done. Remove from oven and invert pan 1 hour, or until cold. Loosen edges with spatula. Frost or eat as it is.

CHOCOLATE ANGEL FOOD CAKE MADE WITH 10 TO 12 EGGS

Follow recipe for white Angel Food Cake. Add 4 tablespoons cocoa to sugar; mix and proceed as for Angel Food Cake.

Make one chocolate and one white cake for company.

AND IF YOU WANT TO MEET . . . ITS NEAR RELATIONS

GOLDEN ANGEL SPONGE CAKE MADE WITH 5 EGGS

For 9-inch tube pan or 12 large muffin tins:

5 egg whites
1 cup sugar
1 tablespoon lemon
5 egg yolks
1 teaspoon vanilla
1 tablespoon grated lemon rind
1 cup cake flour
¼ teaspoon salt

Beat egg whites until stiff but not dry and gradually beat in ⅓ cup of the sugar. Combine lemon with egg yolks, add vanilla and beat until creamy and light in color. Add lemon rind and the remaining sugar and blend well. When well blended, add slowly to the egg whites, folding in the first third with vigorous strokes, then folding the remainder gently until blended. Sift the flour once, add salt, then sift again. Fold gently into the egg mixture, handling the batter very carefully. Pour into ungreased angel food pan or spoon into ungreased muffin tins. Bake 1 hour in slow oven (325 F.). Invert on cooling rack until cool.

CHIFFON CAKE MADE WITH 6 EGGS

For 10-inch tube pan:

2¼ cups sifted cake flour
1½ cups sugar
3 teaspoons baking powder
1 teaspoon salt
½ cup salad oil
6 egg yolks
¾ cup water
1 teaspoon grated lemon rind
2 teaspoons vanilla
½ teaspoon cream of tartar
6 egg whites

Mix and sift first four ingredients. Make a well and add in order salad oil, egg yolks, water, lemon rind, and vanilla. Beat with spoon until smooth. Add cream of tartar to egg whites. Beat until egg whites form *very stiff* peaks. Gently fold first mixture into egg whites until well blended. Fold, do not stir. Turn batter into ungreased 10-inch tube pan. Bake in moderate oven (325 F.) 70 to 75 minutes, or until cake springs back when touched lightly with finger. Immediately invert pan over funnel or bottle to cool. Let stand until cold. To remove from pan, loosen side of cake with spatula.

P.S. This cake may also be baked in 9 x 13-inch loaf pan in moderate oven (350 F.) 40 to 45 minutes. Then slit a triangle out of the top by cutting at an angle on the right side, then on the left to form a trough. Lift this long three-cornered wedge from the top of the cake, spoon some of your favorite frosting into the trough, and press the long triangular wedge down again. You do not need to frost the cake. It is a thing of beauty.

BAKE AN ANGEL FOOD . . . . WITH MIX

Bake angel food mix, following the directions on the package but baking in muffin tins like cupcakes. Make a cone from a double layer of waxed paper; fill it with sweetened whipped cream to which ½ cup thawed, frozen crushed berries has been added for each cup of cream. Force this out of the small end of the cone in an attractive design on each individual cake. Serve immediately.

Bake the cake batter in 2 ring molds. Cool but do not frost. Fill the center with fruit. Arrange whipped cream in big spoonfuls around the base of the cake to form a circle around it. Garnish the whipped cream with fruits or berries.

CRANBERRY ANGEL CAKE

This idea is a pretty party-time cake stretcher. Split the angel cake (or a sponge cake, for that matter) to make two layers. Put them together again with:

CRANBERRY FILLING

1 pound can whole cranberry sauce
1 tablespoon cornstarch
1 tablespoon lemon juice
grated rind of ½ lemon

Keep out a few whole berries to decorate the cake. Then mix the cranberry sauce and cornstarch together. Heat, stirring constantly until thickened. Add lemon juice and grated rind. Cool and spread on the cake as a filling. Then frost whole cake with:

WHIPPED FROSTING

1 teaspoon unflavored gelatin
¼ cup cold water
¼ cup heavy cream, scalded
1¾ cups heavy cream, whipped
¼ teaspoon salt
¼ cup confectioners' sugar
1 teaspoon lemon juice

Soften gelatin in water—you know *that* routine, of course. Then add it to the scalded cream; stir until dissolved. Chill and whip. To the 1¾ cups heavy cream which has been whipped, add the salt, sugar, and lemon juice and fold in the gelatin mixture. Frost the cake and garnish with whole cooked cranberries. This makes a cake that would serve 10 turn into a 12-serving capacity.

RING-AROUND-THE-ROSY CAKES TO BLESS THE BRIDE AND GROOM

The prettiest effect imaginable is one of the easiest. Just bake white cake or angel cake in ring molds or in tube pans. Be sure they are the same size if you have several cakes. Frost with Butter Frosting tinted with vegetable coloring to achieve any array of colors desired.

Then make a garden corsage by tucking flowers through a small lace paper doily. Violets . . . violets with rosebuds . . . rosebuds with the tiny rose leaves showing . . . forget-me-nots . . . white or yellow daisies—any combination you like. Don't cut off the stems until you settle a small glass in the center of the cake and fill the glass less than ⅔ full of water. Trim stems; settle the nosegay into the center of the cake.

Violets or blue flowers or roses in a white cake, yellow roses in the center of a blue-frosted cake.

GOLDEN ANGEL CAKE

1 package angel cake mix
¾ cup sugar
2 tablespoons flour
⅛ teaspoon salt
2 eggs, slightly beaten
1½ cups (No. 2 can) crushed pineapple
juice of 1 lemon
1 cup heavy cream, whipped
½ cup slivered, toasted almonds

Prepare angel cake according to directions on package. Mix sugar, flour, and salt in top of double boiler. Add eggs, pineapple, and lemon juice and mix together thoroughly. Cook over boiling water, stirring constantly until mixture becomes thick, 12 to 15 minutes. Remove from heat. Cool, stirring occasionally. Chill in refrigerator. Whip cream stiff and fold into pineapple mixture. Split angel cake into three layers. Put layers together with pineapple filling, reserving ⅓ filling for frosting top of cake. Garnish with slivered toasted almonds.

FOR ANGEL CAKES . . FROSTINGS MUST BE FESTIVE

Doesn't everyone like to *inhale* angel-light cake, as if he were an angel? No frosting. But they are ravishing, too, frosted. You want a party cover for this dream boat of a cake? These are the ones to think about:

NESSELRODE FROSTING

To cover angel food cake:

Prepare 7-Minute Frosting Elégante, cutting the ingredients in half and beating them 4 minutes. Fold in 3 tablespoons coarsely chopped candied cherries, ⅓ cup coarsely chopped walnuts or pecans, 8 marshmallows cut in sixths. This is particularly beautiful over Golden Angel Sponge or Chiffon Cake, and of course is appropriate for the holidays.

CHOCOLATE BUTTER FROSTING

To cover angel food cake:

3 squares unsweetened chocolate
1½ cups sifted confectioners' sugar
2½ tablespoons hot water
3 egg yolks
4 tablespoons butter

Melt chocolate in top of double boiler. Remove top from boiling water and add sugar and water to blend. Add egg yolks, one at a time, beating well after each addition. Add butter, a spoonful at a time, continuing to beat thoroughly.

FOR ANGEL CAKES . . . . OR ANY CAKE

7-MINUTE FROSTING ELÉGANTE

Covers tops and sides of two 9-inch layers:

2 egg whites, unbeaten
1½ cups sugar
5 tablespoons cold water
1 teaspoon light corn syrup
⅛ teaspoon salt
½ teaspoon orange extract
½ teaspoon almond extract
2 marshmallows

In top of double boiler combine unbeaten egg whites, sugar, water, corn syrup, and salt. Mix thoroughly. Place over rapidly boiling water and beat constantly with a rotary beater until the mixture will hold a peak (7 minutes). Remove from hot water; add the flavorings and marshmallows which have been cut into pieces. Continue beating until cool and thick enough to spread.

8 FLAVORS FROM 7-MINUTE FROSTING ELÉGANTE

• Divide frosting in half, using either white 7-Minute Elégante or Mocha Frosting. Stir ½ cup cut coconut into one half and use for filling. Frost top with the plain half. Stop right there, or go on to press more cut coconut into soft frosted sides, covering it all around.

• Add ½ cup chopped black walnuts to the half of frosting used for filling; use larger pieces or halves to decorate top. Or press chopped nuts into the entire sides of the cake and leave top plain.

• This cake, with sides covered with chopped nuts or coconut, is a good one to use on occasions when a name or date or greeting is spelled out on the top with nuts or with a pastry gun filled with deeper-colored frosting.

• Make a cool-looking cake by using Green Mint Frost. Replace extracts by ¼ teaspoon peppermint and few drops of green coloring. Decorate top with mint candy leaves.

• Peppermint Frosting, tinted pink, using peppermint instead of extracts, is ravishing when bitter chocolate shavings form curls to frame the top.

• Make Coconut Cake by using snowy-white 7-Minute Elégante, adding ½ cup cut coconut to half the frosting. Use it for thick filling. Frost with plain frosting, then press coconut shreds, not cut, all over cake sides and top while frosting is soft.

• Make Banana Cake by covering the filling with slices of banana before placing second layer on top. Frost cake and decorate with dots of banana slices around edge of top while frosting is soft. Make center decoration of seven slices close together resembling flower petals.

FIESTA FROSTING

Make 7-Minute Elégante Frosting, replacing orange extract with vanilla. When cool, fold in 1 cup finely chopped mixed preserved fruit (candied cherries, citron, and dates) and 1 cup chopped pecans.

MOCHA FROSTING

Add 2 teaspoons cocoa and 2 teaspoons instant coffee to 7-Minute Frosting Elégante. Make filling between layers a good ¼ inch thick.

RICH FUDGE FROSTING

Covers two-layer 9-inch cake

3 squares unsweetened chocolate, shaved fine
2¼ cups sugar
¼ teaspoon salt
¾ cup undiluted evaporated milk
6 tablespoons butter or margarine
1½ tablespoons corn syrup
2 teaspoons vanilla

Combine all ingredients except vanilla in saucepan; place over medium heat and bring slowly to a full rolling boil, stirring constantly. Boil 2 minutes. Remove from heat, and when lukewarm add vanilla. Beat until thick enough to spread.

BERRY CREAM FILLING

To fill and frost cake with a light berry cream, whip 1¼ cups heavy cream, fold in ½ cup berries (fresh, sweetened or frozen). Fill and cover.

"NO-COOK" ORANGE FROSTING

To frost two 9-inch layers:

¼ teaspoon salt
2 egg whites
¼ cup sugar
¾ cup light corn syrup
2 tablespoons grated orange rind
food coloring

Add salt to egg whites and beat with rotary beater until mixture forms soft peaks. Gradually add sugar, 1 tablespoon at a time, beating until smooth and glossy. Slowly add syrup, beating thoroughly after each addition, until firm peaks are formed. Fold in grated orange. Tint with food coloring.

COCONUT UNCOOKED FROSTING

Make exactly as above, omitting food coloring. Use 1¼ teaspoons vanilla instead of the grated orange. Sprinkle the whole cake with grated coconut.

SIX FLAVORS . . . . SIX COLORS

MARSHMALLOW FROSTING

Covers top and sides of two 9-inch layers:

¼ teaspoon salt
2 egg whites
¼ cup sugar
¾ cup dark or light corn syrup
1¼ teaspoons vanilla

No marshmallows in this, but you will think there are!

Add salt to egg whites and beat with electric or rotary beater until mixture forms soft peaks. Gradually add sugar, about 1 tablespoon at a time, beating until smooth and glossy. Continue beating and add syrup a little at a time, beating thoroughly after each addition until frosting stands in firm peaks. Fold in vanilla.

BEIGE FROSTING: Omit vanilla and add 2 teaspoons undiluted frozen orange juice. Add 1 tablespoon cocoa with syrup.

COFFEE FROSTING: Omit vanilla; add 1 tablespoon instant coffee with syrup.

LEMON OR ORANGE FROSTING: Omit vanilla; fold in 2 teaspoons grated lemon or orange rind. Add few drops food coloring to give it the lemon or orange look.

SPICE FROSTING: Omit vanilla; add ½ teaspoon ginger, ¼ teaspoon cinnamon, and a few grains cloves with dark corn syrup.

COCONUT FROSTING: Fold in 1 cup shredded coconut with vanilla, or sprinkle 1 cup shredded coconut over top and sides of frosted cake.

BUTTER FROSTING

. . . MAKE ANY FLAVOR . . ANY COLOR

Butter Frosting spreads well, keeps well, freezes well, and is easily managed in a pastry gun or tube for cake decorations. Butter Frosting is extremely adaptable. It not only tastes good but looks good. Make it this way then, with a twist of the right bottle top to make any color you like and any flavor you want.

BUTTER FROSTING

Covers tops and sides of two 9-inch layers:

½ cup (1 stick) butter
1 pound package (2 cups) confectioners' sugar, sifted
⅛ teaspon salt
1 tablespoon cream
1 teaspoon vanilla
1 egg

Cream butter until soft and smooth. Add ⅓ of the sifted sugar and stir until blended. Add salt, cream, and vanilla. Blend. Add unbeaten egg and beat until smooth. Add remaining sugar. Continue beating, adding a little more cream if necessary for spreading consistency.

CHOCOLATE BUTTER FROSTING: Add 2 squares or more of bitter chocolate. Melt in top of double boiler. Add to Butter Frosting.

LEMON BUTTER FROSTING: Omit vanilla and replace cream with 2 tablespoons lemon juice. Add grated peel of 1 lemon.

ORANGE BUTTER FROSTING: Omit vanilla. Add 2 tablespoons orange juice, 2 teaspoons grated orange peel.

STRAWBERRY BUTTER FROSTING: Add ¼ cup strawberries (or raspberries) which have been drained. Add vegetable coloring to tint.

NUTMEG BUTTER FROSTING: Add ½ teaspoon nutmeg to Butter Frosting.

COFFEE OR MOCHA BUTTER FROSTING: Replace vanilla with coffee essence or with 2 teaspoons instant coffee mixed with the cream. Or with 1 teaspoon instant coffee and 2 teaspoons cocoa.

FROSTINGS AND FILLINGS . "FASHION SEPARATES"

For two-layer chocolate cake:

• Almost any of the 7-Minute Elégante Frostings mentioned for the white cakes are also good on chocolate and Devil's Food. White, mint-flavored but not tinted pink as for the white, is a delicious combination.

• Or spread a deep layer of vanilla pudding mix, prepared as for pudding, with milk reduced to 1¾ cups. When thickened and cooled, spread between layers and frost with Chocolate Fudge Frosting or with:

MERINGUE FROSTING

Covers two-layer 9-inch cake:

Beat 3 egg whites until mounds are formed when the beater is raised. Add 6 tablespoons sugar, a spoonful at a time, beating until it has been folded in. Continue beating until the meringue stands in heavy peaks. Coat the entire cake, using a spatula to make an attractive rough swirl on top. Place in a preheated oven (350 F.) for about 10 minutes, or until meringue is delicately browned.

• Fill chocolate cake with Orange Cream Filling and an orange-flavored frosting. Make half recipe to join 2-layer cake:

ORANGE CREAM FILLING

To join three 9-inch layers:

½ cup sugar
3 tablespoons quick-cooking tapioca
¼ teaspoon salt
1¼ cups undiluted evaporated milk
½ cup undiluted frozen orange juice
1 egg yolk
½ teaspoon lemon extract

Combine dry ingredients; mix in top of double boiler. Add milk slowly, stirring until blended, then cook 10 minutes longer, stirring constantly. Combine orange juice and egg yolk; blend. Add to the warm mixture, stirring hard. Cook 2 minutes. Cool; add extract. Chill and spread.

ORANGE-CHOCOLATE FROSTING

Covers two-layer 9-inch cake:

2 squares unsweetened chocolate
1 can (14 to 15 ounces) condensed milk
1 tablespoon water
⅛ teaspoon salt
1 teaspoon grated orange peel

Melt chocolate in top of double boiler. Add condensed milk slowly, stirring constantly. Add water and salt, continuing to stir until blended. Cook 5 minutes over rapidly boiling water, stirring constantly. Remove from heat and cool. Add grated orange peel when you are ready to frost the cake.

- Frost and cover with Lemon Filling and Lemon Butter Cream Frosting.
- Fill with custard filling and frost with white, vanilla-flavored 7-Minute Frosting Elégante.
- Frost with Green Mint Frost after filling with:

CHOCOLATE CREAM FILLING

To join two 9-inch layers:

2 squares unsweetened chocolate
1 cup undiluted evaporated milk
2 tablespoons cornstarch
6 tablespoons sugar
¼ teaspoon salt
1 egg yolk, beaten
½ teaspoon vanilla
2 tablespoons butter

Melt chocolate in top of double boiler; add milk slowly, stirring until blended. Combine cornstarch, sugar, salt; mix and add to chocolate mixture, stirring until thickened. Cook 10 minutes, stirring occasionally. Remove from heat. Add egg yolk, slowly beating it in with rotary beater. When blended, return to heat to cook 2 minutes more, stirring constantly. Add butter and vanilla. Blend. Chill before spreading.

BERRY FESTIVAL CAKE

Make 7-Minute Frosting Elégante or plain 7-Minute Frosting, using strained berry juice instead of water. Just before spreading, fold in ½ cup of the crushed berries which have been well drained.

BERRY FESTIVAL FILLING

Use package of vanilla pudding mix, reducing milk to 1¾ cups instead of the 2 cups designated on the package. For extra-rich filling, use undiluted evaporated milk. Add 2 tablespoons fresh or frozen berries for each cup of filling. Cool and make thick layer of filling between cake layers.

LEMON CREAM CAKE

Make two layers of chocolate or white cake. Split one layer. Using unsplit layer for center of cake, the split one for top and bottom, put layers together with double portion Lemon Filling. Frost cake with sweetened whipped cream. Decorate with grated lemon peel, nuts, or bitter chocolate curls to make border around top. To make the filling:

LEMON FILLING

To use between two 8-inch layers:

¾ cup sugar
2 tablespoons cornstarch
⅛ teaspoon salt
¼ cup lemon juice
grated rind of 1 lemon
3 egg yolks, slightly beaten
½ cup water
2 tablespoons butter or margarine

Combine sugar, cornstarch, and salt in top of double boiler. Add lemon juice and rind and stir until blended, stirring constantly. Add egg yolks, water, and butter, stirring constantly. Place over boiling water and cook until thick, continuing to stir.

PUDDING MIX FILLINGS . . . WHIPPED CREAM FROSTINGS

You want 1¼ cups filling to make a nice deep layer of goodness between two layers.

You need 2½ cups to make 2 layers of filling when your cake has 3 layers.

PUDDING MIX FILLING CHOOSE YOUR FLAVOR

Makes 2¼ cups:

1 package pudding mix, flavor you like
1¾ cups milk (¼ cup less than package directs)
½ cup heavy cream, whipped or ½ cup plus 1 tablespoon evaporated milk, whipped

Follow directions on the package to make pudding mix, using the reduced amount of milk mentioned above. When mixture is thickened and cooled, fold in whipped cream. If evaporated milk is used instead, chill ½ cup until crystals form, about 30 minutes. Turn into chilled bowl and whip with a cold beater until stiff.

• Use vanilla pudding mix. Then fold in ¾ cup well-drained berries or crushed fruit to vary flavor, when cream is being folded in.

• For stronger flavor in a vanilla pudding mix filling to which you intend to add berries, use part of the drained fruit juice to replace milk in cooking pudding.

• Remember, berries increase quantity of filling to about 3 cups. When you make this amount, split one of the layers so there will be three layers of the filling.

WHIPPED CREAM FROSTING CHOOSE YOUR COLOR

Makes about 5 cups:

2 cups heavy cream
¼ teaspoon salt
4 tablespoons confectioners' sugar
1 cup drained berries or chopped fruit or ½ cup prepared chocolate sauce

Whip cream and fold in the salt, sugar, and fruit, omitting sugar if fruit is sweetened. Chill a few minutes and frost one big cake with deep drift of frosting.

Use without fruit or sauce addition for cakes with deep layers of filling. Make it stiffer in texture by scalding ¼ cup of the cream and mixing it with 1 teaspoon unflavored gelatin which has been softened in ¼ cup water. Stir until dissolved. Cool, whip, and fold into whipped cream.

ROLL YOUR OWN . . . . . FILLED CAKE ROLLS

STRAWBERRY CREAM ROLL CHILL ROLLS SEVERAL HOURS BEFORE SLICING

Makes 8 servings:

WHITE CAKE:

¼ teaspoon salt
3 eggs
¾ cup sugar
1 teaspoon almond extract
¾ cup pancake mix

Grease sides and bottom of a 10½ x 15½-inch shallow pan (a jelly roll pan); line with waxed paper and grease again; dust with flour.

Add salt to eggs; beat until thick and lemon-colored. Add sugar a little at a time, beating well after each addition. Add flavoring and pancake mix; stir lightly until batter is smooth. Spread evenly in pan. Bake in hot oven (400 F.) 7 to 8 minutes, or until brown. Sprinkle a towel well with confectioners' sugar. Immediately on taking cake from oven loosen it around edges of pan and turn out on towel. Peel waxed paper carefully from cake. Roll cake in towel and let stand 10 minutes.

FILLING:

2 teaspoons unflavored gelatin
2 tablespoons water
1 cup heavy cream
1 cup sifted confectioners' sugar
1 pint (2 cups) strawberries, fresh or frozen, drained

Soften gelatin in cold water in a custard cup; set in a pan of hot water to dissolve. Cool slightly. Whip cream until stiff; fold in gelatin and ½ cup sugar. Unroll cake; spread whipped cream evenly over cake and lay sliced strawberries on cream. Sprinkle remaining ½ cup sugar over berries (if using sweetened frozen berries, omit this sugar). Roll up cake; glaze with a thin confectioners' sugar frosting and sprinkle with colored coconut. Wrap in waxed paper.

BLUEBERRY CREAM ROLL

Prepare White Cake Roll, substituting ¼ teaspoon lemon extract for almond. Prepare whipped cream filling as directed in Strawberry Cream Roll. Spread whipped cream evenly over cake and top with 1½ to 2 cups blueberries (fresh or frozen, drained). Sprinkle ½ cup confestioners' sugar over berries. Roll up and wrap in waxed paper. Chill.

MAPLE CAKE ROLL

Prepare White Cake Roll, substituting 1 teaspoon vanilla for almond extract. For the filling, cream ⅓ cup butter or margarine. Add 1 egg and ⅓ cup maple-flavored syrup, beating until mixture is well blended. Add ¼ teaspoon salt. Add 2½ cups sifted confectioners' sugar gradually and beat until smooth. Unroll cake and spread with maple filling. Roll up; wrap in waxed paper; chill.

LEMON CREAM ROLL

1 package lemon pudding mix
½ cup sugar
1 egg, slightly beaten
2 cups water
¼ cup heavy cream, whipped
1 cake roll

Put package contents in saucepan. Add sugar; mix well. Gradually add water and egg. Cook over low heat, stirring constantly, until mixture thickens and comes to a boil. Remove from heat. Cool. Fold in whipped cream.

Bake vanilla roll or a chocolate roll. Proceed as for other fillings. Spread with Lemon Cream Filling almost to edge. Roll quickly. Wrap in cloth and cool before slicing.

OLD-FASHIONED JELLY ROLL

And don't forget, all this began with a jelly-filled roll, so good to grow on. After cake cools about 10 minutes, unroll and spread with 1 cup of jelly, the kind you have or the flavor your children like best. Roll again. Dredge top with powdered sugar. Wrap and cool on rack.

CHOCOLATE ROLL . WITH CREAM OR BERRY FILLING

You know, I expect, that the eggs in a cake roll are the ingredients that make it rollable without being breakable. Same with dessert pancakes. Put in enough eggs and you can roll 'em without a break, no matter how thin. But here is how we make a chocolate roll, to fill according to your whim.

CHOCOLATE ROLL WITH 4 EGGS

¼ cup sifted cake flour
½ teaspoon baking powder
¼ teaspoon salt
4 eggs
¾ cup sifted sugar
1 teaspoon vanilla
3 squares unsweetened chocolate
2 tablespoons sugar
¼ teaspoon soda
3 tablespoons cold water

Sift flour once and then measure. Combine baking powder, salt, and those precious eggs in a bowl. Beat with rotary beater, adding ¾ cup sugar gradually. Easiest way is from the sifter. Continue beating until mixture is light-colored and thick. Fold in flour a little at a time and add vanilla.

Melt chocolate over boiling water. Remove from heat and cool. Add the 2 tablespoons sugar, soda, and cold water. Blend. Fold into the batter quickly but thoroughly. Turn into 15 x 10-inch pan which has been lined with paper, then greased. Bake in moderately hot oven (375 F.) 18 to 20 minutes. Turn out on cloth which has been sprinkled with confectioners' sugar. Quickly remove paper and cut off crisp edges. Roll cake, rolling cloth up in it. Let cool on cake rack 30 minutes. Unroll, remove cloth. Spread with one of any number of dreamy fillings and roll again. Secure with waxed paper or cloth and cool on rack.

You can frost this if you want to with a chocolate frosting.

FILLINGS FOR CHOCOLATE ROLL

• A raspberry and cream filling is wonderful rolled up in chocolate cake. Easiest way is to whip 1 cup heavy cream, spread on roll, cover with 2 cups drained and sweetened raspberries.

• Mint filling is divine-looking and you know yourself how good it would be. Make between 2 and 3 cups filling either of these ways: Make the Pudding Mix Filling as described for layer cakes, using vanilla mix. Add ½ teaspoon peppermint extract and few drops of either green or red coloring to tint. Cool and spread on chocolate roll.

Or make Whipped Cream Frosting as described for cakes. Flavor and tint for mint effect. Spread on roll.

• Mocha Filling, Coffee Fillings described for layer cakes are good in this roll.

• Spread softened ice cream; roll and chill.

REFRIGERATOR CAKES MAKE ELEGANT DESSERTS

LEMON REFRIGERATOR CAKE

Makes 12 servings:

24 marshmallows, cut fine
2 cups (1 pint) heavy cream
2 envelopes unflavored gelatin
½ cup cold water
1½ cups sugar
1½ cups water
½ cup lemon juice
24 ladyfingers
7 almonds or pecan halves
1 square unsweetened chocolate

Combine cut marshmallows and cream. Allow to stand 30 minutes, then whip very stiff. Soften gelatin in cold water. Combine sugar and water in saucepan; place over heat and bring to a boil. Cook until sugar is dissolved. Add gelatin and stir well. Add lemon juice and cool before folding in marshmallow-cream mixture. Line an 8- or 9-inch spring-form with ladyfingers. Pour in lemon mixture and chill 6 hours or more. Unmold; decorate top with almonds and curls of bitter chocolate shaved over surface.

NESSELRODE MOLD

Makes 8 servings:

½ cup seedless raisins
2 envelopes unflavored gelatin
½ cup cold water
1 cup hot water
1 cup sugar
¼ teaspoon salt
1 cup diluted frozen orange juice (1 can diluted only enough to make 1 cup)
2 cups heavy cream
1 cup candied fruits
½ cup chopped black walnuts
ladyfingers

Place the raisins in a strainer over boiling water and allow them to steam and become soft. This takes about 20 minutes. Soften the gelatin in the cold water and add the hot water to dissolve. Stir in the sugar, salt, and orange juice. Chill this mixture until it begins to thicken. Meanwhile whip the heavy cream, and when the liquid is thoroughly cooled fold into the cream along with the raisins, chopped candied fruits, and nuts.

Line an 8-inch spring-form pan with ladyfingers. Pour in the Nesselrode and chill until firm. Unmold and serve.

ORANGE VELVET CREAM CAKE

Makes 8 to 10 servings:

1 tablespoon unflavored gelatin
3 tablespoons cold water
1 cup evaporated milk diluted with 1 cup water
2 tablespoons cornstarch
1 cup sugar
2 eggs, slightly beaten
¾ cup orange juice
1 teaspoon grated orange rind
2 dozen ladyfingers or 1 sponge cake
1 cup heavy cream, whipped

Soften gelatin in cold water. Scald 1¾ cups diluted evaporated milk in double boiler. Mix cornstarch and sugar; add to hot milk. Cook 10 minutes, stirring constantly. Add eggs combined with remaining ¼ cup diluted milk. Cook a few minutes longer, stirring constantly. Remove from heat; stir in softened gelatin. Add orange juice and rind. Line a mold with ladyfingers or ½-inch fingers of sponge cake. Fill with alternate layers of cooked mixture and fingers. Arrange fingers on top. Chill a few hours. Serve with whipped cream. Garnish with cherries or sliced orange.

BANANA REFRIGERATOR CAKE

Makes 6 servings:

1 package orange-flavored gelatin
1½ cups hot water
¼ cup sugar
⅛ teaspoon salt
1 tablespoon chopped candied orange peel
½ cup orange juice
¾ cup heavy cream
1½ cups ripe banana slices
18 ladyfingers
1 teaspoon cocoa
½ teaspoon cinnamon

Dissolve gelatin in hot water. Combine sugar, salt, candied peel, and juice; add to gelatin. Chill until consistency of unbeaten egg white. Whip cream until thick but not stiff. Fold in gelatin and bananas. Arrange ladyfingers around sides of mold; pour in gelatin mixture. Chill until firm. Mix cinnamon and cocoa; sprinkle over top and serve.

CHOCOLATE LADYFINGER ICEBOX CAKE

Makes 8 servings:

3 squares unsweetened chocolate
½ cup sugar
⅛ teaspoon salt
¼ cup hot water
1 tablespoon cold water
1½ teaspoons unflavored gelatin
4 egg yolks
1 teaspoon vanilla
4 egg whites, stiffly beaten
½ cup cream, whipped
½ cup finely chopped walnuts (optional)
24 ladyfingers

Melt chocolate in top of double boiler. Add sugar, salt, and hot water. Stir until sugar is dissolved and mixture blended. Add cold water to gelatin. Add to hot chocolate mixture and stir until gelatin is dissolved. Cook until mixture is smooth and thick. Remove from boiling water; add egg yolks one at a time, beating thoroughly after each. Return to top of double boiler and cook 2 minutes, stirring constantly. Add vanilla; cool. Fold into egg whites. Chill. Fold in whipped cream. Add nuts.

Line bottom and sides of mold with waxed paper. Arrange ladyfingers on bottom and sides of mold. Add thin layer of chocolate mixture. Continue arranging ladyfingers and chocolate mixture in alternate layers. Top with chocolate mixture. Trim off ladyfingers around sides of mold and arrange cut pieces in a decorative design on top of the chocolate mixture. Chill 12 to 24 hours in refrigerator. Unmold.

ALOHA PINE-MALLOW DESSERT

This delicious and easy-to-prepare pineapple dessert can be made the day before and chilled in your refrigerator overnight so that you have no last-minute preparation. And if you should have any left over you will find it keeps beautifully in your refrigerator for several days.

Makes 12 servings:

1 pound marshmallows
¾ cup syrup drained from crushed pineapple
½ cup milk
¼ cup strained lemon juice
1½ cups (No. 2 can) crushed pineapple
1 cup (½ pint) heavy cream, whipped
1 cup graham-cracker crumbs (8 to 10)

Heat the first four ingredients together over hot water until the marshmallows are melted and the mixture is smooth. Cool. Fold the crushed pineapple and the whipped cream into the cooled marshmallow mixture. Sprinkle ½ cup graham-cracker crumbs evenly over the bottom of a 9 x 9 x 2-inch pan. Pour marshmallow mixture into pan. Top with remaining ½ cup crumbs. Chill until firm, several hours or overnight. Serve with or without additional whipped cream.

GINGER-APPLESAUCE REFRIGERATOR CAKE

Makes 8 servings:

1½ cups (15-ounce can) sweetened condensed milk
¼ cup lemon juice
2 egg whites
2 cups applesauce
2 tablespoons lemon juice
1 teaspoon vanilla
½ pound ginger wafers or ginger snaps

Combine milk and ¼ cup lemon juice and mix until thickened. Beat egg whites until stiff but not dry. Fold into milk mixture. Combine applesauce, 2 tablespoons lemon juice, vanilla, and blend. Line 8 x 8 x 2-inch pan with waxed-paper strips. Arrange layer of ginger wafers at bottom. Fill pan with alternate layers of milk mixture and applesauce mixture, making top layer of applesauce. Cover with layer of ginger wafers. Chill 12 hours or more. Unmold and serve by cutting into 2 x 4-inch slices. Garnish with whipped cream or not.

On St. Patrick's Day add a few drops of green coloring to the applesauce. It will make a very pretty party mold.

A FRUIT CAKE RECIPE . . USE HALF FOR PUDDING

FRUIT CAKE

Makes about 5 pounds:

½ pound seedless raisins
½ pound finely cut dates
½ pound finely cut candied citron
1 pound finely cut assorted candied fruits: orange peel, lemon peel, pineapple, and cherries
2½ cups sifted all-purpose flour
1 teaspoon baking powder
1 teaspoon salt
1 teaspoon cinnamon
½ teaspoon each allspice, cloves, and nutmeg
1 cup shortening
½ cup brown sugar
1 cup light or dark corn syrup
4 eggs, well beaten
¼ cup orange juice

Weigh and prepare fruit. Mix and sift dry ingredients. Dredge fruit with ½ cup of the dry ingredients. Cream shortening; add sugar; cream until light. Add syrup; mix well. Add 1 cup of the dry ingredients; beat until smooth. Add eggs, beating in thoroughly. Add orange juice; mix well. Add fruit mixture. Fold in remaining dry ingredients. Bake in well-greased loaf pans lined with waxed paper in slow oven (250 F.) 4 to 5 hours, depending upon size of cake. Place shallow pan of water on bottom rack of oven during baking; remove during last hour. (Fruit cake improves with age. Prepare well in advance. Wrap well; store in airtight container.)

OR USE THE 5-POUND RECIPE . . . TO MAKE THESE

STEAMED PUDDING

Makes 1 large or 10 individual puddings:

Use ½ recipe for Fruit Cake with ¼ pound each seedless raisins, chopped dried figs, finely cut dates, and candied citron. Place in well-greased 1-quart pudding mold or individual molds. Cover tightly; steam 3 hours for large molds; 1 hour for small. (Puddings may be prepared well in advance. Reheat for serving by steaming 1 hour.)

FRUIT COOKIES

Makes about 6 dozen:

Use ½ recipe for Fruit Cake; add ½ cup chopped nutmeats with fruit. Drop by teaspoonfuls on greased baking sheet. Bake in moderately slow oven (325 F.) 20 minutes.

PETIT FRUIT CAKES

Makes 2 dozen:

These are so attractive to serve at Christmas time with coffee. Make them early in November, for, like the cake and pudding, these store and improve with age. Use ½ Fruit Cake recipe; add ½ cup chopped nutmeats with fruit. Bake in fluted paper cups in cupcake pans. Bake in slow oven (300 F.) about 1 hour. Remove from oven. Brush tops with egg white and garnish with candied cherries, slivered almonds, or citron. Return to oven and continue baking 15 minutes longer. Cool. To serve, remove paper cups; replace with fresh ones.

LAST-MINUTE FRUIT CAKE . . . EAT OR GIVE AWAY

Makes two 2½-pound cakes or five 1-pound cakes:

You meant to make a fruit cake. Now it is December and you did not make one and there is no time to age one or to make small ones to age and give away. Try this recipe. Make one for the family and give the small ones for presents.

Line your pans with waxed paper (this totals 10 cups, so make it in one big tube or loaf pan or in small pans which together hold that amount).

1 cup evaporated milk
36 marshmallows, cut fine
½ cup undiluted frozen orange juice (or replace with flavoring you prefer in fruit cakes)
8 dozen graham crackers, crushed
½ teaspoon cinnamon
½ teaspoon nutmeg
¼ teaspoon cloves
2 cups seedless raisins (half light and half dark are pretty)
1 cup chopped dates
1½ cups chopped pecans or walnuts
2 cups ready-mixed chopped candied fruits, peel, citron

Combine first three ingredients. Stir and let stand while all remaining ingredients are put into a large mixing bowl or big container. Mix lightly; add milk mixture and stir until crumbs are moistened. Press firmly into pans. Garnish with candied fruits. Chill 2 days before slicing.

CHEESE CAKE WITH A PRESENT . . . AND 3 FUTURES

• The most famous cheese cake in New York is served at Lindy's restaurant, and there the creamy velvet wedges are a good 3 inches deep, with fruit tops in the flavors described here.

• It won't take long to make this superb cheese cake, but you should allow several hours for chilling before the cake is served.

• When you make one, doing things in this order will make it easier. If your cheeses are in the refrigerator, begin by taking them out and putting them in a warm place—not hot, just cozy warm. Then make the crust, the filling, the glaze, in that order.

• Any thickening you like can be used in making the glaze, but the tapioca allows fruit to show off its pure brilliant colors, with no clouding effect.

Makes 8 to 10 servings:

Begin by making a vanilla-wafer or graham-cracker crust, exactly as those described for pies. Press it into the bottom of a 2-quart casserole or a deep cake pan. A spring-form pan is not necessary, but it is convenient.

When making a bigger cheese cake, try using this same size crust in the 2-quart pan; then double the filling to make a *deeper* cheese cake to serve 16 or 20 people. The glaze recipe need not be doubled.

THE CHEESE FILLING:

1 package lemon pie filling mix
⅔ cup sugar
1 cup undiluted evaporated milk
½ pound cream cheese, softened
1 pound (2 cups) cottage cheese
3 eggs, unbeaten
¼ teaspoon salt

Combine the lemon pie filling mix, sugar, and milk in a saucepan. Place over low heat and cook, stirring constantly until thick and smooth. Remove from heat.

Combine the cheeses which have been out of the refrigerator long enough to be a little warm; blend. Add the eggs one at a time, stirring hard after each addition. Add the salt to the cooked pie mix; stir into the cheese mixture and blend thoroughly. Pour over the crumbs in the cake pan. Bake in preheated slow oven (300 F.) 1 hour and 10 minutes. Cool and cover with one of these glazes:

PINEAPPLE, CHERRY, OR PEACH GLAZE

Make glaze of crushed pineapple, black cherries, or with frozen or canned sliced peaches. No. 2 cans are the right size for this recipe.

When making fresh-fruit glazes, crush some of the fruit, cook in 1 cup water for 5 minutes, put through fine strainer, and proceed to add water if necessary to make it equal to 1½ cups.

STRAWBERRY GLAZE

½ cup sugar
2 tablespoons quick-cooking tapioca
1½ cups juice (add water to drained juice to total 1½ cups)
¼ teaspoon salt
1 tablespoon orange juice
2 cups frozen strawberries, drained

Combine all ingredients except berries in a saucepan. Place over moderate heat and stir until blended. Cook, stirring constantly, until juice is well thickened. Remove from heat and cool. Arrange fruit evenly over top of cheese cake and pour the thickened juice on top. Chill several hours before serving.

PUMPKIN DESSERTS . . . . FOR THE HOLIDAYS

PUMPKIN MOUSSE

Make Pumpkin Pie filling, doubling sugar in the recipe. Cool; fold in an equal amount of heavy cream which has been whipped until it holds its shape but not stiff. Chill and serve. P.S. Add chopped nuts to this if you like.

PUMPKIN CAKE

1 teaspoon soda
1 package spice cake mix
canned pumpkin
½ cup water
½ cup finely chopped walnuts

Add soda to cake mix. Substitute pumpkin for liquid called for on package in same amount; combine with the ½ cup water. Mix cake as package directs, using a little over half the pumpkin-water mixture for first addition of liquid. Stir in chopped walnuts last. Bake as package directs. Fill layers and frost top with whipped cream, sprinkling more chopped walnuts between layers. Decorate with walnut halves.

Don't you agree this is a nice one for the holidays?

PUMPKIN WHIP

Makes 8 servings:

2 cups cooked pumpkin, fresh or canned
1 teaspoon salt
½ teaspoon nutmeg
½ teaspoon cinnamon
4 egg whites
½ cup sugar
¼ cup chopped pecans or other nuts

Mix pumpkin with salt, nutmeg, and cinnamon. Beat egg whites with ¼ teaspoon salt until stiff. Gradually add sugar to the egg whites, beating thoroughly after each addition. Fold in spiced pumpkin. Chill thoroughly. Serve in sherbet glasses either plain or with a garnish of chopped nuts.

REGAL DESSERTS . . . . . FOR THE HOLIDAYS

FRUIT BAVARIAN CREAM

Makes 12 servings:

2 tablespoons unflavored gelatin
½ cup cold water
2 cups crushed berries (strawberries, raspberries, apricot purée, crushed pineapple—any type fruit)
2 cups heavy cream
1½ cups powdered sugar
whole fruit to fill center of mold

Soften the gelatin in cold water until absorbed. Place in top of double boiler and stir until dissolved. Add to the berries. Mix well and chill until mixture begins to congeal. Whip the cream till it just begins to form peaks but is still moist. Fold in the sugar and add to the congealed berry mixture. Fill a 2-quart ring mold. Chill until set and serve with a mound of the fruit in the center. If berries are used, arrange whole berries and green leaves as a garnish around the outside of the ring on the platter.

ENGLISH CHRISTMAS PUDDING

Makes 12 servings:

¾ cup sifted flour
1½ teaspoons salt
1 teaspoon allspice
¼ teaspoon nutmeg
1½ pounds mixed dried fruits (figs, white and dark raisins, apricots, prunes, currants, dates) and chopped citron and candied peel
1½ teaspoons vanilla
½ cup fine bread crumbs
1 cup heated milk
¼ cup sugar
3 egg yolks, beaten
8 ounces suet, chopped fine
1¼ cups apple, chopped
3 egg whites, stiffly beaten

Combine flour, salt, and spices and sift together. Add fruits and stir. Combine crumbs and milk and allow to soften. Combine sugar, beaten egg yolks, suet. Stir into the crumbs and add chopped apple. Combine with fruit mixture and blend thoroughly. Fold in the stiffly beaten egg whites. Pour into a well-greased 2-quart mold (pudding should not fill mold more than ¾ full, for it will need room to rise). Cover with its own tight-fitting lid or with greased paper secured over the top with string. Place in deep pan of boiling water and be sure the water continues to boil while pudding is steaming, 3½ to 4 hours. If made in advance, cool but do not uncover. Reheat on Christmas Day by steaming 1 hour.

Perch a spray of mistletoe or holly on the top and serve.

ENGLISH CHRISTMAS PUDDING . . . AMERICAN VERSION!

In this country, more addicted to freezing than to steaming, we might make it this way:

Use the ½-gallon (2-quart) recipe for Hand Freezer Vanilla Ice Cream. Reduce vanilla to ½ teaspoon; add ½ teaspoon almond and ½ teaspoon lemon extract. Turn handle for 15 minutes; open and add 2 cups mixed fruits and nuts made up something like this: ½ cup chopped candied orange and lemon peel, ½ cup seedless raisins which have been steamed and softened, ½ cup mixed chopped candied fruits, ¼ cup chopped citron, ¼ cup chopped nuts. Or compose it of chopped peel, nuts, citron, dates, candied cherries, and raisins. Freeze another 5 to 10 minutes and pack as directed.

Very good this, and it can be made in the freezer trays in half quantity, or in large mold in freezing compartment, following directions for refrigerator freezing.

REGAL 3-LAYER RICE MOLD

Makes 12 servings (about 12 cups):

1½ cups rice
1½ cups water
½ teaspoon salt
3 envelopes unflavored gelatin
⅔ cup cold water
5 egg yolks, beaten
2 cups sugar
4 tablespoons cornstarch
2 large cans undiluted evaporated milk, scalded
2 teaspoons vanilla
2 teaspoons instant coffee
1 can evaporated milk, chilled and whipped
2 squares unsweetened chocolate

This clever way of handling the soft custard each of us has been familiar with since childhood to make an elegant dessert is typical of French ingenuity. So is the addition of rice to make the dessert go farther. Despite its handsome appearance, this is an inexpensive beauty.

Put the rice in a 4- or 5-quart pot. Add 1½ cups water and the salt and cook until tender.

Soften the gelatin in ⅔ cup cold water. Combine sugar and cornstarch in top of double boiler; stir well. Add beaten egg yolks; stir over barely boiling water until the sugar is dissolved and the mixture well blended. Slowly add this to the hot milk which has been heated in a 3-quart or larger saucepan. The size of these pans is important if you are to handle this three-layer mixture with ease. Stir constantly until the custard is thick and smooth. Reduce heat; add the gelatin and stir until dissolved. Add this to the cooked rice; stir well; remove from heat and add vanilla.

Now you are going to divide this into three parts. It will be easy if you use the large pans. Put the instant coffee in a mixing bowl. Add a tablespoon of the warm rice custard mixture and stir vigorously. Add 3 cups of the mixture to this and stir until blended. Fold in ⅓ of the whipped evaporated milk. Pour into the mold to form the first layer and chill until set, about 20 minutes.

Melt 2 squares of unsweetened chocolate in the top of the double boiler (and I hope you didn't bother to wash this). Stir until melted; add ⅓ of the rice custard mixture to it and stir until blended, but do not cook.

Fold in ⅓ of the whipped evaporated milk into the yellow rice custard mixture which remains in the large pan. Pour it on top of the congealed layer to form the second layer. Chill another 15 or 20 minutes, until set.

When the chocolate mixture is lukewarm or cool, fold in the remaining ⅓ of the whipped evaporated milk and pour it on top of the second congealed layer. Chill in refrigerator until ready to serve.

This arrangement means there will be a chocolate layer as the base of the mold, the light layer will be in the center, and the dark coffee custard will be on top. Surround it with more whipped evaporated milk or with cooked fruit, or serve soft custard over it if you like, or eat exactly as it is.

Heavy cream, whipped, is fine in this and you can use it in place of the whipped evaporated milk if you like.

Serve the Mold with Fruit

A beautiful way to serve this is to place the mold on a very large platter surrounded with fresh or drained cooked fruit. An assortment is particularly attractive. Perhaps apricot, pear, and peach halves with a few preserved or drained canned cherries. Serve some of the fruit and some of the rice custard with each serving.

You can serve more than 12 people when fruit is used as garnish.

Vary the colors used after seeing these yellow, brown, and coffee layers. Food coloring can make pastel layers.

CREAM GRAPE BASKET

Makes 6 servings:

1 envelope unflavored gelatin
¼ cup cold water
¾ cup hot water
½ cup sugar
⅛ teaspoon salt
1 can undiluted frozen grape juice
¼ cup lemon juice
⅓ cup water
1 tablespoon lemon juice
⅓ cup non-fat dry milk
1 cup white seedless grapes

Soften gelatin in ¼ cup cold water in mixing bowl for 5 minutes. Pour the hot water over softened gelatin and stir until dissolved. Combine in saucepan the sugar, salt, grape and lemon juice; place over low heat and stir until dissolved. Chill until mixture begins to thicken. Meanwhile pour ⅓ cup water and 1 tablespoon lemon juice in deep 1-quart bowl. Sprinkle non-fat dry milk over top of water. Beat with rotary beater or electric mixer until stiff, about 7 to 10 minutes. Fold whipped non-fat dry milk into thickened gelatin mixture. Pour into 1-quart mold. Chill in refrigerator until consistency of unbeaten egg white. Add white grapes. Chill until firm, about 2 to 3 hours. Unmold on platter of green leaves and arrange sliced banana and strawberry garnish around the mold.

CRANBERRY RICE CREAM

Makes 12 servings:

2 envelopes unflavored gelatin
½ cup cold water
2 cups cold milk
1½ cups cooked rice
2 tablespoons sugar
½ teaspoon salt
2 teaspoons almond extract
2 cups heavy cream, whipped

SAUCE:

2 1-pound cans whole cranberry sauce
2 tablespoons orange juice
½ cup brown sugar

Place gelatin in cup. Add cold water and let stand 2 minutes. Place cup in pan of boiling water until gelatin dissolves. Add to cold milk. Stir in rice, sugar, salt, and almond extract and chill until slightly thickened. Fold in whipped cream. Spoon into sherbets and chill until firm. When ready to serve, heat cranberry sauce, orange juice, and brown sugar until piping hot. Let guests ladle hot cranberry sauce over rice cream.

HARD SAUCES . . . TO SERVE, SAVE, OR FOR GIFTS

VANILLA HARD SAUCE

Makes 2 cups:

½ cup butter
1½ cups confectioners' sugar
½ teaspoon lemon extract
½ teaspoon vanilla extract
2 tablespoons cream

Work the butter until very soft. Add the sugar about ⅓ at a time and continue to mix until well blended before adding more. Add vanilla and lemon extract. Add enough cream to get the consistency you desire.

BANANA HARD SAUCE: Omit flavoring. Add 1 tablespoon lemon juice, ¼ teaspoon nutmeg, and 1 very ripe banana mashed to a pulp.

SPICE HARD SAUCE: Make as Vanilla Hard Sauce, using only vanilla extract and adding ½ teaspoon freshly ground nutmeg and ½ teaspoon cinnamon. Blend.

LEMON OR ORANGE HARD SAUCE: Add 1 tablespoon frozen juice together with 1 teaspoon grated orange or lemon peel to match the juice flavoring in Vanilla Hard Sauce.

Experiment to get any flavor you want for hard sauce, which in Europe has always been heavily loaded with a favorite brandy or liquor. It is quite good when flavored with ¼ cup berries or almost any kind of cooked fruit that has been thoroughly crushed. Any of the candied fruits used at Christmas time for Christmas cakes can be added to hard sauce, about ¼ cup finely chopped cherries, ginger, angelica, citron, candied orange or lemon peel, or preserved ginger.

Hard sauce can be made from half white and half brown sugar. It can also be made from all brown sugar, but is more difficult to blend.

FLUFFY LEMON HARD SAUCE

Makes about 3½ cups:

⅓ cup butter, softened
2¼ cups confectioners' sugar
1 egg yolk, beaten
3 tablespoons lemon juice
1 egg white, stiffly beaten

Combine all ingredients except the egg white and blend until thoroughly creamy consistency. Fold in the stiffly beaten egg white. Chill and serve.

Same variations for flavoring are successful for the Fluffy Hard Sauce as for the Vanilla Hard Sauce.

OLD STANDBY . . . . NEW WRINKLE

BROWN BETTY WITH BANANA HARD SAUCE

Makes 8 servings:

3 cups graham-cracker crumbs
½ cup melted butter
4½ cups tart applesauce
½ cup brown sugar
1 teaspoon salt
2 teaspoons cinnamon
½ teaspoon nutmeg
½ teaspoon cloves
¾ cup seedless raisins
¼ cup lemon juice
¼ cup orange juice
2 teaspoons vanilla

Combine the cracker crumbs and butter. Mix well. Use ⅓ to cover the bottom of the baking dish. Combine the sugar, salt, spices, and raisins. Blend well and sprinkle ⅓ of the mixture over the crumb layer. Combine the lemon juice, orange juice, and vanilla and add ⅓ over this layer. Repeat, alternating the 3 mixtures as layers, ending with crumb mixture on top. Cover and place in moderate oven (350 F.). Bake until done, about 25 minutes. Remove the cover; increase the heat until the pudding is brown. Remove and serve hot with Banana Hard Sauce.

YEAR-ROUND TREATS . FOR YEAR-ROUND COMPANY

QUICK POPCORN BALLS

Makes 6 popcorn balls about
2½ inches in diameter:

¼ cup salad oil
½ cup popcorn
½ cup dark corn syrup
½ cup sugar
½ teaspoon salt

Heat salad oil in a 3-quart covered kettle over medium heat 3 minutes. Add popcorn. Cover, leaving small air space at edge of cover. Shake frequently over medium heat until popping stops. Meanwhile mix together syrup, sugar, and salt. Add to popped corn in kettle and stir constantly over medium heat 3 to 5 minutes, or until corn is evenly and completely coated with mixture. Remove from heat. Form into balls, using as little pressure as possible. Use butter on hands if desired.

Note: Do not double recipe.

CARAMEL CORN: Follow above recipe. After removing from heat, spread on waxed paper and separate the pieces of popped corn. Makes about 2 quarts.

TO BLANCH ALMONDS

Bring water to a rapid boil in a saucepan. Remove from heat. Quickly pour the almonds into the hot water and cover. Leave 5 minutes (no more) and uncover. Drain and "pinch" the skins off by pressing each one with finger and thumb.

HOW TO SLIVER ALMONDS

There are three ways to sliver almonds, so choose your method. One is to blanch them and immediately separate the halves you intend to sliver. Line them up on a chopping board in neat soldierly rows with ends pointing in the same direction and chop each half in two lengthwise once or twice. This is not as tedious as it sounds. Then if you want them toasty brown to serve on beans, fish, etc., brown them as other nuts.

Almonds can be slivered the same way, after blanching, without separating halves.

Almonds can be blanched, browned, and then chopped with a sharp knife, but the long slivers are not as easily achieved this way.

SALTED NUTS

For 2 cups nuts:

Brazil nuts, almonds, walnuts, peanuts, or pecans are treated this way.

Place 2 tablespoons butter, margarine, or salad oil in a shallow pan or cookie sheet. Place in moderate oven (350 F.). Add the nuts, stirring until they are coated. Bake until the nuts are lightly browned, stirring often to ensure even browning. Drain on paper towels and sprinkle with salt.

Nuts can be browned very quickly in a deep-fat fryer, and this is especially practical when other deep frying is being done. Have the nuts ready, drop them into the basket, and submerge them in the 375 F. fat for a minute or two to brown. Drain and salt.

MINTED WALNUTS

For 3 cups walnut halves:

¼ cup light corn syrup
1 cup sugar
½ cup water
1 teaspoon peppermint essence
10 marshmallows

Measure out the first three ingredients into a small saucepan. Cook over medium heat, stirring constantly. When mixture boils, continue cooking until a few drops form a soft ball when dropped into very cold water. Remove from heat; add peppermint and marshmallows and quickly stir until marshmallows have dissolved. Add walnut halves and stir to coat them. Pour onto waxed paper; separate nuts with a fork and cool.

SPICED NUTS

For 1½ cups pecans or walnuts:

1 cup sugar
1 teaspoon cinnamon
½ teaspoon cream of tartar
¼ cup hot water
½ teaspoon vanilla

Mix everything together except the nuts and vanilla. Place over heat and stir until mixture sugars. Continue to stir until syrup forms a ball in cold water. Add nuts and vanilla and turn out on a flat surface. Separate the nuts with a fork and cool.

CHAPTER 6

PIES . . . PIES . . . PIES

LET'S TURN ON THE OVEN . . . AND BAKE A PIE

"Every time I think about making a pie, I get pie-fright," said a young woman from Chicago. She is extremely clever about doing other things, but she—and many others who want to make good pastry but are not sure they can do it—may succeed if they experiment with different fats and different methods. Then it is possible to choose one and have confidence in the outcome.

The flaky melt-in-your-mouth piecrusts made by Grandma were made with leaf lard. Part of the reason for her success in making fine-textured pastry could have been that the lard was never cold. It stayed right there on the pantry shelf until she reached for it, and it blended with the flour with very little liquid. It required a minimum of handling too. And that is important.

The standard recipe for a two-crust pie was 2 cups *sifted* flour—and if you use *pastry* flour, your luck may improve with 1 teaspoon salt. Add ⅔ cup lard or butter and cut it into mixture with a pastry blender. Measure ¼ cup iced water and add it a little at a time, work into a ball, roll it up in waxed paper, and chill it.

That was the way Grandma did it, except she worked skillfully with her fingertips. To turn into a pastry chef when you want to, try this recipe or one of the methods that follow.

Before baking piecrust, read baking suggestions on page 52. Then follow one of these sure-to-be-lucky recipes for flaky crusts.

FOR THOSE . . . . WHO HAVE "PIE-FRIGHT"

A TWO-CRUST PASTRY WITH HOMOGENIZED VEGETABLE SHORTENING

For 9-inch two-crust pie or 9 tart shells:

¾ cup homogenized vegetable shortening
¼ cup boiling water
1 tablespoon milk
2 cups all-purpose flour, sifted once before measuring
1 teaspoon salt

Put shortening in a medium-sized mixing bowl and over it pour the boiling water and milk. Break up the shortening with a fork.

• With rapid across-the-bowl strokes whip until mixture is smooth and thick like whipped cream and holds soft peaks when the fork is lifted.

• Put the measured flour and salt into the sifter and sift onto the contents of the mixing bowl.

• Stir the ingredients quickly with vigorous strokes round the bowl to make a dough that clings together and "cleans" the bowl (takes less than a minute).

• Pick up the dough and work gently until smooth and blended. Shape into a flat round; divide the dough in half and roll each half separately between squares of waxed paper that have been laid on a slightly dampened table. (This is to keep the paper from slipping.) Roll the dough from the center out into the size circle you want. If the paper wrinkles, remove the top one, replace with another square of waxed paper, and turn dough over before beginning to roll again.

• This is called the "water-whip" method of mixing pastry and eliminates the problem of too much flour being worked into the pastry.

• Put the pastry in the pie pan by peeling off the top paper and put pastry side down into the pan. Remove the other paper gently and push the pastry down into the pie pan. Do not trim until the top crust has been put on the pie.

• For a fruit-filled pie, designs or a lattice top of strips of pastry cut with a pastry cutter to make an attractive edge can be placed over the top. For a full-top pastry, a design of the fruit which is inside the pie can be pricked in the dough.

• For a deep brown crust, dip the pastry brush in a mixture of milk or cream and brush the top, then sprinkle with sugar.

• For glazed crust finish, brush the unbaked top crust with egg white which has been beaten until frothy, and sprinkle with sugar.

A SINGLE PIE SHELL

Makes 9-inch pie shell or 6 tart shells:

½ cup less 1 tablespoon homogenized vegetable shortening
3 tablespoons boiling water
1 teaspoon milk
1½ cups all-purpose flour, sifted once before measuring
½ teaspoon salt

Make the pastry as for the two-crust pie but do not divide the dough in half. Instead, shape it into one round ball. Roll between waxed paper. Fit the dough gently down into the pan and trim with scissors about an inch beyond the edge of the pan. Turn the pastry edge back to the pan to make a fold, pinching it lightly with thumb and index finger into a double pastry rim standing about ¼ inch all around.

Make a shell rim by placing the left index finger on the inside of the rim and pinching it outside with right thumb and index finger to get the desired shape.

A fancy edge is easy to make by pushing the rolling pin over the top to remove circle of excess dough. Remove the pan; cut the circle of dough into tiny squares or rounds either with a thimble or with a small cutter. Moisten the rim. Overlap these small pieces of pastry clear around the side; pat them down gently to make them stick.

If pastry is to be baked first, fit it over the pan, prick all over the bottom with a fork, and bake in hot oven (450 F.) about 15 minutes.

When pricking the bottom of the pastry shell, remember this is done to keep bubbles from forming in the lower crust. Prick the sides of the pastry as well. French housewives prevent their pie or tart shells from forming bubbles by weighting them with beans, which are always kept in the kitchen for this purpose.

TO MAKE TART SHELLS

Use recipe for either a double or single crust to make 9 or 6 tart shells, and proceed as for pie pastry. Then roll the dough to about ⅛-inch thickness. Cut into rounds and *fit over the outside of muffin pans.* Pinch the pastry into little pleats to give them an attractive appearance. Bake in hot oven (450 F.) 10 to 15 minutes.

Almost any filling you would put in a pie can be put into tart shells to make individual desserts.

HOW MUCH DO YOU NEED TO FILL THE SHELLS?

Fill a measuring cup with water as many times as necessary to fill the muffin tins you used for making the pastry shells. This will tell you how many cups of creamed chicken, seafood, vegetables, or dessert filling to be served in the shells.

EASY-MIX FLAKY PASTRY WITH SALAD OIL

Makes two-crust pie:

2 cups sifted all-purpose flour
1 teaspoon salt
½ cup salad oil
¼ cup plus 1 tablespoon iced water

Sift together flour and salt. Combine salad oil and iced water in measuring cup. Beat with fork until thickened and creamy. To avoid separation, pour immediately *all at once* over flour mixture. Mix with fork. The dough will be moist. Form into ball; divide in half.

Shape each half into a flat round. Place between 2 sheets of waxed paper about 12 inches square. (Paper will not slip if table is wiped with damp cloth.) Roll out to form circle reaching edges of paper. Remove top sheet of paper; invert dough over pan; peel off paper. Fit pastry into pan. Trim. Roll out top crust. Cut gashes for escape of steam. Fill pastry-lined pan with desired filling. Place top crust over filling and trim ½ inch beyond rim of pan. Seal edge by folding top crust under bottom crust. Flute edge. Bake at temperature required for filling.

FOR ONE-CRUST PIE SHELL: Divide ingredients exactly in half (using 1 cup sifted all-purpose flour, ½ teaspoon salt, ¼ cup salad oil and 2½ tablespoons *iced water*). Combine; roll out; fit into pan as directed. Fold edge and flute. Prick entire surface of crust. Bake in very hot oven (475 F.) 10 to 12 minutes.

A FANCY SHELL . . . . . . TO CHILL, BAKE, FILL

Recipes for 9-inch shells

GINGERSNAP CRUST

Makes 8-inch pie shell:

1½ cups crushed gingersnap crumbs
2 tablespoons sugar
¼ cup butter, softened, not melted

Combine gingersnap crumbs and sugar. Blend in butter with pastry cutter or fingers very thoroughly. Line pie plate with buttered crumbs and pack to fit. Bake in moderate oven (350 F.) 10 to 15 minutes. Cool.

SCALLOPED VANILLA-WAFER SHELL

Roll or grind 30 vanilla wafers to make 1 cup crumbs. Mix with 3 tablespoons softened butter or margarine; blend thoroughly. Press mixture evenly and firmly on bottom and sides of 9-inch pie pan. To form scalloped edge, cut 10 wafers in half and place cut side down around pie plate. Chill in refrigerator until firm, or bake 8 minutes in moderately hot oven (375 F.). Chill before using.

GRAHAM-CRACKER CRUST

1¼ cups graham-cracker crumbs (about 16 crackers)
¼ cup sugar
½ cup butter or margarine

Mix together the crumbs and sugar. Melt the butter or margarine and thoroughly combine with the crumb-sugar mixture. Press crumbs against sides and bottom of a 9-inch pie plate. Removal will be easier if the pie plate is first lined with aluminum foil. Chill in refrigerator until firm, or bake 8 minutes in moderately hot oven (375 F.). Chill before using.

A DELICATE SHELL . . OF MERINGUE OR COCONUT

MERINGUE SHELL

4 egg whites
¼ teaspoon cream of tartar
¼ teaspoon salt
1 cup sugar

Beat egg whites until foamy; add cream of tartar and salt. Continue beating until stiff but not dry. Add sugar gradually, beating until meringue is stiff. Arrange meringue in a large circle about 9 inches in diameter and about ½ to ¾ inches thick throughout on several thicknesses of unglazed paper on a baking sheet. Build up sides with remaining meringue to a depth of about 1½ inches. Bake in a slow oven (250 F.) 2 hours, or until meringue shell is dry and lightly browned. Cool.

NUBBY MERINGUE SHELL

½ teaspoon vinegar
1 teaspoon vanilla
¼ teaspoon salt
4 egg whites
1 cup sugar
½ cup rolled oats, uncooked

Add vinegar, vanilla, and salt to egg whites; beat until frothy. Add sugar very gradually, about a tablespoon at a time, beating well after each addition. Continue beating until mixture is stiff and glossy. Lightly fold in the rolled oats. Place in a mound on greased heavy unglazed paper on a baking sheet. Using a spatula, hollow out the center and build up the sides to resemble a pie shell. Bake in slow oven (275 F.) 45 minutes to 1 hour. Cool for a few minutes, then remove from paper. Cool thoroughly before filling.

MERINGUE TARTS: Place meringue in 8 mounds on the paper. Shape each mound as a little pie. Bake and fill as above.

BAKED COCONUT CRUST

⅓ cup butter
3 tablespoons sugar
1 egg yolk
1 cup sifted flour
1 cup cut coconut

Combine butter and sugar and blend well. Add egg yolk. Mix thoroughly. Add flour and mix again. Add coconut. Pat mixture into greased 9-inch pie pan. Chill 30 minutes. Bake in moderate oven (350 F.) until brown, about 25 minutes.

CHOCOLATE COCONUT CRUST—UNBAKED

2 tablespoons butter
2 squares unsweetened chocolate
⅔ cup sifted confectioners' sugar
2 tablespoons hot milk or water
1½ cups coconut

Combine first two ingredients in top of double boiler. Stir over hot water until chocolate is melted. Combine sugar and milk or water; stir and add to chocolate mixture. Add coconut and stir well. Spread and press on bottom and sides of greased 9-inch pie pan. Chill until firm.

TREATS-OF-THE-YEAR . . . . 6 PIES

CRUMB-TOP PEACH PIE

2½ to 3 tablespoons quick-cooking tapioca
¾ cup sugar
¼ teaspoon salt
4 cups sliced fresh peaches
1 to 2 tablespoons lemon juice
1 unbaked 9-inch pie shell
Crumb Topping

Combine tapioca, sugar, salt, peaches, and lemon juice. Pour into pie shell and sprinkle with the Crumb Topping. Bake in hot oven (425

F.) 45 to 50 minutes, or until syrup boils with heavy bubbles that do not burst.

CRUMB TOPPING

Combine ⅓ cup firmly packed brown sugar, ¼ cup flour, and ½ teaspoon cinnamon. Cut in 2½ tablespoons butter until divided into pieces the size of small peas.

OPEN APPLE PIE

6 tart apples, thinly sliced
1 recipe Easy-Mix Flaky Pastry
1 cup brown sugar
2 tablespoons quick-cooking tapioca
¼ teaspoon salt
1 teaspoon cinnamon
½ teaspoon grated lemon peel
1 tablespoon lemon juice
3 tablespoons butter

Prepare apples by peeling, coring, and slicing them into thin slices. Line a 9-inch pie pan with pastry rolled ⅛ inch thick. Combine sugar, tapioca, salt, spices, lemon peel, and juice. Arrange half the apple slices in layer on the pastry; sprinkle with half the spice mixture. Arrange another layer of the slices and sprinkle with remaining mixture. Dot with butter. Bake in hot oven (400 F.) 1 hour and 15 minutes, or until crust is brown and apples tender.

SNAPPY CRANBERRY-RAISIN PIE

To fill 8-inch gingersnap crust:

1 pound can whole cranberry sauce
1 cup raisins
1 tablespoon cornstarch
¼ teaspoon nutmeg
⅛ teaspoon salt
2 tablespoons orange juice
1 tablespoon lemon juice
1 tablespoon grated orange rind
1 cup heavy cream, whipped

Combine cranberry sauce, raisins, cornstarch, nutmeg, and salt. Cook slowly until clear and slightly thickened. Remove from heat; add orange juice, lemon juice, and orange rind. Cool. Fold in whipped cream and pour into pie shell. Chill for several hours.

FRESH BLUEBERRY PIE

3 tablespoons quick-cooking tapioca
¾ to 1 cup sugar
¼ teaspoon salt
⅛ teaspoon cinnamon
4 cups wild or cultivated blueberries
1 to 2 tablespoons lemon juice
pastry for two-crust 9-inch pie
1 tablespoon butter

Combine quick-cooking tapioca, sugar, salt, cinnamon, blueberries, and lemon juice. Roll half the pastry ⅛ inch thick and line a 9-inch pie pan. Roll remaining pastry ⅛ inch thick and cut several 2-inch slits or a fancy design near center. Fill pie shell with blueberry mixture. Dot with butter. Moisten edge of bottom crust. To adjust top crust, fold pastry in half or roll loosely on rolling pin; center on filling. Open slits with a knife. (Well-opened slits are important to permit escape of steam during baking.) Bake in hot oven (425 F.) 55 minutes, or until syrup boils with heavy bubbles that do not burst.

Sometime try using ½ cup granulated sugar and ½ cup brown sugar.

GOOSEBERRY LATTICE-TOP PIE

4 cups gooseberries
1 cup white sugar
1 cup water
½ cup brown sugar
2 tablespoons quick-cooking tapioca
⅛ teaspoon salt
½ teaspoon cloves
½ teaspoon cinnamon
¼ teaspoon nutmeg
2 tablespoons orange juice
2 tablespoons butter
2-crust pastry recipe
1 tablespoon granulated sugar

Combine berries, white and brown sugar, and water in a saucepan and cook until gooseberries are tender. Combine tapioca, salt, and spices; mix well; add orange juice and add to berries. Stir and allow mixture to cool. Line 9-inch pie pan with pastry; pour in fruit and dot with butter. Cut strips with pastry cutter to form lattice top; press edges and sprinkle lattice with 1 tablespoon granulated sugar. Bake in hot oven (425 F.) about 45 minutes, or until brown.

Serve hot or cold with 1-inch squares of cream cheese for each serving.

PECAN CREAM PIE

1⅓ cups (15-ounce can) sweetened condensed milk
⅔ cup maple syrup
⅛ teaspoon salt
⅔ cup chopped pecans
½ cup heavy cream
1 tablespoon confectioners' sugar
12 pecan halves
1 baked 9-inch pie shell

Combine the sweetened condensed milk, maple syrup, and salt in a saucepan and mix well. Place over low heat and cook until the mixture begins to boil. Stir constantly until it thickens, about 4 minutes. When cool, add about half the chopped pecans to the filling and fill the pie shell. Sprinkle the remaining pecans on top. Whip the cream until stiff, folding in the sugar; pile it on top of the pie. Garnish with pecan halves and chill thoroughly.

PARTY PIES . . . . MAKE MINE CHIFFON

PINEAPPLE CHIFFON PIE

1 envelope unflavored gelatin
¼ cup cold water
1 flat can crushed pineapple
3 eggs, separated
¼ cup sugar
1 tablespoon grated lemon peel
3 tablespoons lemon juice or sherry
¼ teaspoon salt
½ cup sugar
1 baked 9-inch pie shell
chopped nuts

Sprinkle gelatin in cold water. From can of pineapple remove ¼ cup drained fruit and reserve for garnish. Mix egg yolks, ¼ cup sugar, pineapple remaining in can, lemon peel, and sherry or lemon juice in top of double boiler. Cook over hot water, stirring until thick. Add softened gelatin; stir until dissolved. Remove from heat. Cool in refrigerator until mixture begins to thicken. Add salt to egg whites and beat stiff, but not dry. Slowly add ½ cup sugar, beating continually. Fold into cooled pineapple mixture. Pour into cooled baked shell. Chill about 3 hours or until set. Garnish top of pie with chopped nuts and reserved pineapple.

CHOCOLATE-ORANGE SOUFFLÉ PIE

3 squares unsweetened chocolate
1 envelope unflavored gelatin
¼ cup water
4 eggs, separated
1 cup sugar
½ teaspoon salt
1½ teaspoons grated orange peel
1 tablespoon orange juice
1 baked pastry shell made with orange juice instead of water
1 cup heavy cream, whipped

Melt chocolate in top of double boiler. Soften gelatin in 2 tablespoons water. Combine slightly beaten egg yolks, ½ cup sugar, salt, orange peel and juice, and remaining water. Add to chocolate and stir until mixture is thick and smooth. Add softened gelatin and stir until dissolved. Remove from heat. Cool mixture until it begins to thicken. Add remaining sugar to stiffly beaten egg whites and fold into chocolate mixture. Pour into pie shell and chill until firm. When ready to serve, spread whipped cream over top.

LIME CHIFFON PIE

Makes 8 to 10 servings:

1 envelope unflavored gelatin
¼ cup cold water
4 egg yolks
½ cup lime juice
1 cup sugar
¼ teaspoon salt
1 teaspoon grated lime rind
4 egg whites
1 cup heavy cream, whipped
1 baked 10-inch pie shell

Soften gelatin in cold water. Place egg yolks in top of double boiler; gradually add lime juice, ½ cup of the sugar, and salt, mixing until well blended. Cook over hot water until mixture thickens slightly, stirring constantly. Remove from heat; add gelatin and stir until dissolved. Add lime rind. Beat egg whites until stiff but not dry. Gradually beat in remaining ½ cup sugar. Fold into gelatin mixture, then fold in whipped cream. Now tint this a delicate green with vegetable coloring. Pile lightly into baked pastry shell. Chill until firm.

LEMON CHIFFON PIE: Use lemon juice and rind instead of lime.

DE LUXE PEACH CHIFFON PIE

1 envelope unflavored gelatin
¼ cup cold water
1 cup milk
½ cup sugar
⅛ teaspoon salt
3 egg yolks, slightly beaten
1 teaspoon vanilla
3 egg whites
1 baked 9-inch pie shell
1 cup heavy cream

Soften gelatin in cold water. Combine milk, ¼ cup of the sugar, salt, and egg yolks in top of double boiler. Cook over hot water until mixture thickens slightly, stirring constantly. Remove from heat; add gelatin and stir until dissolved. Add vanilla. Chill until mixture begins to thicken. Beat egg whites until stiff but not dry. Gradually beat in remaining ¼ cup sugar. Fold into gelatin mixture. Pile into baked pie shell. Chill. Just before serving, top with whipped cream and garnish with sliced fresh or well-drained canned peaches.

PARTY PIES . . . . . HAVE YOU TRIED THESE?

GOOD PUMPKIN PIE

The ambition of a good pumpkin pie is to have a glazed appearance on top, a firm and unsunken middle, and a light, fluffy texture when eaten. Slow baking helps remove the risk of sinking, and corn syrup ensures the glaze. Try it this way:

2 cups cooked pumpkin, strained
¼ cup corn syrup
1¾ cups milk or milk and cream
½ cup sugar
½ teaspoon nutmeg
½ teaspoon ginger
¼ teaspoon cloves
¼ teaspoon salt
1 tablespoon cornstarch
3 eggs
1 unbaked 9-inch pie shell

Mix pumpkin, syrup, and milk; blend. Combine dry ingredients and mix well. Add dry ingredients gradually and allow to stand in a cool place two hours or more. Add 3 eggs one at a time, beating each one into the mixture until well blended. Fill the unbaked pie shell and bake in hot oven (425 F.) until firm, about 25 minutes.

CRANBERRY-DATE PIE

4 cups whole cranberry sauce (2 1-pound cans)
½ cup chopped dates
1 tablespoon orange juice
3 tablespoons molasses
2 tablespoons quick-cooking tapioca
1 unbaked 9-inch pie shell

Combine cranberry sauce, dates, orange juice, molasses, and tapioca. Fill an unbaked pastry shell. Cover with a lattice topping so that the red can show merrily through. Bake in hot oven (425 F.) about 40 minutes, or until the crust is golden. Cool. Serve with or without ice cream or whipped cream. Serve this on the Fourth of July with vanilla ice cream.

ALMOND BAVARIAN PIE

¾ cup dark corn syrup
3 egg yolks
¼ teaspoon vanilla
1 teaspoon almond extract
1 envelope unflavored gelatin
2 tablespoons water
3 egg whites
⅛ teaspoon salt
1 9-inch crumb shell
½ cup chopped blanched almonds
1 cup heavy cream, whipped

Heat syrup to boiling. Beat egg yolks with rotary beater in top of double boiler; add syrup slowly, beating constantly. Place over boiling water and cook about 5 minutes, beating constantly until mixture is slightly thickened. Remove from heat; add flavoring. Add gelatin, softened in water for about 5 minutes. Stir until gelatin is dissolved. Beat egg whites with salt until mixture stands in peaks. Fold syrup into egg mixture. Chill. When slightly thickened, fold in nuts and whipped cream. Pour into crumb pie shell. Garnish with browned almonds. Chill before serving.

or try these

Makes 8 servings:

FROZEN ALMOND BAVARIAN: Prepare as for Almond Bavarian Pie filling, omitting gelatin and water. After folding in chopped nuts and whipped cream, pour into refrigerator freezing tray. Set cold control for fast freezing and freeze until firm, about 1 hour. Set cold control back to normal until ready to serve.

MARASCHINO BAVARIAN: Prepare as for Almond Bavarian Pie filling, omitting almond extract and chopped almonds. Fold in ½ cup chopped, drained maraschino cherries with whipped cream, and increase vanilla to 1 teaspoon. Chill until slightly thickened. Pile lightly into sherbet glasses. Chill before serving.

PARFAIT PIES . . . . SUMMER SPECIALS

STRAWBERRY-RHUBARB PARFAIT PIE

1 package lemon-flavored gelatin
¼ cup hot strawberry juice
1 cup hot rhubarb juice
1 pint vanilla ice cream
1 cup sugared, sliced strawberries, drained
¾ to 1 cup cooked, sweetened rhubarb, drained
1 baked 9-inch pie shell, cooled

Dissolve gelatin in hot fruit juice in 2-quart saucepan. Add ice cream by spoonfuls, stirring until melted. Then chill until thickened but not set (15 to 25 minutes). Fold in drained strawberries and rhubarb. Pour into pie shell. Chill until firm (about 1 hour). Garnish with strawberries if desired.

BLUEBERRY PARFAIT PIE, NEW ENGLAND STYLE

1 package lemon-flavored gelatin
2 tablespoons brown sugar
hot blueberry juice plus water to make 1¼ cups
2 tablespoons lemon juice
⅛ teaspoon cinnamon
1 pint vanilla ice cream
1 cup canned blueberries, drained
1 baked 9-inch pie shell, cooled

Dissolve gelatin and brown sugar in hot blueberry juice and water in 2-quart saucepan. Add lemon juice and cinnamon. Add ice cream by spoonfuls, stirring until melted. Chill until thickened but not set (25 to 35 minutes). Fold in drained blueberries. Turn into pie shell. Chill until firm (15 to 25 minutes). Garnish with whipped cream.

COFFEE DELIGHT PARFAIT PIE

1 package orange-flavored gelatin
1¼ cups hot water
½ cup sugar
2 tablespoons instant coffee
1 pint vanilla ice cream
½ to ¾ cup coarsely chopped walnuts
1 teaspoon grated orange rind
2 tablespoons raisins
1 tablespoon chopped maraschino cherries
1 baked 9-inch pie shell, cooled

Dissolve gelatin in hot water in 2-quart saucepan. Add sugar and instant coffee and stir until dissolved. Add ice cream by spoonfuls, stirring until melted. Then chill until thickened but not set (15 to 25 minutes). Fold in nuts, orange rind, raisins, and cherries. Turn into pie shell. Chill until firm (20 to 30 minutes). Garnish with whipped cream.

PEPPERMINT PARFAIT PIE

1 package lemon-flavored gelatin
¼ cup finely crushed peppermint stick candy
1¼ cups hot water
few drops red food coloring
1 pint vanilla ice cream
1 baked 8-inch pie shell, cooled

Dissolve gelatin and candy in hot water in 2-quart saucepan. Add food coloring. Add ice cream by spoonfuls, stirring until melted. Chill until thickened but not set (15 to 25 minutes). Turn into pie shell. Chill until firm (15 to 25 minutes). Garnish with whipped cream and shaved chocolate.

TROPICAL PARFAIT PIE

1 package orange-flavored gelatin
1¼ cups hot orange juice
1 pint banana ice cream
1 cup cut coconut
1 baked 8-inch pie shell, cooled

Dissolve gelatin in hot orange juice in 2-quart saucepan. Add ice cream by spoonfuls, stirring until melted. Chill until thickened but not set (30 to 40 minutes). Fold in coconut. Turn into pie shell. Chill until firm (15 to 25 minutes). Garnish with whipped cream and additional coconut.

BLACKBERRY PARFAIT PIE

1 package raspberry-flavored gelatin
hot berry juice plus water to make 1¼ cups
1 pint vanilla ice cream
1½ cups fresh, canned, or quick-frozen blackberries, sweetened and drained
1 baked 9-inch pie shell, cooled

Dissolve gelatin in hot liquid in 2-quart saucepan. Add ice cream by spoonfuls, stirring until melted. Chill until thickened but not set, 10 to 20 minutes. Fold in drained blackberries. Turn into pie shell. Chill until firm (15 to 25 minutes). Garnish with whipped cream.

ICE CREAM PIES . . . . . . MADE-IN-ADVANCE

Make 9-inch Chocolate Coconut Crust and fill it with one of these:

• Orange ice or lemon milk sherbet spooned into the shell in mounds.

• Green-tinted mint-flavored ice cream, spread on evenly to cut like Cream Cheese Pie.

• Mix ½ cup chopped citron and candied fruits with 1 cup heavy cream which has been whipped and sweetened to taste. Fill the crust and chill in freezer 25 minutes before serving.

• Chocolate ice cream, stirred until soft enough to spread evenly in the shell, then top with whipped unsweetened heavy cream and serve. For fancy effect, shave unsweetened chocolate over top of cream.

• Spread layer of vanilla ice cream in bottom of pie shell.

PUDDING PIES . . . . IN A COCONUT SHELL

Make 9-inch Baked Coconut Crust and fill it with one of these:

• Lemon pie or pudding mix. Garnish with maraschino cherries.

• Vanilla custard made with undiluted evaporated milk for rich cream filling. Sprinkle top with white shreds of coconut.

• Chocolate pudding mix made with undiluted evaporated milk for a rich filling. Beat pudding with rotary beater to make it light; garnish with walnut or pecan halves to make it beautiful.

• Chocolate cream. Spread with heavy cream, whipped but only slightly sweetened.

• For a tropical pie, pit and chop 2 cups dates. Add 1 cup water, 1 tablespoon lemon juice, and 1 tablespoon quick-cooking tapioca. Place over low heat and simmer, but do not allow it to boil, until it is thickened. Cool. Fill the coconut shell and chill. Cover with whipped cream just before serving.

CHOCOLATE FILLINGS . . FOR MERINGUE SHELLS

CHOCOLATE MOCHA CREAM FILLING

Makes 3½ cups:

1 package (¼ pound) sweetened chocolate
3 tablespoons hot water
2 teaspoons instant coffee
1½ cups heavy cream, whipped

Melt chocolate in top of double boiler. Add water and instant coffee; stir and cool. Fold into the whipped cream. Fill meringue shell and chill at least 2 hours before serving.

VANILLA-CHOCOLATE LAYER FILLING

Makes 4½ cups:

3 squares unsweetened chocolate
3 tablespoons hot water
⅛ teaspoon salt
2 cups heavy cream, whipped
6 tablespoons sugar
1 teaspoon vanilla

Melt only 2 squares of chocolate in top of double boiler; add water and salt. Stir and cool a little. Fold in half the whipped cream. Pile into meringue shell. Add sugar and vanilla to remaining cream. Spread over top of chocolate layer. Sprinkle with shaved or grated square of chocolate. Chill 2 or 3 hours before serving.

CHOCOLATE-MINT FILLING

Makes 5½ cups:

2 packages chocolate pudding mix
⅓ cup chopped peanuts
few drops peppermint flavoring

Make the pudding according to directions on the package. Add mint flavoring to taste. Cool and fill the meringue shell. Sprinkle chopped peanuts in a narrow band around the edge. Chill before serving.

FRUIT AND BERRIES . . . FOR MERINGUE SHELLS

FRUIT CREAMS

Makes 6 cups:

2 cups heavy cream
⅛ teaspoon salt
2 cups sweetened fresh or frozen raspberries, strawberries, or peaches

Whip cream; sprinkle with salt; fold in berries. Makes bountiful fillings for meringue shells.

MILK WHIP FILLING

Makes 5 cups:

½ cup water
1 tablespoon lemon juice
1 teaspoon vanilla
½ cup non-fat dry milk
3 tablespoons sugar
2 cups sweetened fruit or berries

Put water into a 1-quart mixing bowl. Stir in lemon juice and vanilla. Sprinkle dry milk over top of liquid; beat with rotary beater or electric mixer until stiff, about 10 minutes. Sprinkle sugar on the surface. Beat until sugar is blended and mixture is stiff enough to hold peaks, about 5 minutes. Fold in sweetened fruit and fill meringue shell. Or make a layer of the fruit on the shell, then pile sweetened whip in a mound at the center.

FRUIT CREAM WHIP

Makes 5 cups:

1 can (14½ ounces) evaporated milk, chilled 30 minutes
2 cups raspberries, strawberries, or peaches, sweetened

Pour undiluted evaporated milk into freezing tray (or into a mixing bowl if you have a freezer). Chill and whip until it holds peaks. Fold in the sweetened fruit. Spread to fill or frost cake.

PIES, PIES, PIES . . . . FILL A 9-INCH SHELL

REFRIGERATOR PINEAPPLE-CHEESE PIE

Makes one 9-inch pie shell:

4 cups corn flakes
2 tablespoons sugar
4 tablespoons melted butter or margarine

Crush corn flakes fine. To do this the easy way, fold them up in clean tea towel, roll up tightly, and crush with hands. This amount makes 1 cup. Add sugar and melted butter or margarine; mix well. Press into 9-inch glass pie pan, reserving 3 tablespoons of crumbs for topping. Chill thoroughly.

FILLING:

1 envelope unflavored gelatin
¼ cup cold water
3 eggs, separated
⅔ cup crushed pineapple, not drained (a buffet or No. 1 flat can)
1 teaspoon grated lemon peel
2 tablespoons lemon juice
¾ cup sugar
1 cup cream-style cottage cheese
¼ teaspoon salt

Add plain gelatin to cold water; set aside. Beat egg yolks slightly in double boiler or heavy saucepan; add crushed pineapple, grated lemon peel, lemon juice, and ¼ cup of the sugar; cook, stirring until thick.

Add gelatin; stir until dissolved; remove from heat. Force creamy cottage cheese through wire strainer; add to hot mixture; cool until beginning to thicken. Beat egg whites with salt; when stiff, gradually beat in ½ cup sugar and fold into pineapple-cheese mixture. Heap into chilled crust; sprinkle with the reserved crumbs and chill 3 hours or longer.

CREAM CHEESE PIE

1⅓ cups (15 ounces) sweetened condensed milk
¼ cup lemon juice
1 3-ounce package cream cheese
2 eggs, separated
1 cup sliced strawberries, raspberries, crushed pineapple, ripe sliced bananas, or red sour cherries—all fruit, no juice
¼ teaspoon cream of tartar
4 tablespoons sugar

Combine the milk and lemon juice in mixing bowl and beat until thickened. Soften the cream cheese and beat until it is soft and smooth. Add egg yolks one at a time, beating after each addition until thoroughly blended. Add the fruit and mix well. Now add the milk mixture, folding it in. Pour into cooled pastry shell. Add the cream of tartar to the egg whites and beat until almost thick enough to hold a peak. Add the sugar gradually, beating until the whites are stiff and glossy but not dry. Pile the egg whites on the pie and bake in a slow oven (325 F.) until lightly browned, about 15 minutes. Cool before serving.

STRAWBERRY PIE

4 cups (1 quart) strawberries
¾ cup sugar
4 tablespoons cornstarch
½ teaspoon salt
½ cup orange juice
¾ cup heavy cream, whipped

Wash, drain, and hull strawberries; cut in half. Combine sugar, cornstarch, and salt in top of double boiler. Gradually add orange juice, mixing until smooth. Add half of the strawberries. Place over boiling water and cook, stirring constantly until mixture thickens (about 5 minutes). Cover and continue cooking 10 minutes, stirring occasionally. Remove from heat; cool. Fold in remaining strawberries. Pour into baked pie shell. Chill. Just before serving, top with whipped cream sweetened to taste.

EVERYBODY LOVES . . . . . . A DEEP-DISH PIE

May is here and cherries are ripe. Even when they aren't you can make a deep-dish pie with canned cherries. A deep-dish pie can be made to fill any casserole or big baking dish you want to use. This makes it a handy dessert when you cook for the crowd (or when you have a family that eats like one).

A deep-dish pie is a creation . . . yours . . . for the fruit and berries vary in sweetness, not only from one season to the next, but depending upon whether you use fresh, canned, or frozen fruit, the last two usually having sugar added. This doesn't need to make it difficult. Fruit and berries full of themselves, not too delicate, heavily laden with flavor to coax out into the juice around them, full of steaming goodness under the flaky crust, make the best pies. Cherries in May through July, blackberries and blueberries those months too, and that suitably wedded pair, strawberries and rhubarb—suitably wedded in a pie at least—are May and June delights. Then comes autumn and apple deep-dish pies.

- Serve them hot or cold with hard sauce . . . hot or cold with whipped cream.
- Cover them with a pastry in which you have cut a daisy or some design worthy of the fruit, through which steam can escape.
- Make the pies this way, always remembering the only joker is—you must taste to test the sweetening. No complaints about that?
- Add a tablespoon of orange juice to the berry pies. Try half brown sugar or maple sugar with apple or peach pies. And always be sure the "steam vents" in your pastry top are open.

BLUEBERRY DEEP-DISH PIE

Makes about 7 cups:

Proceed as for Apple Deep-Dish Pie below, using the following seasonings for each 4 cups of fresh, uncooked blueberries. Frozen or canned blueberries require less sugar and should be drained, adding water to the juice to make 2 cups.

1 cup sugar
4 tablespoons tapioca
⅛ teaspoon salt
2 cups water
1 tablespoon lemon juice
4 cups blueberries, uncooked
1 tablespoon butter
1-crust pastry recipe

Combine dry ingredients and stir. Add water and lemon juice and mix thoroughly. Arrange berries in greased casserole, sprinkling the liquid over them until the baking dish is filled, being sure to pile the fruit a little bit higher in the center. Cover with pastry and bake in moderate oven (350 F.) about 60 minutes. Serve with heavy cream, whipped cream, or hard sauce.

APPLE DEEP-DISH PIE

Makes 6 cups:

½ to 1 cup brown sugar
½ teaspoon cinnamon
½ teaspoon nutmeg
3 tablespoons quick-cooking tapioca
¼ teaspoon salt
4 cups tart apples
2 teaspoons lemon juice
2 tablespoons butter
1 cup water
1-crust pastry recipe

Mix dry ingredients. Arrange apples in greased baking dish. Sprinkle lemon juice and the dry ingredients over the apples, alternating until the dish is filled. Be sure to pile the apples a little higher in the center as you would for a shallow apple pie. Sprinkle the remaining sugar and spices over the top and dot with the butter. Cover with pastry. Bake in moderate oven (350 F.) 55 minutes, or until apples are tender.

CHERRY DEEP-DISH PIE

Makes about 5 cups:

¼ cup sugar
3 tablespoons quick-cooking tapioca
⅛ teaspoon salt
½ cup water
4 cups pitted fresh cherries
2 tablespoons butter
1-crust pastry recipe

Combine dry ingredients; stir; add water. Arrange a layer of fruit in greased baking dish, then sprinkle with the sugar mixture, adding another layer of fruit and sprinkling with the remainder of the mixture. Dot with butter. Cover with pastry and be sure slits are opened. Bake in moderate oven (350 F.) until cherries are cooked, about 45 minutes. It's that easy. (Double or triple recipe to fill larger baking dish).

CHAPTER 7
FRUIT AND BERRY DESSERTS

STRAWBERRY RHAPSODY . . PLEASURES OF SPRING

All over the world strawberries share with the first robin the joy of ushering in the spring. In this country the big ripe sweet berries appear in April and are plentiful through May and June. There is no end to eating them with pleasure when picked fresh from underneath a leaf where they were hiding, bought in baskets at the market, bursting with juice a few hours later when submerged in sweetened cream, in shortcakes or fruit rolls, or spooned over or into ice cream.

The Queen of England selected some of the first strawberry crop to serve at her spring garden party. These English berries are unlike the English; for the berries are enormous show-offs—the biggest strawberries man has ever seen. Not a morsel of flavor is lost in their growing to such a size. They are filled with perfume and fine flavor. Anyone could buy them from peddlers on the street, and few who bought got home with the baskets intact. Mine never saw the sight of cream but were eaten as if they were candy, nibbled off the stems.

Then came June in Paris. Strawberries again, tiny ones no larger than my thumbnail, deep maroon in color, delicious beyond belief. The little yellow dots on these lend a crusty texture to each bite of juice-filled berry. The French pick these little berries and nestle them lovingly inside leaves to avoid any of the strawberry juice or flavor escaping into the air. The leafy baskets are sold by vendors in the street; the berries are the pride of every restaurant. The French set a good example for all who would be happy. They know when their *petites fraises* ripen. They anticipate enjoying them, and then they expand with pleasure when the moment—and the berries—are ripe.

Another year these little strawberries were ripe in Spain in March. There the sun shines earlier, longer than anywhere else, and has a special blessing for all fruit—an obvious thing anyone who visits Spain will know. All their fruit is drenched with flavor, distilled essence of perfection, whether a berry or an orange.

A FRUIT AND BERRY ALMANAC . . . . ANTICIPATE THESE

But we are at home. Ours is a land laden with fruit, the supply abundant the year round in canned and frozen packages. These are done with such care that the quality is excellent, the flavor fine. But anticipating the first appearance of each fruit and berry, enjoying them in season, serving them in dozens of ways, is part of the good life.

The berry season begins in April (and never stops until summer does) with STRAWBERRIES . . . BLUEBERRIES . . . HUCKLEBERRIES . . . DEWBERRIES . . . BLACKBERRIES . . . RASPBERRIES appearing in constant procession. Before the modern fruit supply these berries used to make a change from winter apple pies.

This is the season to make Fruit Rolls of biscuit dough, brushed with butter, spread thick with berries sprinkled with sugar and cinnamon. Roll up as if it were a jelly roll, and bake in a pan with more sweetened berries all around it. The berries outside the roll reduce to juicy sauce to pour over the steaming slices of Berry Roll when it comes, browned and wonderful, from the hot oven. Of course you eat it hot. Who could wait for it to cool?

When fruit was enjoyed only in its season, the first cherry pie appeared on the table in May and showed up for rosy repeat appearances until September in Cherry Rolls and in lattice-top pies, in cobblers and in deep-dish pies. Sweet and warm from the tree, a few handfuls were stemmed and pitted to toss into a freezer of custard ice cream. There might be Open Cherry Tarts for dinner. Next morning the day began all over again with small sweet Cherry Rolls for breakfast. And a few were always candied to go into Christmas cakes. Since then we have learned how attractive cherries are to beautify salads, to surround a Cherry Bavarian Cream. Nothing could be lovelier than a bowl of cherries, with nothing done to them, served with stems on for dessert.

All the berries and fruit were popped into muffins, made into preserves, and stewed to eat with angel cake.

May is the merry month of the MANGO. Luscious fruit best enjoyed if you're able to slip over to Mexico to eat them, eat them, eat them. Who cares if the juice dribbles a bit, spotting a necktie or a dress? Mangoes are perfumy fruit when dead ripe; lose character when canned, alas. But then—they had plenty to lose.

CURRANTS join the array in June, become abundant in July. Tedious to pick, delicious to eat, they are wonderful in jelly. Don't fail to make some. The butterflies used to light on the branches during currant-picking time when I was a little girl. Watching their gay maneuvers made the time pass quickly.

Combine currants with black or red raspberries to make jelly. Put the berries into biscuits, breads. And of course you know that in all of Europe currants must be in puddings and in *Stollen* at Christmas time. Red currants are also beautiful on hats—artificial currants.

GOOSEBERRIES in June and July. Biscuit Cobbler is where they belong, or in a lattice-top pie. Sprinkled with granulated sugar on top. Fact is, gooseberries are good in about everything—conserves, tarts, preserves too. Make them sweet and thick but don't take their sting away.

APRICOTS are their ripe best from June through July. They are so beautiful served whole. Use them whole, too, for decoration on desserts or salads.

NECTARINES, first cousin to a peach, appear in June too. Eat them ripe. Put them in compotes until they disappear in August.

PEACHES are ripe by July, with us from late May lasting into October, and there is no end of enjoying them. Remembered raptures of tree-ripe fragrant peaches should make those frozen sliced peach sales pick up the year round. There is no place you cannot put a peach, beginning with fuzzy-beautiful in the center of the table, to simmering it in the Peach and Blueberry Cake Compote I told you about, that a peach is anything but superb.

SEPTEMBER SONG . . . . . . AUTUMN FRUIT

PRICKLY PEARS are "September Songs" sure enough. Quarter them, then remove the threatening peel, and serve slices or wedges.

ENJOY FRUIT IN ITS OWN SEASON . . . AUTUMN

PLUMS are in the markets by May but are abundant from July through September. Eat the red ones, the purple ones; by all means gently stew a few to cool and eat for breakfast. These plush, purple beauties are ripe until October.

POMEGRANATES, with their dull red surface hiding those jewel-like seeds, should always be cherished through October and November. The seeds scattered over other fruits in a compote or salad are undeniably marvelous.

PEARS in August, with plenty of them through September and October. Then there are winter pears all through December, juicy and wonderful fresh-peeled or baked in syrup.

October is the month for autumn leaves and bright PERSIMMONS. The orange blobs of fruit last until Christmas. Serve these plain, split open and seeds removed, with a mound of cream cheese softened with sweet cream atop. Sprinkle with cinnamon, serve on a lettuce leaf. What a sight!

GRAPES! What beauties these are. Decorative on the table too, graceful October, November centerpieces.

TANGERINES come in November, abundant in December, still around in January. Remember to enjoy these for breakfast.

KUMQUATS, plentiful in November, more so in December and January, still with us in February, and easing off the market in late March. Don't forget to preserve some of these yourself. Use them in table decorations, including the leaves, or just eat a few as if they were candy.

A FRUIT ALMANAC . . . . . . WINTER BLESSINGS

BANANAS are every-month-in-the-year fruit, and isn't that lucky, since they are so full of what gives us *oomph* that they are very nearly the perfect food. Shake up with milk, and there is no match for the pair. And did you know that bananas ripen for us exactly as they do for people who live where they grow? They are cut off the trees in those tremendous bunches while very green and allowed to ripen, which is exactly the way they are cut and shipped all over the world.

LEMONS and LIMES are summertime fruits from choice. Nevertheless, the supply is a year-round one, and the other round-the-calendar fruits include COCONUTS, GRAPEFRUIT, ORANGES, and those old familiars we have been so accustomed to in dried form that we hardly knew they had their own birthdays—FIGS . . . DATES . . . PRUNES . . . APRICOTS—and they actually are around all the year in freshly put-up packs. Well, not exactly. Apricots are June and July delights, but who cares? They are desirable fresh, dried, or canned. Same with PINEAPPLES. They are slightly better in Cuba and Hawaii fresh from the field. But the canned pineapple is a near-nature treat we can have any old time.

APPLES—around the year round—also have a special season of their own from October through March. That is their peak. Their peak in flavor is such that everybody loves them, so they are pale or blushing with good cause. In February there is an Apple Week, in case the apple, which used to be stowed away in cellars with the first frost and brought up on winter evenings to munch before going to bed, might lose out to more new-fangled fruit.

With shipping what it is, this calendar of sorts is really not a necessity, perhaps it will be a pleasure. Fresh, frozen, or canned abundance is always with us. There is small need, really, to learn about any other desserts. Just eat fruit. Beside the pies and pastries and cobblers and all those things fruit has already appeared in, here are a few exclusive fruit desserts. So quick and so good they are. You will run into them in a minute.

MELONS ARE A JOY . . . . WHEN TO EXPECT THEM

MELON ANTICIPATION CALENDAR

May	through August	Watermelons are ripe.
June	through July	Honeyballs are ripe.
July	through August	Cantaloupes beguile us.
July	through October	Cranshaws are here.
July	through October	Honeydews, those heavenly honeydews.
August	through October	Persians take over.
October	through December	Casabas stay till Christmas.

There are those who think people fools who tamper with a fragrant, juicy ripe melon. There are others who love to "fix" things. It is not my idea to encourage the latter but to console them. For their sakes, here are four things to do with melons before eating them.

MELON FRUIT BOWLS

Chill melons (except watermelons) and cut in halves or in wedges; scoop out the seeds and fill them with contrasting fruit—blueberries, big black cherries, orange wedges, or with balls of various melons. These are pretty as all get out and make a table look divine.

MELON ICE CREAM COMPOTE

Prepare the melons as for the bowls, then fill them with an ice or a scoop of ice cream. Small scoops of ices and ice creams in different flavors add to the floral effect.

CANTALOUPE BAKED ALASKA

Fill cantaloupe halves with ice cream; cover with sweetened meringue, piling it clear to the edge of the melon. Arrange the halves on chopped ice in a deep tray and shove under the broiler to brown in a hurry. Remove and serve.

MELONS WITH LIDS ON

In France, delicious little melons are served one for each person. The top is cut off as for a jack-o'-lantern, the seeds scooped out, and the lid put back. Perch a cantaloupe or a honeyball fixed this way, with a green leaf under it, on a party plate, and serve.

FREEZE MELONS FOR NEXT WINTER . . HERE'S HOW

Did you ever eat enough watermelon? Or enough cantaloupe? Probably not. It wasn't possible during their brief stay. Now you can have a year-round melon spree if you have a freezer handy. This includes Persians . . . Cranshaws . . . Casabas . . . and Watermelons.

TO PREPARE LIGHT SYRUP: Combine 1 cup sugar with 3 cups water in saucepan; bring just to a boil. Makes 3½ cups. Chill in the refrigerator. When ready to use, add 3½ teaspoons lemon juice (fresh, frozen, or canned).

TO PREPARE BALLS: Cut melon in half; remove seeds, using tip of teaspoon. Spoon out balls, using melon ball cutter (small or large) or ¼- or ½-teaspoon measure. Place in freezer containers; cover with syrup; put crumpled strip of waxed paper in top to hold fruit under syrup; seal.

TO PREPARE WEDGES: Slice melon in quarters; remove seeds, using tip of teaspoon. Cut quarters lengthwise into ¾-inch slices; cut crosswise into wedges. Place in freezer containers; cover with syrup; put crumpled strip of waxed paper in top; seal; label.

TO FREEZE: Fast-freeze balls or wedges and store at 0 F.

HOW TO DEFROST MELONS FOR USE

In refrigerator—approximately 8 hours.

At room temperature—approximately 3 hours.

Keep in refrigerator until ready to use—serve frosty, to have at their natural delicious best.

OLD-FASHIONED—DELICIOUS . 3 BISCUIT COBBLERS

CHERRY BISCUIT COBBLER

Makes 8 servings:

4 cups (2 No. 2 cans) sour pie cherries
½ cup brown sugar
½ cup white sugar
⅛ teaspoon salt
3 tablespoons quick-cooking tapioca
⅛ teaspoon cloves
¼ teaspoon cinnamon
2 tablespoons orange juice
2-cup recipe of biscuit mix

Pour the cherries into a large saucepan. Combine the dry ingredients, mix well and stir them into the fruit. Place over medium heat and bring to a boil and continue cooking another 5 minutes. Remove from heat and pour into a buttered 2-quart casserole. To make the cobbler extra-rich, use undiluted evaporated milk in preparing the biscuit top. Drop the batter by spoonfuls on top of the fruit, making 8 mounds of biscuit. Bake in preheated oven at 400 F. about 20 minutes, or until biscuits are browned.

PINEAPPLE-CHERRY COBBLER

Makes 8 servings:

½ cup granulated sugar
2 tablespoons cornstarch
¼ cup brown sugar, firmly packed
½ teaspoon ginger
3½ cups (No. 2½ can) pineapple chunks, not drained
½ cup cherries, drained

Mix first four ingredients together thoroughly in an 8 x 8 x 2-inch baking dish. Stir in pineapple chunks and syrup and the cherries. Place in preheated oven set at 400 F. while preparing:

BISCUIT TOPPING:

1½ cups sifted all-purpose flour	*½ teaspoon salt*
3 teaspoons baking powder	*¼ cup shortening*
2 tablespoons granulated sugar	*½ cup milk*

Sift dry ingredients together; cut in shortening until well distributed. Stir in milk. Turn dough out on a floured board and knead gently several strokes to smooth dough. Roll out to an 8-inch square. Prick dough in several places and put it on hot fruit. Continue baking at 400 F. for about 25 minutes. Serve warm.

• Or make topping with 2-cup recipe of biscuit mix, adding 2 tablespoons sugar.

BLUEBERRY BISCUIT COBBLER

On Cape Cod, blueberries are plentiful through the summer, and it was there that the steamed biscuit-top Blueberry Grunt originated. Times have changed—although the blueberry supply has not, nor our taste for these berries in a pie or cobbler. Now we do not steam the tops, but bake our cobblers brown and crisp to contrast with the purple velvet richness underneath.

Makes 8 servings:

4 cups fresh blueberries combined with ¾ cup water or 2 No. 300 cans blueberries
½ cup brown sugar
½ cup white sugar
3 tablespoons quick-cooking tapioca
¼ teaspoon salt
2 tablespoons lemon juice
½ teaspoon cinnamon
2-cup recipe biscuit mix topping
2 tablespoons sugar

Combine all ingredients except topping and 2 tablespoons sugar in saucepan. Bring to a boil and cook 5 more minutes for canned berries, about 10 minutes for fresh. Add 2 tablespoons sugar to biscuit mix.

Pour blueberry mixture into casserole. Cover with biscuit topping or make dough for Drop Biscuits and drop on top of the fruit. Bake as directed on the package until biscuits are brown.

TOP BILLINGS . . . . FOR THESE SWEETHEARTS

PEACH AND BLUEBERRY CAKE COBBLER

Makes 6 servings:

2 cups (No. 303 can) peaches
2 cups (No. 300 can) blueberries
3 tablespoons quick-cooking tapioca
½ cup sugar
½ cup brown sugar
⅛ teaspoon cinnamon
¼ teaspoon salt
1 tablespoon lemon juice
1 tablespoon butter
½ small package (1 pound, 1 ounce) white cake mix

Lightly butter a casserole—it should be nice and deep, for this needs depth—and pour the fruit into it. Combine dry ingredients; sprinkle over the top of the fruit and lift the fruit gently with a fork to let the dry flavoring seep into it. Sprinkle with lemon juice and dot with butter. Prepare half the contents of a *small* white cake mix. Spoon the batter over the fruit and bake in a preheated oven as directed on the package, until the cake is *thoroughly* done.

BLACK CHERRIES-PALE PEARS COBBLER

Makes 12 servings:

2 cups (No. 303 can) bing cherries
3½ cups (No. 2½ can) pear halves
3½ cups apricots
4 to 5 tablespoons quick-cooking tapioca
½ cup sugar
¾ cup brown sugar
⅓ cup orange juice
1 tablespoon lemon juice
¼ teaspoon salt
⅛ teaspoon cinnamon
2 tablespoons butter
1 small package (1 pound, 1 ounce) white cake mix

Prepare as for the Peach and Blueberry Cake Cobbler, except a deep, long casserole or pan is needed for this one, with more fruit and a larger surface of cake. Don't make the cake deeper.

ORANGE AND GRAPEFRUIT CAKE COBBLER

Makes 8 servings:

1 No. 303 can grapefruit slices
1 No. 303 can grapefruit and mandarin orange slices
½ cup brown sugar
½ cup granulated sugar
½ cup raspberries, drained
¼ teaspoon salt
1 tablespoon butter
3½ tablespoons quick-cooking tapioca
½ small package (1 pound, 1 ounce) white cake mix

Pour fruit into a deep, lightly buttered casserole. Proceed as for Peach and Blueberry Cake Cobbler.

SHORTCAKES . . . . CRISP, DRIPPING WITH FRUIT

CRISP INDIVIDUAL BERRY SHORTCAKES

Makes 8 hungry-man servings. No use making these little, or everyone will want two.

4 cups biscuit mix
1⅓ cups undiluted evaporated milk
2 tablespoons brown sugar
¼ teaspoon salt
½ cup butter, softened
4 cups berries, sweetened
2 cups heavy cream, whipped

Combine first four ingredients and blend with a fork. Drop large spoonfuls onto greased cookie sheet to make 8 biscuits. Use a fork to flatten and shape. Bake in hot oven (450 F.) about 15 minutes. Split open, butter, and fill with berries. Put on tops; load with whipped cream and more berries. Serve warm. If you like, let each person split, butter, and fill his own shortcake from bowls of cream and berries on the table.

Use any fresh sweetened or frozen berries you like, or sliced peaches for shortcakes. Try No. 2½ can whole cranberry sauce too.

6-LAYER SHORTCAKE

Makes 12 servings:

shortcake batter
4 cups berries
3 cups heavy cream, whipped

Make batter as for Crisp Individual Shortcakes. Use fork to spread into three rounds on baking sheet, or bake in three greased 8-inch cake or pie pans. Split the cakes with a long sharp knife; place one layer on large serving plate; cover with cream and fruit and add biscuit top, continuing until the pile is high. Serve hot, and slice as for layer cake.

• If the cake is to be served cold, do not fill until ready to serve, or the crispness will be lost.

• Thing to watch is, the layers must not be *thin*. Biscuit dough comes out of the oven about twice the size it went in. So remember that and mix more if your pans are larger than 8 inches.

BANANA SHORTCAKE

Makes 12 servings:

2 tablespoons cocoa
shortcake batter
⅔ cup sugar
2½ cups heavy cream, whipped
3 cups banana slices

Add cocoa to biscuit batter. Bake three 8-inch biscuits, and proceed as for 6-Layer Shortcake. Add sugar to whipped cream. Fill layers with cream and banana slices.

23 COMPOTES . . . . . . HAVE YOU TRIED THESE?

• Combine fresh fruits or berries with fruit or berries from chilled cans or from frozen packages to make colorful ready-chilled compotes.

• Regard the vitamins as highly as the flavor of fruit and keep them intact. When combining canned fruits in a chilled compote, chill cans unopened; combine when ready to serve. Store unused fruit in covered containers, for vitamins elope via air and you never see them again. When cooking, use low heat and minimum cooking time.

• In opening 3 cans or 3 frozen packages of fruit or berries, use half of each for a compote. Reserve the rest to serve over breakfast cereal, to fold into sweetened whipped cream, to serve as a fruit mousse or, on lettuce with dressing, as a fruit salad.

• Combine the contents of 3 canned fruits or berries and chill. Serve as you want it, for compotes improve as they stand. Anyhow, they will soon be eaten up.

• Add a few dashes of Angostura to the syrup of almost any fruit or fruit combination being served as a chilled dessert.

• Make a sugar syrup of 1 cup sugar, ½ cup frozen orange juice, undiluted, and ½ cup water. Place over low heat and stir until the sugar is dissolved. Cool; add a dash of Angostura bitters, ⅛ teaspoon cinnamon, and serve over bowls filled with ⅔ blueberries and ⅓ banana slices. Garnish with chopped crystallized ginger for a fancy dish or sprinkle with about ¼ teaspoon powdered ginger.

• From May until August lovely berries are in season. Combine strawberries . . . blackberries . . . dewberries . . . blueberries . . . huckleberries or fresh raspberries with frozen or canned fruit to compose colorful compotes.

• Canned pears, frozen peaches, ripe raspberries can be sweetened to taste for compotes. Drain the canned pears, pouring the juice into a saucepan. Add a little sugar if necessary. Boil about 5 minutes. Add a tablespoon of lemon juice and pour hot sweetened juice over the fruit combination. Cool, then chill before serving.

• Pineapple chunks, banana chunks, and pitted bing cherries can be combined by draining the cherries and the pineapple separately. Reserve the bing cherry juice for a fruit drink. Add sugar to taste to the pineapple juice, boil to reduce, and pour over the 3 fruits which have been combined. Chill and serve.

• Spice a No. 2 can of any fruit in light syrup (peaches, apricots, pineapple, cherries) by draining the juice into a saucepan and adding 10 cloves, ½ teaspoon cinnamon, ½ teaspoon nutmeg. Boil for 5 minutes. Remove the cloves; add 1 tablespoon lemon juice and 1 teaspoon grated lemon peel. Pour the syrup over the fruit; cool and chill.

Serve plain or with a sprinkling of coconut or with a little blob of hard sauce.

• Combine young berries and bananas, half and half. Drain and spice the juice from the berries; pour back and chill.

• Boysenberries, apricots, and grapefruit slices make a beautiful compote. Drain boysenberry juice separately into a saucepan. Place over heat and boil until reduced to half original amount. Add to the undrained fruit and juice. Chill.

• Combine canned gooseberries, orange slices, and the juice from each. Add inch-long chunks of banana which have been sprinkled with lemon juice. Chill and serve with sprinkling of cinnamon on top.

• Don't bother giving Kadota figs any company; just open a chilled can of the fruit, sprinkle with a little orange or lemon juice, top with a blob of cream cheese softened with a bit of sweet cream.

• Cook heavily sweetened apricots until they are well done and syrupy. Put through a sieve and return to saucepan. Add chunks of banana; cover and cook over low heat about 8 minutes. Remove from heat but do not remove cover. Allow to cool slowly and then chill thoroughly and serve with cheese as a dessert.

• Kumquats (preserved) add a decorative touch when combined with strawberries and peaches, frozen or fresh. These rarely need sweetening, but sprinkle 1 or 2 tablespoons of orange juice over them to bring out the flavor.

• Mangoes and pineapple (canned) can be drained and the juice sweetened to taste and boiled about 5 minutes to reduce to half. Flavor is heightened with a tablespoon of lime juice. Pour over the fruit while juice is still hot. Cool and garnish with a sprinkling of blueberries or coconut.

• Nectarines, blueberries, and bing cherries are a pleasant combination. Drain the cherries, saving the juice for a fruit drink. Cover the fruit with orange juice to which enough lemon juice has been added to give a pleasant tartness.

• Orange and grapefruit slices are delicious and easy to combine. Get them canned in light syrup. Combine, chill, and garnish with strawberries if you like.

• October and November are pomegranate season. Sprinkle the beautiful red seeds from a pomegranate over combinations of peaches with pears, pineapple with pears, or over the orange and grapefruit combination. This is a truly exotic effect.

• Combine banana and pineapple chunks which have been drained. Put the juice in a saucepan; add a few drops of green food coloring and ½ teaspoon freshly grated nutmeg. Cook over low heat until the juice is reduced to thick syrup, about 5 minutes. Pour over the fruit chunks; cool and serve.

• Bananas cut into chunks are most attractive and delicious with almost any fruit combination. Combine with tart apricots, sour pie cherries, or bing cherries.

BAKED FRUIT COMPOTE

Makes 4 to 6 servings:

1 cup light corn syrup
⅓ cup orange sections
½ cup uncooked cranberries
3 fresh pears, quartered, peeled, and cored
6 whole cloves
1 3-inch stick cinnamon

Combine ingredients in a casserole. Cover and bake in moderate oven (350 F.) about 1 hour, or until pears are tender. Chill thoroughly before serving.

• Make up other fruit compotes for easy baking. Sweeten with syrup and put in the oven.

APPLE FRUIT COMPOTE

This is beautiful and delicious, depending upon how careful you are to cook the apples enough, yet not too much, so that they will be whole rather than mushy.

Makes 8 servings:

2 cups sugar
2 cups water
8 apples
⅛ teaspoon mace
¼ teaspoon cloves
1 tablespoon coarsely chopped lemon peel
a delicious orange, cubed

Combine the sugar and water in a saucepan and cook until the sugar is melted. Add the apples; reduce heat and cook until they are tender. Remove apples; add spices, lemon, and orange. Cook the syrup until it is thick. Pour over the apples and serve warm or cold.

IT'S EASY TO BAKE FRUIT . . FOR PARTY DESSERT

PARTY BAKED APPLES

Makes 4 servings:

½ cup dark corn syrup
½ cup water
¼ teaspoon cinnamon
1 teaspoon grated lemon rind
1 tablespoon butter
2 tablespoons sugar
4 baking apples
1 egg white
2 tablespoons sugar
14 almonds, blanched, shredded
4 maraschino cherries, chopped

Combine syrup, water, cinnamon, lemon rind, butter, and sugar in small saucepan. Bring to a boil. Remove from heat. Core apples; pare upper half. Place in shallow baking dish. Pour hot syrup mixture over apples. Bake in moderate oven (350 F.) about 1 hour, or until tender, basting frequently. Remove from oven. Beat egg white until foamy; gradually beat in sugar. Top each apple with meringue. Insert almonds in meringue. If desired, dot with chopped, drained maraschino cherries. Return to oven and bake 15 minutes, or until topping is delicately browned.

FRUIT FLOATS . . . . . PRETTY AS A PICTURE

Do you own a big crystal bowl? Even a big silver one would do. Or a big one made of sunny yellow pottery. If it is big enough to hold 3 quarts or more, you'll like filling it with one of these desserts to serve in pretty soup bowls. It will be a beautiful sight for the family . . . so don't keep these just for company.

MANGO FLOAT

Makes 13 cups:

1 14-ounce can mangoes
1 No. 303 can grapefruit and mandarin orange sections
1 No. 303 can grapefruit sections
1 12-ounce can apricot nectar
¼ teaspoon salt
½ teaspoon cinnamon
¼ cup lemon juice
1 teaspoon Angostura bitters
1 cup raspberries, drained
1 quart to 6 pints orange ice

Put the cans in the refrigerator to chill. When ready to serve, put the salt, cinnamon, lemon juice and bitters into the bowl and pour contents of each can into the bowl as you open it. Add raspberries. Stir gently. Spoon the orange ice into the bowl, making at least as many mounds as there are people to be served. It's ready!

STRAWBERRY FLOAT

Makes 13 cups:

4 cups (1 quart) fresh, stemmed strawberries
1 can frozen orange juice, thawed, undiluted
1 quart ginger ale
1 quart vanilla ice cream

Do not chill the berries, but be sure everything else is cold until ready to fill the bowl and serve. If you think the berries need sweetening, sprinkle them lightly with sugar after cleaning them.

GREENGAGE FLOAT

Makes 13 cups:

1 No. 2½ can greengage plums
1 No. 2½ can apricots
2 tablespoons lemon juice
1 No. 303 can black cherries, drained, or 2 cups fresh, pitted cherries
1 quart vanilla ice cream

Chill the cans until serving time, then open and fill the big bowl. Let the ice cream form a big white island in the center. Spoon off helpings when serving.

GRAPEFRUIT FLOAT

Makes 8 cups:

2 No. 303 cans grapefruit sections
1 package frozen raspberries
⅛ teaspoon salt
1 quart lemon ice

Chill until serving time. Combine and serve.

RHUBARB-BERRY FLOAT

Combine cooked rhubarb with equal amount of cooked strawberries and half the amount of whole blueberries, or the recipe could read this way:

1 package frozen rhubarb, cooked
1 package frozen strawberries, unthawed
½ package frozen blueberries, unthawed
1 can frozen orange juice, unthawed
½ cup lemon juice
¼ teaspoon salt
1 quart vanilla ice cream

Combine fruit and juices in a bowl and let stand at room temperature until thawed enough to stir gently with a fork. Return to refrigerator to chill. At serving time, place vanilla ice cream in center of bowl, to be spooned up with the fruit.

CHERRY-PINEAPPLE FLOAT

Combine canned pineapple chunks and canned bing cherries in equal quantities. Chill and serve for dessert.

This can be chilled and made even more beautiful than it already is by placing a big mound of lemon ice or pineapple ice in the center of the bowl. This will do the chilling, and a bit of it can be spooned off with each portion as the compote is served.

CHAPTER 8
COOKING AT THE TABLE OR ANYWHERE

PANCAKES . . . . FOR DESSERT

BANANA DESSERT PANCAKES

Makes 5 pancakes:

2 tablespoons sugar
½ teaspoon cinnamon
few grains nutmeg
¼ teaspoon salt
3 very ripe bananas, thinly sliced
1½ tablespoons fresh lemon juice
¾ cup milk
¼ teaspoon salt
½ cup sifted flour
2 tablespoons sugar
1 egg, well beaten
¼ cup butter or margarine

Combine sugar, cinnamon, nutmeg, and salt. Add to bananas. Add lemon juice, mixing carefully. Set aside. Stir milk, salt, flour, and sugar into eggs, beating only until smooth. Lightly grease a 10-inch frying pan, using enough butter or margarine to coat bottom and sides of pan. Heat pan. For each pancake, pour in ¼ cup batter. Turn and tilt pan, spreading batter to form a large, thin pancake. When delicately brown on under side, turn and bake on other side. Slip onto a hot platter. Spread lightly with butter or margarine. Spread about 6 tablespoons of banana mixture over surface of each pancake, leaving 1 inch uncovered around edges. Roll pancake. Sprinkle with confectioners' sugar or serve with a hot fruit sauce, syrup, or honey if desired. Serve immediately . . . very hot.

• Do you know why dessert pancakes have eggs in them? The eggs make the thin-as-paper pancakes fold without breaking.

• You can make the silver-dollar-sized pancakes in advance if you like. I made a hundred one time and served them several hours later drenched in the hot sauce, and good as if they had just come off the griddle. A fun way to prepare pancakes for dessert is to make them on a grill at the table, or take everyone to the kitchen and let each person cook his own.

• One thing to remember is that the plates they are served on should be *hot,* as well as the cakes and the sauce.

DESSERT PANCAKES

Makes 6 large or about 24 small:

3 eggs, beaten
½ cup milk
½ cup pancake mix
½ teaspoon grated lemon peel

Combine eggs and milk. Beat until smooth. Add pancake mix and lemon peel. Stir lightly until mixed, but don't worry about a few lumps—this makes the cakes tender, and the lumps disappear in cooking. Use a greaseless griddle or a small amount of butter in a skillet. When the butter bubbles, pour in enough batter to make the pancakes the size you want. This batter should be thin, and if it isn't thin enough to make thin cakes, add a teaspoon of milk. Brown on both sides.

• If you are going to serve a sauce over these, roll up each cake as it comes off the griddle and place in a hot serving dish until all the cakes are cooked. Then pour the sauce over the pancakes and serve.

• If you are going to fill the cakes, add the spoonful of filling in a line down the center, fold each side over, and put folded sides down in the serving dish. Then sprinkle generously with confectioners' sugar.

• If you make dollar-sized pancakes, cook as many as you want to serve, stack them as you cook them in an overlapping arrangement around the serving plate, and pass the sauce with the cakes.

TO MAKE FLAMING CRÊPES SUZETTE: Soak sugar cubes in pure lemon or orange flavoring (80% proof) for approximately 1½ hours. Arrange cubes around rolled Dessert Pancakes. Light the cubes just before taking to the table.

THE FINISHING TOUCHES . . . . FOR PANCAKES

Makes sauce for 6 cakes:

ORANGE SAUCE

Grate the peel of 1 orange and 1 lemon. Combine with ½ cup orange juice, 3 tablespoons sugar, and ⅓ cup melted butter. Heat in a small saucepan that can be used when serving. In a little bowl have 6 cubes of sugar and the lemon or vanilla extract bottle nearby. Serve the pancakes, spoon sauce over them, and drench sugar cube with extract. Ignite the cube with a lighted candle. Let it burn, and enjoy the results.

CHERRY SAUCE

Heat 1 package frozen dark cherries or 1 No. 2 can cherries. Mix thoroughly ½ cup sugar and 2 tablespoons cornstarch. Add gradually to cherries, stirring constantly. Cook until thickened. Add 1 tablespoon lemon juice.

FRESH FRUIT FILLINGS

Almost any fruit you have is delectable when wrapped round with a thin hot pancake and dredged with sugar. Sauté apple slices in butter a few minutes and fill your pancakes. Or fill them with drained canned pears which have been diced and sprinkled ever so lightly with ginger.

ICE CREAM PANCAKES

Fill the hot pancakes with ice cream, fold quickly, dredge with sugar, and serve immediately. Or spread a half dozen pancakes with ice cream, piling them up like a gorgeous miniature cake of many layers. Cover with sauce or whipped cream. Serve.

JAM OR JELLY FILLINGS

Lingonberries are the most delicious filling—the Swedes began that—but strawberry jam, currant jelly, whatever you like, is good. Apricot jam is marvelous too.

CHEESE FILLING

Grated Swiss cheese or Cheddar is very good inside pancakes. The cheese can be enclosed by itself or accompanied by a pitted cherry or a pear slice. Cover rolled pancakes with fruit syrup.

PETITE PANCAKES

Make the dollar-sized pancakes after stirring in 1 cup of blueberries. Serve dredged with sugar and with or without more berries for sauce.

FUN COOKING AT THE TABLE . . . HOT FRITTERS

THE BATTER IS THE BEGINNING DEEP FRY AT 375 F.

Makes 24 fritters:

½ cup butter
1 cup boiling water
1 cup all-purpose flour
4 eggs, unbeaten

Add butter to the boiling water in a sauce pan and beat until butter melts. Dump the flour into this mixture quickly and beat like all get out until the batter leaves the sides of the pan. Remove from heat and let cool about 5 minutes. Add 1 egg; beat hard. Add second egg and beat hard, continuing to beat after each egg is added, until the four are blended.

• Add ½ cup grated Swiss cheese to this batter; stir a minute and drop by spoonfuls into hot fat to brown. They cook in about 5 minutes and *turn themselves over* with no help from you to brown on the other side! Remove to drain on paper towels, and serve hot. Cold fresh fruit is nice with these, but not necessary.

• Add 2 tablespoons sugar to the batter and 2 tablespoons chopped nuts. Drain and dredge with sugar.

• Add ¼ teaspoon nutmeg, ½ teaspoon cinnamon, and 2 tablespoons sugar to batter. Serve with hot or cold apricot sauce or nutmeg sauce spooned over them, or any thinned fruit or ice cream sauce.

• Add ⅓ cup finely chopped candied fruit and peel and 1 tablespoon sugar to the batter. Brown, drain, dredge with confectioners' sugar.

• Add ½ cup chopped shrimp to batter, for shrimp fritters. Fry in deep fat at 375 F. until golden. Drain and serve.

Make these for lunch. It takes only a minute.

DIP BATTER FOR FRITTERS

Makes 2 cups:

1 cup all-purpose flour
1 teaspoon baking powder
¼ teaspoon salt
1 egg white
1 tablespoon sugar
¼ teaspoon cinnamon
1 egg yolk
⅔ cup milk
1 teaspoon melted butter

Combine first 3 ingredients. Sift together. Beat egg white until stiff and add sugar and cinnamon. Beat yolk until thick and lemon-colored. Add milk and butter; stir into flour mixture. Fold in egg white.

The batter should be *thin,* yet thick enough to *coat* whatever you dip into it.

• Drain apricot halves, peach halves, and bing cherries. In cherry season, select bunches of cherries and leave the stems on when dipping. Peel and remove sections of tangerines or drain mandarin orange slices. This assortment is a delight, but of course you can stick to a single fruit. Dry fruit thoroughly by additional draining on paper towels. Test with one first to be sure the batter "holds" (the weather and not just your measuring affects cooking, you know). If one browns and comes out sufficiently coated, then dip all of them. Drain as the browned fritters are removed from the fat; keep hot and serve with confectioners' sugar sprinkled over them. Any sauce you like or whipped cream happily accompanies them too.

SAVORY FRITTERS

• Use the batter above, omitting sugar and cinnamon. Dip sage leaves, tender celery leaves on the celery stem. Serve with meat. And our grandmother used to dip flowers in the batter and serve them with meat, crisped and delectable and hot. Very hot. These are good appetizers too.

These aren't desserts—but they are so good with meat I have to tell you about them.

CHAPTER 9

ICE CREAM FOR COMPANY . . . OR ICES . . . OR CHEESE

ALL YOU NEED . . . . IS MAGIC

ICE CREAM SNOWBALLS

Nothing new about these, but this is just to remind you.

Snowballs of vanilla ice cream—or of that Pineapple-Coconut Ice Cream—are just three times as good when two more things are added. Roll the ice cream balls in chopped nuts (black walnuts or English walnuts, pecans or peanuts are good), in grape-nuts, in very fine crumbs made by crushing vanilla wafers, gingersnaps, or corn flakes. Then serve one of the Sundae Sauces or serve several for a selection to pour over the nut-crusted balls.

FROST A BRICK TO MAKE AN ICE CREAM CAKE

Buy a three-flavored, three-colored quart brick of ice cream or two pint ones. Chill in the freezing compartment while you whip 2 cups heavy cream. You won't need sugar in it, but a teaspoon of vanilla is nice.

Frost the brick with the whipped cream, making the top smooth and saving some of the whipped cream to fill your pastry gun. If you use two bricks, they can be put end to end and treated as one, or frost them separately with identical or contrasting colors and designs. Tint the cream before filling the gun, and while you are doing this, put the frosted brick back where it will keep frosty-cold. When all is cool, including the cream in the gun, decorate the top by making a rippled edge, crisscrosses, or whatever you fancy in the way of a design. Return to freezer until ready to serve. (There's that gun again, I tell you, you simply cannot cook without it.)

BIG NEWS IN ICE CREAM . . . . IS THESE

7 LUCKY LAYERS

"It is the best dessert on our menu," the waiter at Sardi's in New York told us. And it must have been. The layers were thin, 7 of them, beautiful and cold and as good as he promised. Cut into slender wedges, as if from a round cake, the layers actually can be made either round or in an oblong pan. These are easy to make, marvels to store in the freezer, wonderfully colorful to bring out for company. Choose your own flavors and colors, or make it this way with thicker layers than the Sardi cake:

Makes 12 servings:

1 pint raspberry ice
1 pint orange ice
1 pint vanilla ice cream
1 pint (2 cups) heavy cream, whipped
¼ teaspoon salt
1 white loaf cake (10 x 5 x 3)
1 tablespoon sugar
1 teaspoon vanilla extract
½ teaspoon lemon extract

Soften the ices and the ice cream enough to spread. Add salt to cream and whip until it holds its shape. Cut cake lengthwise into 3 layers. Spread the ice cream and the ice between the layers, making one red and the other white, ending with a golden top. Chill. Add sugar and extracts to the whipped cream, blend, and frost all sides of the loaf. Chill until cream is firm. Slice in plain slices or in pie-shaped wedges. It will slice easily and evenly if you dip your knife in hot water before each slicing.

SPICED NECTAR ICE CREAM

Makes 6 cups or 1½ quarts:

1 envelope unflavored gelatin
½ cup cold water
1 cup honey
1½ cups canned or fresh, cooked pumpkin
½ cup sugar
2 tablespoons cornstarch
1 teaspoon cinnamon
½ teaspoon ginger
½ teaspoon ground mace or allspice
2 cups evaporated milk, heated
4 egg yolks, beaten
1 tablespoon grated orange rind
1 cup coarsely chopped pecans
2 egg whites, beaten stiff
½ teaspoon salt
1½ cups heavy cream, whipped

Soften gelatin in the cold water. Combine honey and pumpkin. Stir until blended. Combine sugar, cornstarch, spices and blend well. Add the heated milk to dry mixture and stir in egg yolks and gelatin. Cook over low heat, stirring constantly until thick and smooth. Add pumpkin mixture. Stir until heated through. Remove from heat; add orange rind and chill before adding the remaining ingredients. When the mixture is cold but not frozen, add the pecans and fold in the egg whites to which the salt has been added before beating. Fold in cream which has been whipped until thick but not stiff.

BOMBES

A Bombe is a parfait grown up. You need a covered mold, 1½ to 2 quarts, or a pan that size which can be covered with aluminum foil. If using a 1½-quart melon mold, let 1 quart vanilla, chocolate, or coffee ice cream soften just enough for you to press it against the sides of the mold to make an even layer. Fill the center hole with 1 pint of orange, lemon, or raspberry ice. Or fill it with tinted and fruit-flavored whipped cream. Add some whole fruit to the cream for a nice touch. An ice is best because of the contrast in texture enjoyed when eating the layers. Seal or wrap. Freeze as long as you like. To unmold, wrap mold with a Turkish towel wrung from very hot water. Leave until you can count ten and remove it. Uncover ice cream; put a plate over the top and turn the mold upside down on the plate. Remove the mold and serve the cream.

BAKED ALASKA

Anyone who can whip egg white for a pie meringue can make Baked Alaska. It is that easy. Make a big one on baking day by baking white cake batter in a ring mold. Plain white cake, chocolate cake, or angel food will do, but usually white cake is used for the base. And a sponge cake from the store does nicely too. But let's make one with a ring-mold cake, because it is new and different. This one makes 12 servings.

When the cake is cool, put it on a serving plate that can go into the oven. Any old pan covered with aluminum foil will go from oven to freezer to the table, as this must do.

Heap vanilla ice cream or a mixture of two ice creams in the center of the cake and spread over the outside to frost it thickly. Place in the freezer until very firm.

When about ready to serve, turn on your oven to 400 F. Then beat 5 egg whites to which ¼ teaspoon of salt has been added. Add 8 tablespoons sugar (½ cup, really, but you should add a spoonful at a time) to the egg whites and beat until stiff. Cover the entire ice cream cake and scoot it into the hot oven to brown, about 5 minutes. Serve immediately, slicing clear through to the middle.

LOAF-SHAPED BAKED ALASKA: Easier than the ring mold. Make an oblong base of sponge cake. Heap ice cream on it or top it with a brick of ice cream. Cover with sweetened meringue and brown in the hot oven.

INDIVIDUAL BAKED ALASKAS: Easy to handle, using 4 squares of sponge cake heaped with ice cream and covered by meringue—about 3 egg whites and 5 tablespoons of sugar to cover these for 4 people. Brown them as you did the big one.

EASTER EGG MOUSSE

Makes 6 servings:

6 canned apricot halves
1¼ cups heavy cream
1 tablespoon sugar
⅓ cup apricot juice
¼ teaspoon salt

Drain the canned apricots. Whip the cream, and when fluffy but not stiff beat in the sugar and salt. Whip until thick but not stiff. Fold in the apricot juice, adding more if you prefer a strong flavor. Fill 6 sherbet glasses and place an apricot half roundside up on the top of each dish of white mousse. Place in refrigerator to chill or in freezing compartment to freeze for 1 hour before serving.

REFRIGERATOR-TRAY ICE CREAMS . . . . WITH VARIATIONS

REFRIGERATOR-TRAY VANILLA ICE CREAM

Fills 1 tray:

½ cup light cream
1 teaspoon unflavored gelatin
⅓ cup sugar
⅛ teaspoon salt
¼ cup light corn syrup
1½ cups light cream
1 teaspoon vanilla

Place cream in saucepan, sprinkle gelatin over cream, and stir. Let stand 5 minutes. Place over low heat, stirring constantly until gelatin dissolves. Remove from heat. Add sugar, salt, syrup. Stir until blended. Add light cream and vanilla; blend thoroughly. Pour into ice tray. Place on refrigerated shelf or floor of freezer compartment. Freeze until firm (about 1 hour).

Use blunt knife to cut ice cream into small pieces; place in chilled bowl and beat with rotary or electric beater until smooth *but not melted.* Return to ice tray to freeze until firm (about 1 hour).

VARIATIONS

BUTTERSCOTCH ICE CREAM: Cook sugar in small saucepan with 2 tablespoons butter or margarine. Stir until browned. Add to ice cream mixture.

BUTTERSCOTCH ALMOND: Make as above and add almonds (or peanuts) which have been chopped and browned in a small amount of butter.

GREEN CHOCOLATE MINT: Add few drops green vegetable coloring, 5 drops mint flavoring, and shavings of 1 square bittersweet chocolate.

COFFEE ICE CREAM: Add 1 tablespoon instant powdered coffee to sugar when mixing the ice cream.

STICK CANDY ICE CREAM: Crush ½ pound peppermint candy sticks and add instead of sugar in the recipe.

MOLASSES ICE CREAM: Replace corn syrup with 2 tablespoons fine-flavored molasses; reduce sugar to ¼ cup.

PEACH ICE CREAM

Makes 4 cups (1 quart):

1¼ cups chopped fresh peaches
½ cup sugar
1 tablespoon lemon juice
2 egg yolks
½ cup light corn syrup
¼ teaspoon salt
1 cup milk
1½ teaspoons gelatin
1 tablespoon cold water
1 teaspoon vanilla
⅛ teaspoon almond extract
2 egg whites
1 cup light cream

Wash about 1½ pounds fully ripe peaches. Peel and pit. Put through food chopper, using medium knife. Add ¼ cup sugar and lemon juice and let stand. Beat egg yolks in top of double boiler; add syrup and salt. Slowly stir in milk. Place over boiling water and cook, stirring constantly, about 5 minutes, or until mixture is slightly thickened. Add gelatin softened in cold water. Stir until gelatin is dissolved. Cool until thickened. Add flavoring. Beat egg whites until stiff but not dry; gradually beat in ¼ cup of the sugar. Fold into custard mixture. Gradually stir in cream. Fold in peach mixture.

Pour into refrigerator freezing tray. Freeze with control set at coldest point until mixture is almost firm, about 2 hours. Place in chilled bowl and beat with rotary beater. Return to freezing tray and continue freezing until ice cream is firm, beating mixture once with a spoon.

• If frozen peaches are used, thaw before using and reduce sugar in recipe if they are already sweetened.

PINEAPPLE-COCONUT ICE CREAM

Makes 5 cups (over 1 quart):

2 eggs
¾ cup sugar
1 tablespoon cornstarch
1 cup milk
1 cup pineapple syrup drained from a No. 2 can crushed pineapple
1 cup heavy cream
2 drops lemon extract
1½ cups drained crushed pineapple
¾ cup moist shredded coconut

Turn the freezer control on your refrigerator to its coldest setting. In a saucepan mix thoroughly the eggs, sugar, cornstarch, milk, and pineapple syrup. Cook over moderate heat, stirring constantly, until smoothly thickened. Chill thoroughly. Whip the cream with the lemon extract until stiff. Fold into the chilled pineapple custard. Pour into refrigerator tray and freeze until very firm (several hours). Turn out into a large bowl and beat with rotary beater or electric mixer until creamy. Stir in the drained crushed pineapple and the coconut. Return to tray and refreeze.

BANANA-DATE ICE CREAM

Makes 6 cups (3 pints):

½ cup coarsely chopped dates
½ cup water
1 cup mashed very ripe bananas (2 to 3)
2 teaspoons lemon juice
¼ cup firmly packed light brown sugar
¼ teaspoon salt
⅓ cup milk
2 egg whites
1 cup heavy cream
2 egg yolks
1 teaspoon vanilla

Combine dates and water and simmer 10 minutes. Cool. Mix bananas, lemon juice and add sugar, salt, and milk, stirring until blended. Beat egg whites until stiff. Whip cream until thick but not stiff. Beat egg yolks until thick. Combine all ingredients, including the cooled date mixture. Fold together and turn into freezing trays, and freeze with indicator at coldest setting. Stir every 30 minutes until mixture begins to hold its shape. Freeze until firm.

BISCUIT TORTONI

Makes 4 cups (1 quart):

1 package vanilla pudding mix
⅓ cup sugar
2 cups milk
1 cup heavy cream, whipped
¾ teaspoon almond extract
½ cup finely rolled macaroon or vanilla cookie crumbs

Put package contents in saucepan. Add sugar; mix well. Gradually add milk, mixing until smooth. Cook over medium heat, stirring constantly until mixture thickens and comes to a boil. Remove from heat. Cool. Pour into refrigerator freezing tray; chill until just firm, setting control for fast freezing. Remove chilled mixture to bowl; combine whipped cream and almond extract, fold into pudding mixture. Fold in cookie crumbs, reserving about 2 tablespoons to sprinkle over top. Fill 8 to 10 little paper cups; freeze 2 to 3 hours. Set control midway between fast freezing and normal for storage.

NO SECOND BEATING . . . . FOR THESE

PEPPERMINT OR CHOCOLATE FROST

Makes 8 cups (2 quarts):

1⅔ cups (14½-ounce can) undiluted evaporated milk
3 tablespoons lemon juice
2 egg whites
½ cup light corn syrup
1 cup crushed peppermint stick candy or 1 cup crushed chocolate mints

Chill milk in refrigerator tray about 30 minutes, until crystals form. Pour into a cold bowl and whip until foamy. Add lemon juice and continue beating until stiff, about 2 minutes. Beat egg whites until soft peaks are formed. Stir syrup and egg whites into milk mixture. Fold in candy or chocolate mints. Pour into freezing trays or containers. Chill until firm. Serve with chocolate sauce or just eat it all up as it is.

CHOCOLATE MALTED ICE CREAM

Makes 6 cups, or 3 pints:

4 tablespoons sugar
1/8 teaspoon salt
2/3 cup chocolate malted milk powder
2 eggs, beaten
1 teaspoon vanilla
1 1/3 cups undiluted evaporated milk, chilled

Combine sugar, salt, and malted milk powder and stir. Add beaten eggs and vanilla. Blend well. Chill milk in freezer tray until ice crystals form around edges (about 30 minutes). Whip in cold bowl with cold beater until milk is stiff. Fold gently into egg mixture. When thoroughly blended, pour into ice-cube trays or container for freezing unit and freeze.

APRICOT VELVET CREAM

Makes 6 cups:

3 1/2 cups (No. 2 1/2 can) apricot halves
1/4 cup confectioners' sugar
1/8 teaspoon salt
1 cup evaporated milk, chilled and whipped

Mash apricots, reserving a few for garnish, and add sugar and salt. Whip chilled evaporated milk until thick. Fold in apricot mixture. Freeze in freezing tray 2 hours.

S.O.S. . . . ALL HANDS TO THE ICE CREAM FREEZER

No better way in the world to wear out overenergetic children than to fill up the freezer. But a strong adult hand is necessary at the end when it says: "Allow to stand 2 to 3 hours before using." Let's begin with:

FREEZER VANILLA ICE CREAM

Makes 16 cups (2 quarts):

1 cup sugar	*1 cup water*
1 teaspoon salt	*2 eggs, beaten*
1 tablespoon cornstarch	*1 tablespoon vanilla*
1 cup evaporated milk mixed with	*2 cups undiluted evaporated milk*

Combine sugar, salt, and cornstarch in top of double boiler. Add milk-water mixture; cook over low heat until slightly thickened, about 10 minutes. Stir small portion of milk mixture into beaten eggs; blend with rest of mixture. Cook over hot water for 2 to 3 minutes. Remove from heat; add vanilla and undiluted milk. Pour into ½-gallon freezer; cover. Use mixture of chopped ice and salt to pack freezer. Turn about 20 minutes, or until ice cream is fairly thick. Pack with additional ice and salt. Cover and allow to stand 2 to 3 hours before using.

MAKE OLD FAVORITES THIS WAY

PEANUT BUTTER ICE CREAM: Chop 8 tablespoons peanut butter coarsely. Add to mixture last. Serve chopped peanuts on top of this one.

CHOCOLATE CURL MINT: Shave curls from unsweetened chocolate, using 4 squares. Add 2 teaspoons mint flavoring and omit vanilla. Add few drops of green coloring for a pretty effect.

ORANGE ICE CREAM: Omit vanilla. Add 1 teaspoon grated orange peel and replace water with 1 can frozen orange juice, undiluted.

FRESH STRAWBERRY OR RASPBERRY ICE CREAM: Omit vanilla. Add 2 cups crushed berries lightly sweetened (about ¼ cup sugar) and 2 tablespoons frozen orange juice. Use frozen berries without the sugar.

BANANA ICE CREAM: Reduce vanilla to 2 teaspoons; add 2 cups crushed bananas sprinkled with 1½ tablespoons lemon juice. Add ¼ teaspoon nutmeg and ¼ teaspoon cinnamon.

BLUEBERRY ICE CREAM: Cook 2 cups frozen berries in ½ cup water until berries are soft. Crush and add 1½ tablespoons lemon juice before folding into mixture. Or cook fresh blueberries, adding 1 cup sugar and ½ cup water. Brown sugar is good with the blueberries.

PEACH ICE CREAM: Add 2 cups sliced peaches and 1 tablespoon lemon juice; reduce vanilla to 2 teaspoons.

A MONTH OF SUNDAES . . 30 ICE CREAM SAUCES

A different sauce for every day of the month, to pour over ice cream from the store or over ice cream you make. These are good, too, to pour into little jars and give away.

It is reckless to give a recipe for fruit juices, because the idea is to use the juice you have, drained from fruit or left over from breakfast, to make a delectable sauce. Orange juice is best added to strawberry or raspberry juice, but lemon is better with blueberries or peach juice. Use your own judgment and begin this way, remembering that the total in your saucepan is about ⅓ less when cooked.

Juices good for this are: loganberries, rhubarb, pineapple, cherry, mango, raspberry, blueberry, strawberry, apricot, to name a few. You go on from there and concoct your own concoctions.

9 FRUIT JUICE SAUCES

Makes 2 cups:

2 cups sweet fruit juice or 2½ cups tart fruit juice
2 tablespoons orange or lemon juice
⅛ teaspoon salt
1 cup water
2 tablespoons quick-cooking tapioca
½ cup sugar, white or brown

Combine all ingredients in saucepan; bring to a boil and stir constantly until the sauce thickens, about 8 minutes. Taste to test for sweetness. Chill or serve hot over ice cream. Good over puddings too.

PAPAYA SUNDAE

Makes 8 servings:

Combine 3 tablespoons cornstarch, ½ teaspoon each of allspice and ginger, and 1 teaspoon lemon juice in a small saucepan. Stir in the syrup drained from 2 No. 2 cans sliced papaya. Cook, stirring constantly, until sauce is thick and clear. Dice the slices from one can of papaya and add to the syrup. Fold slices from the other can into 1 quart softened vanilla ice cream. Return to freezing compartment and freeze until firm enough to serve. Chill sauce, and spoon over the frozen cream when served.

PINEAPPLE-MINT SAUCE

Makes 1¾ cups:

¾ cup light corn syrup
1 cup (9-ounce can) crushed pineapple
¼ teaspoon peppermint flavoring
few drops green food coloring

Combine all ingredients. Blend, cover, and chill thoroughly. Use as a sauce for ice cream or puddings.

MELBA SAUCE

Makes 1 cup:

½ cup currant jelly
1 tablespoon cold water
⅛ teaspoon salt
½ cup raspberry jam
1 tablespoon lemon juice

Combine all ingredients in saucepan. Cook over medium heat, stirring constantly, until mixture just comes to a boil. Remove from heat. Strain and cool.

FLUFFY TROPICAL TOPPING

Combine 1 can frozen undiluted orange juice with 1 cup heavy cream, whipped. Fold in 1 can moist shredded coconut, 1 teaspoon grated orange or lemon rind. Fold together and serve as topping on ice cream.

• Use same mixture, chilled, to frost sponge or angel food cake from the store.

• Another time chill or serve immediately as a mousse.

FRUIT CREAM SAUCE

Makes 2 cups:

⅔ cup (½ can) sweetened condensed milk
3 tablespoons lemon juice
1 cup fruit, crushed pineapple or bananas, strawberries or raspberries, pitted drained cherries
cold water

Combine sweetened condensed milk and lemon juice. Place over low heat and stir until the mixture thickens. Remove from heat and add crushed fruit. Blend well. If a thinner sauce is wanted, add 1 tablespoon of water at a time until the consistency desired is secured.

WHIPPED CREAM STRETCHER

When you don't have heavy cream for whipping and do have light cream (20% fat content this has instead of 40% in your usual heavy cream for whipping), light cream can be whipped this way: Chill your cream. Dissolve 1 teaspoon unflavored gelatin in 1 tablespoon cold water, holding the container in hot water and stirring. When dissolved, add to cream in chilled bowl and whip. In an electric blender this takes only about 15 seconds.

DESSERT TOPPING

Here is the way you whip evaporated milk to use in place of Whipped Cream Frosting, or fold in fruit or flavorings to make an ice cream sauce.

Makes 3 cups:

1 cup evaporated milk, undiluted
2 tablespoons lemon juice
¼ cup confectioners' sugar
1 teaspoon vanilla

Chill milk thoroughly in ice-cube tray or in freezing compartment until ice crystals begin to form, about 30 minutes, unless you keep an unopened can in the refrigerator, which decreases cooling time after it is opened. Pour into a cold bowl and whip until stiff. Add lemon juice and continue whipping to blend. Add sugar and vanilla and mix.

MAPLE SUGAR SAUCE

Fold ½ cup coarsely chopped maple sugar into Dessert Topping. Serve over ice cream.

ORANGE SAUCE

Thaw frozen concentrated orange juice. Fold into Dessert Topping, allowing ⅓ can for each cup.

ORANGE SPICED SAUCE

Add ½ teaspoon cinnamon, ½ teaspoon nutmeg, and 2 tablespoons undiluted frozen orange juice to Dessert Topping, and serve over ice cream.

BERRY SAUCE

Fold ½ cup berries, crushed and sweetened, into Dessert Topping.

PEANUT BRITTLE SAUCE

Crush ½ cup peanut brittle into coarse bits; fold into Dessert Topping just before using.

FLUFFY MARSHMALLOW SAUCE

Makes 2 cups:

1 cup light corn syrup
1 egg white
1/8 teaspoon salt
1/2 teaspoon vanilla

Place syrup in small saucepan. Bring to a boil over medium heat. Cook until small amount of syrup forms soft ball in cold water. Meanwhile add salt to egg white. Beat until stiff but not dry. Slowly add hot syrup to stiffly beaten egg white, beating constantly with rotary beater. Add vanilla. Beat about 1 minute. Sauce may be stored in the refrigerator. If sauce thickens too much on cooling, thin with a little hot water.

BUTTERSCOTCH CREAM SAUCE

Makes 2 cups:

3/4 cup sugar
1 1/3 cups brown sugar
3/4 cup corn syrup
1/2 (1/4 cup) stick butter
1 cup undiluted evaporated milk
1/2 teaspoon vanilla
1/2 teaspoon lemon extract

Combine first 4 ingredients and 1/2 cup milk. Cook, stirring constantly, until sugar is dissolved and the sauce well blended. Add remaining milk and cook about 1 minute, stirring constantly. Cool; add flavoring.

TOFFEE

Makes 2 cups:

Get a 1-pound bag of caramels and put them in the top of the double boiler. Keep the water under them hot but not boiling. Cover and let the caramels melt. Stir in 1/2 cup hot water; blend. Serve hot or cold.

SPICED MOLASSES SAUCE

1/8 teaspoon salt
1 cup heavy cream
2 tablespoons molasses
1/8 teaspoon cinnamon
1/8 teaspoon nutmeg

Add salt to cream and whip until cream is just thick enough to hold its shape. Fold in molasses and spices and serve immediately over coffee or vanilla ice cream.

MINCEMEAT SAUCE

Thin mincemeat to use as a sauce on vanilla ice cream with dark molasses. Serve it in a bowl to be spooned onto vanilla ice cream. Pass sugar cubes and a little dish of lemon extract so that each guest can submerge the sugar cube in the lemon extract, place it on top of the ice cream and mincemeat mound, and light his own.

COFFEE SAUCE

Makes 2¼ cups:

2 teaspoons instant coffee
⅛ teaspoon salt
1 cup heavy cream
⅓ cup corn syrup

Add coffee and salt to syrup; stir until blended. Whip the cream and add about 3 tablespoons to the syrup mixture. Stir vigorously. Fold into remaining whipped cream.

HOT FUDGE MINT SAUCE

Makes 2½ cups:

3 squares unsweetened chocolate
1 cup sugar
1 cup light or dark corn syrup
½ cup light cream
¼ teaspoon salt
2 tablespoons butter or margarine
1 teaspoon vanilla
¼ teaspoon peppermint (optional)

Combine all ingredients except vanilla in saucepan. Cook over medium heat, stirring constantly, until mixture comes to a full rolling boil. Boil briskly 3 minutes, stirring occasionally. Remove from heat. Add vanilla. Serve hot. Sauce may be stored in refrigerator. To reheat, place in pan of hot, not boiling, water until sauce has thinned to pouring consistency.

LIGHT CHOCOLATE SAUCE

Makes 2 cups:

1 cup cocoa
½ cup sugar
¾ cup light or dark corn syrup
¼ teaspoon salt
1 cup cold water
2 teaspoons vanilla

Combine all ingredients except vanilla in small saucepan. Place over heat and bring to a boil, stirring constantly; boil 3 minutes. Remove from heat. Add vanilla. Cool.

CHOCOLATE HONEY SAUCE

Makes 1¾ cups:

1 6-ounce package semi-sweet chocolate bits
½ cup honey
¾ cup evaporated milk, undiluted

Melt chocolate bits in top of double boiler. Add honey and evaporated milk. Stir until well blended.

LEMON MILK SHERBET

Makes 1 quart:

2 egg whites
¼ cup sugar
1 cup light corn syrup
2 cups milk, whole or made with non-fat dry milk
⅔ cup lemon juice
½ teaspoon grated lemon rind

Beat egg whites until stiff but not dry. Gradually add sugar. Slowly add remaining ingredients, beating constantly. Pour into refrigerator freezing tray. Freeze with control set at coldest point until mixture is almost firm. Place in chilled bowl and beat with rotary beater until smooth. Return to freezing tray and continue freezing until sherbet is firm. Set cold control midway between fast freezing and normal for storage.

FIESTA SHERBET

Makes 1 quart:

2 cups mashed very ripe bananas
¼ cup lemon juice
⅓ cup orange juice
½ cup dark corn syrup
⅛ teaspoon salt
1 egg white
⅓ cup sugar
1 cup milk
¼ cup maraschino cherry juice
½ cup coarsely chopped maraschino cherries
1 teaspoon grated orange rind

Mash bananas thoroughly with lemon juice. Add orange juice, syrup, and salt. Beat egg white until stiff but not dry; gradually beat in sugar. Fold into banana mixture. Add milk, stirring slowly. Add maraschino cherry juice, chopped cherries, and orange rind. Turn into refrigerator freezing tray. Freeze with control set at coldest point until mixture is almost firm. Place in chilled bowl and beat with rotary beater. Return to freezing tray and continue freezing until firm, beating mixture once with a spoon. Set cold control midway between fast freezing and normal for storage.

ORANGE-APRICOT FLIP

Makes 6 ⅔-cup servings:

1 envelope unflavored gelatin
1 cup orange juice
⅔ cup lemon juice
6 tablespoons sugar
⅛ teaspoon salt
⅓ cup water
1 tablespoon lemon juice
½ teaspoon vanilla
⅓ cup non-fat dry milk
½ cup strained apricots or 4¾-ounce jar strained baby fruit

Set refrigerator control at coldest point. Soften gelatin in ¼ cup orange juice in mixing bowl 5 minutes. Scald ⅔ cup lemon juice and remaining orange juice. Pour slowly over softened gelatin, stirring until dissolved. Mix in sugar and salt; stir until dissolved. Chill until mixture begins to thicken. Meanwhile put water, lemon juice, and vanilla in deep 1-quart bowl. Sprinkle dry milk powder over water and beat with rotary beater or electric mixer until stiff, about 10 minutes. Fold apricots and whipped milk into gelatin mixture. Pour into 2 small freezing trays of refrigerator. (Freezing in 2 small trays hastens freezing and makes dessert smoother.) Cover with waxed paper. Freeze to a firm mush. Turn into chilled bowl and beat with rotary or electric beater until fluffy but not melted. Quickly return to freezing trays and cover with waxed paper. Return to freezing unit. Freeze until firm, about 2 hours.

LOW-CALORIE DESSERTS . FOR WEIGHT WATCHERS

No one wants to be fat, but everyone likes dessert . . . or gravy . . . or sweet potatoes dripping with brown sugar . . . or fried chicken with biscuits. Is there anything as good that will slim you down a bit? One woman said she would have no trouble if she just knew about desserts with low calories that her family would like. The subject of low-calorie recipes could fill a book but must not fill this one.

Desserts are easy if fresh fruit is plentiful, melons ripe. When these are not available but water-packed fruit is, drain the fruit and sweeten and spice the juice with artificial sweetener of your choice. The spice won't add pounds—just flavor. Douse the fruit in this as for the Fruit Compotes described.

Serve water and milk ices. Serve colorful molds given graceful shape and texture by unflavored gelatin. Add non-fat whipped milk for lovely-looking molded Whips. Serve these on a platter encircled with fresh fruit or drained canned fruit decoration to make them triply appetizing.

Here are four recipes which are given not because they are unusual or new, but because almost everyone would find them pleasing, the calorie count is given, and—most important—because each of the recipes is adaptable to other fruit or flavor combinations. With them as a beginning you could make more than 30 low-calorie desserts.

APRICOT SPONGE

6 portions, 21 calories each:

1 envelope unflavored gelatin
½ cup cold water
½ cup sieved apricot pulp
1 tablespoon grated lemon peel
1 tablespoon lemon juice
4 non-caloric sweetening tablets, or to taste
3 egg whites, stiffly beaten

Soften unflavored gelatin in cold water in top of double boiler. Dissolve thoroughly over hot water. Stir in apricot pulp, lemon peel and juice. Chill thoroughly. Add sweetening. Whip with rotary beater until fluffy. Fold in beaten egg whites. Turn into 6 individual molds. Chill until firm. Unmold and serve decorated as desired.

VARIATION: In place of the apricot pulp in the above recipe, any of the following fruits may be used: canned, drained crushed pineapple; peaches, raspberries, or fresh orange sections—sieved or puréed; or applesauce.

LEMON SNOW

6 portions, 10 calories each:

1 envelope unflavored gelatin
1½ cups water
¼ teaspoon cinnamon
¼ teaspoon nutmeg
1 teaspoon grated lemon peel
¼ cup lemon juice
1 egg white, stiffly beaten
24 non-caloric sweetening tablets

Soften gelatin in ½ cup cold water. Dissolve thoroughly in 1¼ cups very hot water, stirring until clear. Add spices. Add lemon peel and juice. Chill until of unbeaten egg white consistency. Whip until light. Add the beaten egg white. Place the bowl in ice water. Continue beating until mixture begins to hold its shape. Beat in the non-caloric sweetening tablets which have been dissolved in a little of the mixture. Turn into 6 individual molds. Chill until firm. Unmold. Serve decorated as desired.

VARIATION: Coffee or other fruit juices may be used in place of the hot and cold water and the lemon juice in the above recipe.

ORANGE ICE

4 portions, 31 calories each:

1 envelope unflavored gelatin
1½ cups water
2 teaspoons grated orange peel
¾ cup orange juice
2 tablespoons lemon juice
12 non-caloric sweetening tablets

Soften gelatin in ½ cup cold water. Boil remaining water and orange peel 2 minutes. Remove from heat. Add softened gelatin and stir until thoroughly dissolved. Mix in strained orange and lemon juices. Add sweetening tablets. Blend. Pour into freezing tray and set control for coldest, fastest freezing until firm, stirring every 15 minutes, until mixture begins to hold its shape. When frozen, spoon into serving dishes.

CHOCOLATE WHIP

4 portions, 84 calories each:

1 envelope unflavored gelatin
2 cups skim milk
1 square (1 ounce) unsweetened chocolate
⅛ teaspoon cinnamon
¼ teaspoon vanilla
4 non-caloric sweetening tablets

Soften gelatin in cold skim milk in top of double boiler; mix well. Add chocolate and cinnamon. Place over hot water and stir until chocolate is melted and gelatin is thoroughly dissolved. Beat with rotary beater, if necessary, to blend. Add vanilla. Chill to unbeaten egg white consistency. Mix crushed sweetening tablets with a little gelatin mixture until dissolved. Add to remaining mixture and whip with rotary beater until fluffy and fine-textured. Turn into 2-cup molds or 4 individual ones and chill until firm. Unmold and serve decorated as desired.

CHEESE AND CRACKERS . . . WITH FRESH FRUIT

Cheese was one of the chief foods of mankind long before the time of Christ, and making it has not changed much in all these hundreds of years. In much of Europe cheese is still regarded sufficient for a meal, together with crusty bread, good butter, and a jug of milk.

In America most of us grew up with yellow store cheese or home-made cottage cheese and knew few others. For we did not make a different cheese in every village as is done all over the old countries, from which we imported cheese and enjoyed them but never got to know them very well.

Now we import them, manufacture them, and eat cheese night and day. We cook with it, take it on picnics, and know that cheese—several kinds—is a fine finish for a meal.

CHEESE BOARD FOR DESSERT

The more varied the cheeses on a wooden cutting board, the better. The board enables the cheeses to be sliced off as wanted, and they continue to give a pretty effect, flocked together until consumed. Accompany the cheese with cored apples or pears cut into wedges and with peel left on. Crackers, or crusty bread slices, or bread in a whole loaf should be on the board or served nearby.

CHEESE PLATTER

Fingers of Swiss cheese or paper-thin slices of it can surround a red Gouda, and crackers or bread can be available in another bowl.

CHEESE AND FRUIT CART

For a crowd, set up a serving cart (maybe the enamel one you ordinarily use in the kitchen) with a round of bleu cheese, a slab of Swiss cheese to show off the attractive holes, a few wrapped wedges of Camembert or Roquefort cheese.

Slices of a variety of breads, white and dark, a bowl of butter, a big bowl of fresh fruit complete the picture and the abundant delightful dessert. No serving problem except knives and small plates on the second shelf.

BLEU cheese is a cheese this country can be very proud of making. It is a Roquefort-type cheese, the creamy wheels veined with bleu "mold" so palatably that it has an unusual but appealing flavor for almost everyone. Buy it in wheels; put it on your table as it is to cut off slivers for appetizers or dessert. Crumble some into French dressing when making green salad, mix it with cream for an exciting spread or to fill the white curves of celery.

CAMEMBERT cheese, as made in France, is considered one of the finest cheeses of the world. Camembert has a soft, creamy inside protected with a light brown outside crust. It is about four inches across and one inch thick. It is often available here in six wrapped triangles fitted into a box the size of the original wheel. These vary in quality, are usually white on the outside. Camembert must always be left at room temperature at least an hour before serving, for best flavor.

CHEDDAR, too, is world-famous as well as about the finest cheese England produces. It is yellow, is best when aged enough to have a "sharp" bite to it, and excellent Cheddar is made in this country as well as in England. Since its age determines the amount of sharpness, decide whether you like it best mild or sharp, and buy accordingly. Buy it in wedges or in a thick cylinder. Wrap sides with a napkin and put on the table as it is. Cheddar is excellent served in squares, fingers, slices, and is superb in cooking and in rabbits. Americans love it on our wonderful juicy apple pies.

EDAM and GOUDA are the red balls of cheese from Holland. Their flavor is mild, their appearance decorative and cheerful, the devotees legion. Edam- and Gouda-type cheeses are in our markets from Wisconsin and from South America. Everyone likes these cheeses served as they are, with slivers cut off as needed as you would cut wedges from an apple.

SWISS cheese is one of the world's finest cheeses, with good reason. Made in Switzerland for hundreds of years, it is recognized by the big holes in the slice of cheese and loved for its nutty, creamy flavor. It is also famous for its size, for Switzerland Swiss cheese wheels are the biggest in the world, measuring as much as 4 feet across and approaching 200 pounds in weight. The last time I visited the cheese warehouses in Switzerland, row upon row of these big wheels made an impressive sight. Buy a wedge of genuine Swiss cheese made in Switzerland—the red marking saying *Switzerland Swiss* appears on all wheels made in Switzerland—and compare it with a wedge made in this country. Each is delicate, but the imported has a finer flavor than the domestic. Use Swiss cheese for grating over creamed dishes, for Cheese Fritters, Cheese Soufflé, Rabbit, and to make Cheese Soup or Bacon Crumble Cheese Pie. And of course serve it in fingers, squares, or paper-thin slices for dessert.

OKA is a Canadian cheese, which is neither hard nor soft in texture; nor is it as strong as LIMBURGER. It is delicious, but its strong flavor transfers so that it needs to be sealed when stored. A fine cheese for dessert, canapés, or in sandwiches.

MUNSTER cheese is a German cheese, mild in flavor and very good in sandwiches, served in slices or fingers, and can be used in cooking.

PARMESAN is Italian, a pale, yellow, hard cheese with a sharp flavor which makes it tops for grating and is used in cooking.

GRUYÈRE cheese comes from both France and Switzerland, is fine-flavored and excellent for eating or in cooking. The Gruyère made in this country is processed cheese, comes in foil-wrapped wedges, and is very different in flavor from the foreign wheels for which it was named.

Most of the cheeses mentioned here are ancient specialties of the countries that make them. Denmark, where some climate or pasture trick of fate enables the Danes to make the finest butter known to man, has developed a cheese industry, as we have, since the war interrupted the usual flow of cheese from Switzerland, France, Holland, Germany, and Italy. This comparatively new cheese industry is chiefly aimed at making cheese similar to the Old World favorites. But it means an abundant supply of cheese in all price ranges and also brings up new types of bricks and useful cheeses for every household.

part three

INFORMATION CENTER

CHAPTER 10
KITCHEN CALENDAR

You can't be "uppity" and dress better than your neighbors or they may hate you. You can't have more money than they have or they'll envy you. But when it comes to consideration of others—which is what good manners are—you can afford to be the best in town. And if you're the best cook for miles around, you can't possibly get into trouble, for everyone will want to come to see you.

• One thing—well, there are several really—that helps in case there are more people to feed than there are dollars for food is non-fat dry milk. A canister of it within reach improves flavor, stretches the proteins and food value of everything from meat loaf to sauces, and helps out generally wherever it is needed, which is about as often as salt.

• The meat tenderizer has come into its own (and into my home) only in the past year or so. What a discovery that was. Although you can get the tenderizer in both seasoned and unseasoned powder, you may prefer your own seasoning and like the non-seasoned tenderizer best. Sprinkle it on the least expensive piece of meat you can buy, including liver, and leave it there about half an hour before cooking. The tenderizing effect is sensational—or do you already know?

• MONOSODIUM GLUTAMATE (MSG)—I don't need to mention that probably, but it is a *must* along with salt and pepper.

• Herbs are such delicate little things, they need to be kept in bottles, sealed except when you are helping yourself to their offerings of exquisitely touched-up food. Remember to go easy on them. They steep like tea, getting stronger with a little time and bitter instead of enhancing if cooked too long. Use ⅛ teaspoons at first, increase it a little, but don't miss the pleasure of herbs in cooking to make almost anything taste better. Add them at the last about 15 minutes before long-cooking food is done.

• A wonderful seasoner is orange juice. Anywhere you think orange juice, just a tablespoonful or two, might improve a fruit flavor, try it out and see. Lemon juice brings out quality flavor in shy berries such as blueberries. And sugar, just ½ teaspoon, to the bottom of the roasting pan, to the skillet before browning meat, to gravy—does things you can hardly believe to meat flavor.

• Orange juice acts on many fruits as the good wife who helps her husband excel himself, to be even better than he thought he could be. That is what orange juice does to other fruits. What it won't do, lemon juice will.

• People who do not like fruit drinks as sweet as they are, who like a change from straight ginger ale or cola drinks or pop, can add a few dashes of Angostura bitters.

• A dash of Angostura perks up clam juice too, either hot or cold clam juice.

• You know, probably, that banana slices will stay their creamy color and not turn dark if you sprinkle them with lemon or orange, grapefruit or lime juice.

• Did you ever try running a fork the full length of a peeled banana, making lines down its whole length all round it? Then slice it and see the little fluted pattern the fork notches produced.

• One thing I should hate to be without: a timer. One of those kitchen alarms that can be carried to other parts of the house, ticking away the time something is in the oven and ringing a bell when time comes to take it out.

• And will you tell me why cranberries happened to be considered Christmas berries? Cranberries are so nippy and wonderful, they should be invited to the table on the Fourth of July in that Cranberry Ice Cream Pie. Pour 'em over ice cream in August. Salads, sweets, relishes—there isn't a thing they aren't good with unless it's potatoes.

• Word came the other day that we in this country throw away so much good food that about 5 pounds of it per person are wasted each week. Nothing around this kitchen ever escapes the soup pot, especially now that the electric blender age is here. The few leftover vegetables and meats, plus a can of creamed soup, and there is a new soup every other day. Each one good, too.

• Evaporated milk is another thing that comes in handy. A can of it in the freezer, several cans on the shelf. What non-fat dry milk and it can't do—well . . .

• How do you and parsley get along? And onion? Parsley is decorative, of course, but it lends a fine flavor to other vegetables, to the green salad, and is pretty, too, when chopped and scattered on top of the soup bowl. Why don't you eat more soup anyhow? It's good for you and so good. Especially with little buttered squares of toasted bread with garlic salt on them.

• Raisins have been around a long time, but how many things do you do with them? Perhaps you might like to toss a few into the steamed squash. That's good. And add them to hot cereal for breakfast, making a lot so some will be left over for slicing and sautéing as if it were fried mush. Raisins still there, of course. Add raisins to apples when you bake them, along with chopped nuts in the center. Put a few in the meat loaf; add them to muffins; fill butter cookies with them.

A CHEERFUL KITCHEN . . . . HERBS IN THE POT

The kitchen should be a pretty place, as cheerful and as convenient as you can make it. Give it the *look* of being valued. Plant herbs in little boxes in your window, to be clipped for use and to appear pleasantly green as they grow there. Those most suitable for kitchen growing are chives, rosemary, parsley, sage, and thyme.

Their presence will encourage you to experiment with them, clipping a few to drop in the soup as it warms, to flavor vegetables, meanwhile making their own bouquet for you.

Do you have a record player in the house? One of those automatic ones that play a stack of records will cheer you while you work in the kitchen, and they won't interrupt you by requiring constant attention.

If you spend a lot of time in your kitchen, find a way to get those hooks you have meant to put up for the last ten years so that your measuring cups can be within reach, your coffee cups hung from the top of the shelf to save space—and to save breakage—and buy a kitchen stool to sit on part of the time when you are working.

A geranium plant wouldn't hurt either. In Switzerland one of the delights visitors long remember is the rows of geraniums on the window sills, on barn ledges, along the front of a small store, arranged in a circle around the flagpole! Which reminds me of the bear which is the emblem of Bern and which is the white frosting design on the wonderful Swiss honey cakes.

Swiss bears are in a roomy pit and are not apt to roam around, but in New York City one of the bears from the Bronx Zoo got a bit of wanderlust and looked for his chance to escape. Eventually the moment came and he went romping off to see the sights. Naturally the keepers were frantic. So were the residents, who did not care for a visit from the bear. They hoped to find him before he did harm and before he was harmed. And how do you think they got him back?

One of the worried keepers remembered that a bear wandering around the city might get hungry, so he prepared a super bear meal and placed it where the bear could get at it. The end of the story you can guess. The bear got hungry, sought his feeding place, ate the meal, and was so content he was willing to stay home. There is a moral in this story if you care to look for it!

• A carrot is split lengthwise, an onion halved or quartered, a stalk of celery left complete with leafy ends, a few sprigs of parsley . . . These are the first things to go into the pot when meat or fowl is to be simmered. The *bouquet garni* you read about is fine, but it originated because the French used garden herbs and rightly wanted to put them in the pot at the right moment and to be able to fish them out at the right moment. For herbs go in for brief cooking when you want the marvel of their flavor. Remember, dried herbs, carefully kept sealed, will do as well and are easier. Besides, the *bouquet garni* should be one thing for fowl, another for beef, another for veal, another when seafood goes into the pot.

• When beef is to be boiled or beef broth wanted from cracked bones and odds and ends of meat, add the vegetables, simmer slowly, barely cooking for a couple of hours. (Bones can simmer all day.) Fifteen minutes before you intend to take it from the stove, add 1 bay leaf, 2 or 3 cloves, ½ teaspoon of thyme or marjoram. These are in addition to the salt and pepper used.

• When chicken is to go into the pot, add ½ teaspoon tarragon for that final flavoring. Or add ½ teaspoon ground nutmeg in addition to salt and pepper.

• Strain the broth and there you are. If you don't want to strain it, tie up all the things you put into the pot, except the meat, in cheesecloth. Straining is easier.

• When seafood is to be cooked, herbs go in at the beginning, for seafood requires little cooking. See Seafood Celebrities for herbs used with it, as well as cooking time.

ABOUT CANNED FOODS . . . . DID YOU KNOW?

• You store your cans, I hope, on a shelf away from the heat of the stove or steam pipe.

• Keep your canned food supplies on the coolest shelf available, and if possible place glass jars of food in a fairly dark place.

• Cans that have been opened are perfectly safe for containing food until it is used, but keep them cool and covered.

• If you are opening canned juices, shake the can before you attempt to open it. It pays to have a good can opener, a puncture-type opener for juices and a special jar opener that pries up the lids from glass jars with such ease and speed that the top is not injured and can be reused on the jar. Keep it on the magnetic knife rack or some other convenient place where you can find it when you need it.

• In heating canned vegetables, there are smart things to do just as in heating frozen foods. Remember that the contents of canned vegetables or fruits have been cooked and are ready to serve as they are. For this reason the food itself should be cooked very little. Pour off the juice into a saucepan and boil it until it has been reduced to half the original amount. Only then should the vegetable be added for quick heating, with the salt, pepper, butter, and other flavorings you wish to combine with the vegetable.

• Naturally, reducing the juice by heating it before adding the vegetable increases the amount of flavor in the liquid and in the vegetable served in it. But if you are not serving the juice with the vegetable, never throw it away. Save it to use instead of water for diluting canned soups, or add it to gravies or to White Sauce. It has food value and its flavor.

• Remember, too, that if you don't like canned fruits or vegetables it may be because you aren't buying the best quality. Nothing in the world is going to replace quality in any fruit or vegetable, whether fresh, frozen, or canned.

FROZEN OR CANNED . . . . VERSUS FRESH

What's all this nonsense that you can't be a good cook if you use canned or frozen foods when fresh is right under your nose? That belief is no more sensible than maintaining that a bicycle built for two is the only way to go to church, and is just as out of date.

In our country packers and canners of frozen and canned quality brands vie with each other to produce the most fresh-tasting, the most vitamin-whole fresh vegetables and fruits. In excelling each other they surpass most of us, not to mention the vegetable man we buy from. What do you know about him?

He may pick them, desert them, revive them, and sell them to you and me—or he may bring them in, fresh as the morning, to a spot where you get them almost as dewy crisp as when he picked them.

Then how do you cook them? I mean are you as careful as packers are to cook fresh vegetables and fruits so that they lose none of their valuable flavor or nutritious ingredients? You buy them in the first place because you know they are good and like their flavor, but your family flourishes on them satisfactorily according to your wisdom in handling them.

The packers use fresh fruits and vegetables grown especially for packing; freeze or can them with the greatest care to preserve both their natural abundant flavor and vitamin content. There is a law that keeps its eagle eye on all plants where food is packaged, so that you are protected from any manufacturer who is inclined to be careless. This law not only prevents any spoiled or damaged food from being processed, but the plant itself must be spotlessly clean and the workers in it carefully supervised. The packages they produce for you must be free of any material or preservatives that would be harmful, the ingredients must be stated on the label, and the package or can must never be deceptive in size or shape. Everyone likes this, including the packers. It assures them that, while their back is turned putting extra flavor beyond and above the call of duty into their own products, someone down the road isn't going to put out a poor-quality package with deceptive labeling and turn into a ruinous competitor.

Nice thing, too, is that each package of frozen food is labeled, telling you how to carry on between opening it and putting the contents on your table.

I'll get a word in here, too, if you don't mind. There are numerous brands in your grocery store of both frozen and canned foods. It doesn't take any woman very long to find out that the best quality she can buy is the only quality to buy. Flavor does vary among the different brands.

Stock your shelves with a supply of the various cans needed to produce perhaps as many as half a dozen different dishes. No one can tell you what these cans should be because it depends upon the personal taste of you and of your family and certainly upon its size. These cans on the shelf or cartons in the freezer will ensure your having the makings of a good meal on those occasions that otherwise turn into frantic hours, if you are ill or delayed or are surprised just before mealtime and required to produce more than you have the strength or minutes to cook the long way.

There are also a few little cans or jars that will serve you well in flavoring and in varying the food you put on the table. These are pretty sure to be valuable for everyone. When preparing your list of the main-course-dish shelf supply, consider a selection of flavoring aids too. These are to keep within reach to use in daily cooking, not up on the top shelf where those Reserve-for-Mad-Moments cans are waiting to rush to your rescue.

Each person has his own favorites. Surely, among them, will be MSG, peppercorns for crushing or grinding, dried parsley or chives, both sweet and hot paprika, Bovril, Worcestershire, a can of dry mustard, Tabasco Sauce, and please—a few herbs along with poppy and caraway seeds.

CHAPTER 11

SAUCES

WHITE SAUCE . . . . . IN THE REFRIGERATOR

Cream Sauce or "White Sauce" in the refrigerator, ready to be mixed with other flavorings, means endless interesting variety in the flavoring of food you eat day after day. Mix ½ cup Cream Sauce with 4 tablespoons grated cheese, heat, and pour over broccoli, tomatoes, over sliced hard-cooked eggs. Thin heavy sauce with a little cream, add a pinch of curry powder, heat 5 minutes, and serve over chicken sliced off the bones.

A large supply of White Sauce can provide creamed soup in a minute by adding almost any green vegetable, chopped fine, heated to appetizing steaminess.

If Cream Sauce is there to use, you will find daily use for it and will be apt to make a 4- to 6-cup supply. Make your creamy White Sauce this way, in the thickness you like, trying each one in this amount. Afterward, make only the one you find most useful.

Makes 2 cups:

THIN WHITE SAUCE:

2 tablespoons butter
2 tablespoons flour
2 cups rich milk or undiluted evaporated milk
½ teaspoon salt

MEDIUM WHITE SAUCE:

4 tablespoons butter
4 tablespoons flour
2 cups rich milk or undiluted evaporated milk
½ teaspoon salt

THICK WHITE SAUCE:

6 tablespoons butter
6 tablespoons flour
2 cups rich milk or undiluted evaporated milk
½ teaspoon salt

Melt butter, add flour, and blend until smooth. Add cold milk and cook until thickened, stirring constantly. Add salt; cool and store, or add any other desired seasonings for immediate use. White sauces (or cream sauces) are naturally creamy when made with undiluted evaporated milk or very rich whole milk.

SAVORY CHEESE SAUCE

Makes 2½ cups:

1½ cups Medium White Sauce
⅛ teaspoon pepper
1 teaspoon prepared mustard
¼ teaspoon Worcestershire sauce
1 cup grated American cheese

Heat White Sauce, add seasonings, and stir until smooth. Add cheese and cook as little as possible, stirring until sauce is smooth. Serve on vegetables or hard-cooked sliced eggs.

SEAFOOD SAUCE

This is another one of those elegant sauces which is better and better with several leftovers added such as bits of cooked fish or any seafood. Actually it is 1 cup White Sauce with ½ cup (or more) of chopped cooked shrimp stirred into it. But you can also add the other seafood, as I mentioned. And when you chop the shrimp, keep it in chunks, not too fine a chopping job on it. A little curry in this if you like it when it is to be served over fish. But I like it best just shrimp sauce over seafood or chicken croquettes.

CAPER SAUCE

Thin 1 cup Thick White Sauce with ⅓ cup fish broth (if this is to be served on fish) or ⅓ cup cream if it is to be served on any other dish. Add 2 tablespoons lemon juice and 2 tablespoons capers. This is superb company for salmon, fresh, cooked, or out of a can.

CARAWAY SAUCE

Make a creamed caraway sauce for vegetables (this is especially good on Brussels sprouts) by thinning White Sauce with a little cream and adding 1 to 2 teaspoons caraway seeds for each cup of sauce. This is very good on potatoes too. Or simply add the caraway seeds to melted butter; cover and let stand for 5 or 10 minutes, then drench the potatoes, Brussels sprouts, or cabbage.

CURRY SAUCE

Add 1 teaspoon curry powder to 1¼ cups White Sauce. Throw in ¼ cup raisins and stir while heating over very low flame. Then astonish yourself with how good this sauce makes any chicken, meat—either beef or lamb—or seafood you can lay your hands on. Just add about 2 cups of whatever it is to the sauce. Salt and pepper to taste, and is it good! Try each one if you haven't already. I like the weest sprinkling of ground ginger on top of each serving, and you may too.

MUSHROOM SAUCE

Good on almost anything. You use this on vegetables, meat, seafood, everything except desserts. Cook ¾ cups sliced mushrooms—stems and all—about 5 minutes in 2 tablespoons butter, margarine, or peanut oil. Add 1 tablespoon chopped onion to this and let it cook along with the mushrooms. Add 1 cup White Sauce and stir gently until blended and heated through. Use a small pan for making your sauces, then you won't waste any. You can always add a little cream or milk, just a tablespoon or two, to make a sauce thinner.

Cooking Mushrooms

If mushrooms can be cleaned without washing them, so much the better. Brush them off with a damp cloth. Do not peel. Slice the stems as well as the tops when you are going to cook them to use in a sauce. If you want the large thin slices of the top of the mushroom for decorative purposes, then cook the sliced tops and the chopped stems separately in salted water which has a little lemon juice or vinegar added to keep them from turning dark. Cover and allow them to simmer 5 to 10 minutes.

Mushroom caps which are going to be stuffed should be cooked in this way no longer than 5 minutes. Remove and drain before filling and heating under the broiler. Chop the stems and cook them in the same juice used for preparing the tops.

When slicing mushrooms, slice from top down (as if slicing bread) not across. This gives you shapely slices.

MUSHROOM ANGOSTURA SAUCE

Thin 1 cup Thick White Sauce with a little cream; add ½ cup mushrooms (stems too) sliced and sautéed in butter. Stir in 1 teaspoon Angostura bitters. Very good over cold meat or chicken, on hot fish, or over sliced hard-cooked eggs.

BEGIN WITH MAYONNAISE . . . TO MAKE THESE

LEMON MAYONNAISE

Makes 2½ cups:

1 egg
¼ cup lemon juice
1 teaspoon dry mustard
1 teaspoon salt
1 tablespoon sugar
dash of pepper or paprika
2 cups olive or salad oil

Combine all ingredients except salad oil. Add oil almost a drop at a time while beating it in with rotary or electric beater, until 2 cups are blended.

For fruit salads, try thinning this with orange juice, or fold in whipped cream with nutmeg sprinkled over it.

It is a good idea to double this recipe in a family where dressings are constantly used. It is the beginning for:

THOUSAND ISLAND DRESSING

Makes 2½ cups:

1½ cups Lemon Mayonnaise
¾ cups chili sauce
2 tablespoons chopped celery
2 tablespoons chopped green pepper

Combine and stir well.

GINGER MAYONNAISE

Stir ¼ teaspoon ground ginger into 1 cup mayonnaise. Add 1 tablespoon chopped preserved ginger. This is wonderful on fruit salad.

GREEN SAUCE

Add 2 tablespoons finely chopped parsley, 1 tablespoon finely chopped scallion tops, and 2 tablespoons onion juice to 1 cup Lemon Mayonnaise. This is so good hot or cold over fish. It is especially good served cold with cold salmon.

PASTEL CREAM DRESSING

½ cup mayonnaise
¼ cup currant jelly
¼ cup cream, whipped

Place mayonnaise and jelly in a small bowl. Beat with rotary beater until smooth and well blended. Fold in whipped cream. Chill before serving. Delicious on fruit salad.

FRENCH DRESSINGS . . VARIATIONS ON A THEME

FRENCH DRESSING

Makes 1½ cups:

1 cup olive or salad oil
½ cup vinegar or lemon juice
1 teaspoon sugar (optional)
1 teaspoon dry mustard
1½ teaspoons salt
½ teaspoon pepper
¼ teaspoon paprika
2 cloves garlic (optional)

Combine all ingredients in a bottle or cruet and shake vigorously until blended. Everyone differs in the French dressing recipe liked best. Omit the sugar and the garlic if you prefer. Try adding ¼ teaspoon dill seeds or ½ teaspoon dried tarragon. A favorite of mine is the recipe as you see it above, with only about ½ teaspoon sugar and with ½ teaspoon dried basil and 1 tablespoon chopped chives.

ROQUEFORT FRENCH DRESSING

Crumble Roquefort cheese, adding about 2 tablespoons to 1 cup of your favorite French dressing, and serve on green salad.

TARRAGON FRENCH DRESSING

This is a French dressing from France! Although the French rarely have dried herbs as used here. Their seasonings are from the garden or the market.

Makes 1¼ cups:

1 teaspoon salt
¼ teaspoon chervil
1 teaspoon finely chopped chives
1 tablespoon chopped onion
1 teaspoon finely chopped parsley
¼ cup tarragon-flavored vinegar or wine vinegar with ½ teaspoon tarragon added
½ teaspoon mustard
½ teaspoon sugar
⅔ cup olive or peanut oil

Combine herbs and vinegar, mashing them together well. Pour into bottle or cruet. Cover tightly, allowing them to blend for at least an hour before adding the olive oil and seasonings to the bottle. Shake thoroughly and serve on any green salad. Try this on plain red, ripe tomato slices. If you have fresh chervil or chives, chop them and sprinkle a little over the top for garnish.

CELERY SEED DRESSING

Makes about 1¼ cups:

1 teaspoon salt
1 teaspoon dry mustard
½ teaspoon paprika
1 teaspoon celery seed
½ cup light corn syrup
¼ to ⅓ cup vinegar
1 cup salad oil
1 tablespoon grated onion

Place all ingredients in a small bowl. Beat with rotary beater until well blended and thickened. Place in covered container. Chill several hours. Shake before serving.

SPECIAL SAUCES . . . . USE OFTEN

HUNGARIAN CREAM DRESSING

Makes 1½ cups:

1 cup undiluted evaporated milk
1 tablespoon vinegar

Chill milk 30 minutes in refrigerator tray. Whip until slightly thickened. Stir in vinegar. Chill and serve over any fruit or berries, fresh, canned, or frozen. Serve on gingerbread or other cake squares. Serve blobs of this on borsch or other cold soup.

BLACK BUTTER SAUCE

½ cup butter
3 tablespoons lemon juice

Melt butter in a small saucepan, watching it carefully until it is well browned—but not burned. Immediately add a teaspoon of cold butter and stir in the lemon juice.

Try this over cooked broccoli or lima beans. And next time you cook trout, drench the white flakes in Black Butter Sauce. Delicious.

COTTAGE CHEESE DRESSING

Makes 1 cup:

3 tablespoons lemon juice
6 tablespoons cottage cheese
6 tablespoons evaporated milk
½ teaspoon salt
2 teaspoons honey
⅛ teaspoon paprika
1 tablespoon chopped chives

Combine and beat until smooth. Serve on fruit or on green salad.

part four

LUNCHEONS, FIRESIDE SUPPERS, AND FOOD FOR THE FAMILY

CHAPTER 12

MENUS

CARD PARTIES . . . . FUN AND FOOD

There never was a brighter idea than those bridge-playing club members had who decided to play for money and then give it to the winner. It was then her privilege to donate it to her favorite of the four charities the club had decided to sponsor. Just an idea. The fun of winning is for some reason more important when money is involved . . . and the ornery part of it all is removed entirely by the good works benefited.

Tell me something. Did you know that there is nothing strange about the idea of telling fortunes with cards? The playing cards you use for bridge, canasta, poker, whatever, descended from *torok,* the cards used by the gypsies for fortunetelling. Each card in the *torok* was a symbol of mysterious power outside human ken. Our cards are not exact duplicates, for the original *torok* cards could scare you to pieces. The ace of spades was the death card, picturing a forbidding skeleton. The joker descended from a card in the *torok* picturing the Foolish Man. He was dressed in rags and tags, blithely walked toward a crocodile ready to eat him, a dog ready to bite him, a precipice ready to trip him. All this time he was singing happily. If he survived all these traps and was still alive at the foot of the precipice, there was a bonfire ready to end the whole matter.

Playing games of all sorts is one of the important accomplishments in life. Developing skill in a few and enjoying them add a great deal of pleasure to life. Also, games prevent gossiping among friends who see each other so often they haven't anything new to say. Then, too, playing cards do keep you alert. Being alert fifty, sixty, seventy years, maybe longer, is rather difficult. Toward this valuable mental quality cards engagingly do their bit.

However, what you and your friends like to eat before or after cards is the important thing. Maybe some of the alert bridge players would like these.

SOUP 'N' SALAD LUNCHEONS

Borsch
Salmon Mousse Molds
Coffee Eggnog
Mints

Quick Crab Bisque
Cranberry-Grapefruit Salad
Spiced Viennese Coffee

Peanut Butter Soup
Rainbow Salad
Chocolate Calypso

Cheese Soup
Melon Ginger Ale Salad
Hot Chocolate or Cold Cola

Fresh Currant Raspberry Soup
Cheese Salad in Tomato Cups
Cold Cola

Fresh Vegetable Chowder
Herb Croutons
Chicken Salad
Mocha Java

Curried Bean Soup
Fruit Rolls
Marinated Vegetable Salad
Hot Coffee or Coffee Cooler
Mints

SALAD 'N' SANDWICH . . . . PLATE LUNCHEONS

Frozen Fruit Salad
Beef Open Sandwich
Spiced Nuts
Coffee Cooler

Tuna Salad
Watercress Sandwiches
Lemon or Maple Cream Roll
Iced Coffee Trinidad

Cranberry-Grapefruit Salad
Delicious Nut Bread
(buttered and filled with jams or marmalade)
Iced Tea

Shrimp Salad
Apricot Puff Loaf Slices
Cinnamon Drops and Corn Candy
Coffee Float

Red and White Cole Slaw
Salad Roll Sandwiches—Cranberry Sandwiches
Brownies—Hot Tea

Melon Ginger Ale Salad
Assorted Danish Open Sandwiches
Chocolate Mints
Spiced Viennese Coffee

FOR ST. PATRICK'S . . . . . . OR BEFORE CARDS

Irish Stew
Fruit Salad with Whipped Cream Dressing
Devil's Food Cake
with Green Mint Filling and Frosting
Coffee

Frozen Melon Ball Cocktail
Meat and Potato Ring Mold
Irish Biscuit Pie
Green Salad made with every possible green combined
and tossed in French Dressing
Almond Bavarian Pie
(with green vegetable coloring added)
or
Lime Chiffon Pie
Coffee

Kebabs
French-Toasted Sandwiches
Avocado, Romaine, and Celery Salad
Roquefort Dressing
Angel Pie with Lime Filling
Coffee

Sweet-Pungent Pork
Peas and Lettuce   Carrots and Herbs
Ginger-Applesauce Refrigerator Cake
Coffee

SHOWERS . . . . LUNCHEON MENUS

"Swallow a thimbleful of salt before you go to bed," they said, "and you will dream of your future husband." That was the advice given long ago to unmarried damsels. It is much more fun to serve a beautiful dessert and coffee in honor of the bride-to-be (who dreams of him night and day anyway) or to give a shower luncheon.

Menus for these showers are probably just the thing you want for any pretty luncheon or filling suppers when men are present. Use the one you like most for the sewing-circle luncheon . . . for the shower given for both bride and groom . . . for supper before the men play cards. . . . Easy, colorful, these menus give you a place to begin. Change them to suit your whim so long as the colors are inviting, the food appropriate for the weather.

SHOWER LUNCHEON OR VALENTINE MENU

Chicken South Seas
Tomato Aspic Hearts on Lettuce
Biscuits with Orange Peel
Olives Celery Radishes
Cranberry Angel Cake
Chocolate Mints
Coffee

SHOWER LUNCHEON AND FOR EASTER TOO!

Cheese Soufflé
Orange Slices Sprinkled with Cinnamon
or French Dressing
Salami Muffins
Biscuit Tortoni
Coffee

Ham Rolls
Broccoli and Herb Sauce
Mustard Biscuits
Easter Egg Mousse
Coffee

Eggs Benedict
Crisp Fresh Spinach served with Celery Heart Leaves
French Dressing
Regal 3-layer Rice Mold
or
Angel Cake Hatbox
Coffee

4 SHOWER SUPPERS . . . . MEN PRESENT

Hawaiian Punch
Cheese Rabbit à la Suisse
(In Chafing Dish)
Toast
Frozen Fruit Salad
Frost-a-Brick Ice Cream Cake
Coffee

Batter-Dip Fried Chicken
Potato Chips
Biscuits Wedding Ring
Fresh Fruit—Cheese Board
or
Rainbow Coconut Kisses
Coffee

Western Fish and Avocado Strips
Deep Red Tomato Slices
(salt and pepper, no dressing)
Hot Potato Chips Sprinkled with Paprika
Ice Cream Pie in Chocolate Coconut Shell
Iced Tea

Shrimp Salad
Pineapple Muffins
Small Whole Pickled Beets
Chocolate Mint Heavenly Pie
Coffee

COOKING AT THE TABLE . ON GRILLS OR GRIDDLES

Pretty enough for a shower when couples are invited, good for filling meals at any hour, perfect for square-dance fare. Choose your time and let everyone make his own or appoint two cooks to serve:

Apricot Eggnog (while the cooking goes on)
Cheese Pancakes
Hungarian Cream
Cranberry Relish
Greengage Fruit Float
Coffee

Mexican Corn Meal Stacks
Sausage Cakes or Fried Scrapple
Hot Syrup
Mango Fruit Float
or
Ring-around-the-Rosy Angel Cake

Pancakes Filled with Creamed Chicken
Green Beans with Tarragon Sauce
Cranberry Apple Salad
Assorted Ice Cream Sundaes

Buckwheat Cake Stacks and Sausage
Maple Syrup and Butter
Cantaloupe Baked Alaska
Coffee

De Luxe Lobster Newburg
Toast Triangles
Sliced Tomatoes with Curried Mayonnaise
Dessert Pancakes
Coffee

Pecan Waffles   Blueberry Griddle Cakes
Maple Syrup and Butter
Black Cherries-Pale Pears Fruit Float

Hot Spiced Cranberry Punch
Waffled French Toast   French-Toasted Sandwiches
Maple Syrup and Butter
Pineapple-Coconut Ice Cream
Coffee

Spiced Hot Tomato Cider
Swiss Cheese Omelet
Green Salad with French Dressing
White Senegalese Cake
with Pink Mint Filling and Coconut Frosting
Coffee

2 DEEP-FRY COOK 'N' SERVE MENUS

Shrimp Savory, Cheese Fritters
Crisp Green Salad with Tomato Wedges
Aloha Pine-Mallow Dessert
Coffee

Chicken-Pecan Croquettes
Tomatoes with Spinach
Garden Biscuits
Ring-around-the-Rosy Angel Cake
Coffee

SPECIAL-OCCASION LUNCHEON OR SUPPERS

Hawaiian Fruit Punch
Western Fish and Avocado Strips
Savory Rice
Herb Tomatoes
Peach and Blueberry Cake Cobbler
Coffee

Chicken Luau
Banana Muffins
Crisp Green Salad
Lemon Refrigerator Cake or Golden Angel Cake
Coffee

SEAFOOD MENUS . . . . MAKE YOUR OWN

Seafood Cakes . . . Kebabs . . . Steaming Crusty Pies . . . Seafood broiled, boiled, or barbecued—are best with good company of:

CRISP SALADS	Cole Slaw Green Salad Fruit Salad with tart dressing
POTATOES	French Fries Crusty browned pan-fried Potato Chips
FRUIT DESSERTS	Fruit Floats Deep-Dish Fruit Pies Cake or Biscuit Cobblers Biscuit Shortcakes Sherbets Fruit and Cheese

FIRESIDE SUPPERS . . . . . . FINE AND FILLING

Swiss Pork Chops
Spinach and Herbs
Onion Soufflé
Cloverleaf Rolls
Chocolate Cream Raspberry Roll

Shrimp and Pork Philippine
Cauliflower Dundee
Carrots with Mustard
Fluffy Biscuits
Deep Dark Chocolate Cake
with Tropical Filling and Coconut Frosting
Coffee

SPANISH MAIN COURSES . . . . AND WONDERFUL

Hot Spiced Cranberry Punch
Paella
Hearts of Lettuce—Thousand Island Dressing
Orange Ice
Coffee

Lemon-Grape Ade
Spanish Cocida
Pecan Cream Pie
Coffee

6 DINNERS . . . . WITH SOUP FEATURED

Swedish Cabbage Soup—Caraway Dumplings
Tossed Green Salad with Tart French Dressing
Crumb-Top Peach Pie
Coffee

Jambalaya
Biscuit Crisps
Ginger Ale Salad
Toasted Corn Bread Squares
Chocolate Ladyfinger Icebox Cake
Coffee
Spiced Nuts

Chicken-Oyster Gumbo
Peanut Butter Toasted Loaf
Cranberry-Apple Salad
Chocolate Senegalese Cake
with Lemon Filling and Frosting
Coffee
Pillow Mints

Hot Mulled Cider
Cheese Spreads—Cereal Nut Crisps
Crab Bisque
Fresh Fruit Salad with Lemon Mayonnaise
Tiny Corn Bread Muffins
Blackberry Parfait Pie
Coffee

New England Clam Chowder
Crisp Hard Rolls
String Beans with Herb Sauce
Baked Spiced Sweet Potatoes
Deep-Dish Blueberry Pie
Iced Tea

Shrimp Butter—Stuffed Celery
Crackers—Radishes
Potato-Fish Chowder
Toasted Finger Loaf
Asparagus with Black Walnut Sauce
Cold Pickled Beets
Watermelon or Cantaloupe
Iced Coffee

CHAPTER 13

SOUP—CANNED BUT DIFFERENT

The stock pot is out of style, too time-consuming, but who cares? The stock-pot supply is within fingertip reach in cans, rich, well flavored, convenient. Use it as you would the stock made in your own kitchen, to dilute canned soups instead of water or to replace part of the water when thinning soups. And let's admit it . . . there are few people today who can make soup as good as the soup we can fortunately enjoy from cans.

There is no end to the variety in serving them as they come or in combining two or three to suit the occasion.

PEANUT BUTTER SOUP

Makes 5 cups:

3 tablespoons butter
2 tablespoons chopped onion
4 tablespoons peanut butter
1 can (10½-ounces) cream of mushroom soup
1 can (12½-ounces) chicken broth
1 cup water
1 tablespoon chili sauce

Melt butter in saucepan; add onion and cook until lightly browned. Add peanut butter. Stir. Pour in mushroom soup and slowly add the chicken broth and water, stirring constantly until blended and thoroughly hot but not boiling. Serve garnished with chopped parsley.

CREAMED CURRY SOUP

Makes 6 cups:

2 tablespoons butter
1 tablespoon curry powder
1 teaspoon Worcestershire
1/8 teaspoon cayenne
1 can (10½ ounces) cream of mushroom soup
1 can (10½ ounces) cream of pea soup
2 cans (12½ ounces) chicken broth

Melt butter in 2-quart saucepan. Stir in curry powder and seasonings. When blended, pour in mushroom and pea soups, adding the liquid slowly and stirring constantly. Rinse out the cream soup cans with the chicken broth before adding it. Cover and allow to stand a few minutes before serving. Reheat to boiling point before filling soup bowls. Garnish with chopped peanuts and sprinkling of instant coffee.

6 SOUPS TO USE . . . . AND TO TREASURE

SWEDISH CABBAGE SOUP*

Makes 10 to 12 cups:

1 small head white cabbage
3 tablespoons fat
1 medium onion, chopped
2 quarts rich meat stock
1 carrot, diced
¼ teaspoon thyme
¼ teaspoon marjoram
¼ teaspoon pepper
2 tablespoons syrup

Choose a firm cabbage and cut in very small strips. Brown in the fat with onion. Add meat stock and simmer gently 2 hours. Strain a little of this stock into a small saucepan with the carrot, herbs, and pepper and boil 15 minutes. Combine the two mixtures and add syrup. Bring to boiling point and serve very hot.

Easy to increase this for a crowd, still easier to eat often—at home.

*House of Herbs.

FRESH VEGETABLE CHOWDER

Makes 6 to 8 cups:

¼ cup rice
4 cups water
1 teaspoon salt
1 cup chopped raw carrots
½ cup chopped celery
½ cup tomatoes
½ cup miscellaneous raw vegetables (onions, turnips, green pepper, parsley)
2 cups undiluted evaporated milk
½ teaspoon freshly ground pepper
⅛ teaspoon paprika
¼ teaspoon marjoram

Boil rice in salted water until almost tender. Add the prepared vegetables and seasonings. Continue cooking until vegetables are just tender. Add milk and cook very slowly until thoroughly heated.

AVOCADO-CHICKEN SOUP

Makes 4 cups:

3 cups chicken broth
¼ cup finely chopped celery
1 cup avocado purée (1 medium-sized)
1 tablespoon margarine or butter
¾ teaspoon salt
⅛ teaspoon ground black pepper
½ teaspoon finely chopped onion

Cook chicken broth and celery in covered saucepan until celery is tender. Beat in avocado. Add remaining ingredients. Heat and serve.

CHEESE SOUP

Makes 8 to 10 cups:

4 tablespoons butter
2 medium-sized onions, sliced
1½ cups diced crusty rolls or bread
4 bouillon cubes
8 cups boiling water
4 egg yolks, beaten
1 cup cream
8 ounces (2½ cups) grated Swiss cheese
salt, pepper, and nutmeg to taste

Melt butter in 3-quart saucepan; brown onions lightly; add bread and brown 5 minutes. Dissolve bouillon cubes in boiling water and add to bread. Simmer 10 minutes. Strain; return to saucepan and keep over low heat. Combine egg yolks with cream; add cheese. Stir well and slowly stir into hot soup. Blend, season, and serve.

BORSCH

Makes 5 to 6 cups:

4 tablespoons butter
1 carrot, cut fine
1 onion, cut fine
3 cabbage leaves, cut
2 sprigs parsley
1 stalk celery, cut
2 cups boiled beets, grated
1 pint beef broth
½ teaspoon marjoram
¼ teaspoon egg-cheese-herb blend
2 teaspoons sugar
2 teaspoons flavored-for-salads wine vinegar
1 cup raw beets, grated

Heat butter and simmer carrot, onion, cabbage, parsley, celery, and grated cooked beets. Add the broth and all seasonings and cook gently 25 minutes. Add juice of grated raw beets squeezed through cheesecloth. Serve very hot. Pass the sour cream at the table.

FRESH CURRANT-RASPBERRY SOUP

Makes 8½ cups:

1 quart currants
1 pint red raspberries
2 cups water
1 cup minus 1 tablespoon sugar
6 tablespoons quick-cooking tapioca
¼ teaspoon salt

Stem and wash currants. Wash raspberries. Place fruit and water in saucepan. Bring to a boil and cook 1 minute. Strain. Combine sugar, tapioca, and salt in saucepan. Add strained juice. Cook over medium heat until mixture comes to a boil, stirring constantly. Remove from heat. Cool 15 minutes, stirring occasionally. Chill and serve with a spoonful of whipped cream. Garnish with a sprig of parsley.

3 WAYS TO MAKE POTATO SOUP . . . EACH IS GOOD

Potato Soup is internationally famous as fine-flavored, you know, and it is so very inexpensive. To be its most superb it must be smooth as velvet, a texture acquired from beating. An electric blender makes this soup—or others—perfect in about 2 minutes. Always serve Potato Soup garnished with finely chopped chives or parsley.

RICH POTATO SOUP

Makes about 8 cups:

3 cups diced raw potatoes
½ cup finely chopped onion
½ teaspoon salt
3 cups potato water
3 cups chicken broth (canned or your own)
1⅓ cups evaporated milk, undiluted
¼ teaspoon marjoram
⅛ teaspoon cayenne
3 tablespoons melted bacon fat
2 tablespoons chopped chives or parsley

Cook potatoes and onions in 3 cups salted water until tender. Drain; save the water, combining with chicken broth, evaporated milk, and marjoram. Force potato and onion through ricer or sieve. Add cayenne and fat. Slowly add the liquid to the sieved potatoes, stirring constantly until velvety consistency. Heat thoroughly. Garnish with chopped chives or parsley.

BUDGET POTATO SOUP

Make this like the recipe above, except use 6 cups of water and no chicken broth.

WEIGHT WATCHER'S POTATO SOUP

Prepare exactly as first recipe, omitting heavy milk. Add 1½ cups non-fat dry milk powder to cool chicken broth before it is combined with potato water. Naturally, the chicken broth makes potato soup more full-flavored, and when used it should be clear and not brown enough to discolor the soup.

CHAPTER 14
PARTY SANDWICHES

FRENCH-TOASTED SANDWICHES

Make these with white bread, but use any kind of filling you like, so long as it is soft and sticky enough to hold the slices of bread together. Use cheese, peanut butter, or a combination of peanut butter and honey, ground meat of any kind you like with mayonnaise, or chopped olives or pickles. To add flavor, use seafood which has been mixed with enough Thick White Sauce to hold it together; add a little curry powder to the creamed seafood, or ⅛ teaspoon of ginger to 1 cup of ground pork.

After filling the bread slices with all the good things you can think of, cut them into triangles or squares of whatever size you want and dip each one in a mixture made by combining 1 well-beaten egg with 1½ cups milk and ⅛ teaspoon salt. Now fry the sandwiches in melted butter, letting them brown evenly at a moderate temperature.

You can prepare and freeze these the day before, or long before you want to use them, when needed, bring them out and place on the table beside a table grill or barbecue. Then let each person dip his own sandwich in the batter and cook it on the grill. Fruit Kebabs are wonderful with these hot sandwiches.

SALAD ROLL SANDWICHES

Slice a loaf of white bread lengthwise, then trim off the crusts. Spread each oblong slice with softened butter or margarine and place a mound of filling on one end. This can be the creamy salad mixture, such as you used in the French-fried sandwiches, or a crisp salad mixture composed of crunchy, wonderful greens and radishes, and even shredded turnip held together with mayonnaise. Put big spoonfuls of salad at one end of each slice and roll it up enough to hold the salad in place—not too tightly. Place these on a plate and cover with a damp, cold towel. Leave them for 5 or 10 minutes to get accustomed to their shape. Serve garnished with pickles, olives, or greens.

Waldorf Salad sandwiches, made of apples, nuts, and dressing as filling, are wonderful when served with fingers of several kinds of cheeses.

CRANBERRY SANDWICHES

Makes 10:

20 slices bread (1 loaf)
softened butter
1 can jellied cranberry sauce
2 cups chicken salad, well seasoned
cream cheese, approx. 1 pound

Trim bread crusts. Butter the first slice of bread. Spread with a generous layer of cranberry sauce. (Butter prevents cranberry sauce from soaking into bread.) Top with second slice of bread buttered on both sides. Cover with a layer of chicken salad. Top with third slice of bread, buttered on both sides. Spread with cranberry sauce. Cover with fourth slice of bread, butter side down. With a sharp knife cut each stack in half. Cover sides and top with cream cheese moistened with milk to spreading consistency. Garnish with cranberry sauce cutouts.

DANISH OPEN SANDWICHES . FASHIONABLE, FILLING

The Danes—as who doesn't?—dearly love good food; especially their Open Sandwiches. Unlike the American sandwich with a slice of bread fore and aft, these are built on top an ample slice of fresh bread —usually dark whole-grain, and delicious—buttered or spread with rich mayonnaise, then decorated with whole-meal-on-top. The selection for this top is done with considerable thought to achieve contrast in texture and flavor, but also to produce an alluring sight with a variety of colors.

Serve these as the Danes do, for lunch. Serve them as they were first served to the Danes, when the men were hungry in the evening after cards.

Serve them buffet in an array of bowls filled with spreads, bread slices, butter or mayonnaise, for each person to spread his own.

Make them up as near the time for serving as is possible; cover with aluminum foil and chill until serving time.

Or stand at the buffet or behind a table with the makings in front of you and create each one to order—which is fun if you are artistic and arrange them beautifully, each on a half slice of bread.

• Beef Tartar is one of the biggest surprises, one of the tastiest too. Make it by mixing everything, then spreading it thickly on the buttered bread. Combine 1 cup best beef put through grinder twice, 2 tablespoons each of Lemon Mayonnaise, prepared horseradish, grated onion, capers. Add 2 raw eggs, salt, and pepper. Beat hard and spread. In Denmark each ingredient perches on top the bread-butter-meat foundation, no egg white is used and the whole yolk is in the center of each sandwich. But one Danish woman mixed everything as it is done in this recipe. Tastes the same and is quick and easy. Makes 2 sandwiches that will convert anybody to raw beef.

• Slice cooked lobster meat paper thin. Lay on buttered slices in overlapping arrangement similar to fish scales. Put a thin strip of pimiento down the center; sprinkle with lemon juice.

• Or chop cooked lobster meat, stir in 1 tablespoon Lemon Mayonnaise, spread, and decorate with half lemon slices, rounded portions meeting in center to form a butterfly.

• Lay sardines in rows across the bread, neat as soldiers; make a cross of chopped onion to the edges of the bread.

• Spread with Beef Tartar, make a cross of green chopped sweet pickle.

• Spread with salmon folded into Lemon Mayonnaise; decorate with paper-thin slices of onion and edge with thin slices of cucumber.

• Perch a fried egg on the center of a Beef Tartar sandwich.

• Slice smoked oysters and alternate with rows of overlapping oyster and cooked shrimp curled on top the buttered bread.

• Thin slices of vegetables, red ripe tomato, onions, radishes, which have been marinated in French Dressing, can cover another.

• Slices of chicken liver, well seasoned, is a good one. Make neat rows of the liver separated by a line of chopped onion.

• Beef jelly is added for a trim to the sandwich covered with spooned mounds of goose liver. The jelly is chopped and forms bright cubes.

• Cover one with cream cheese; edge it with currant jelly.

• Make diagonal strips across the bread with chopped pickled beet, slices of white cooked fish, and chopped dill pickle.

• Arrange slices of chicken over mayonnaise flavored lightly with curry. Make a center row of stuffed-olive slices.

• Make rows of hard-cooked eggs, the whites grated, the yolks sieved, red caviar, and slices of radish.

• Alternate roast pork slices with unpeeled apple slices.

In Denmark there are about 200 different sandwiches. You can make up as many of your own.

DANISH OPEN SANDWICHES . . . MAKE YOUR OWN

Offer variety with different breads as well as by having cheese to slice, bowls to dip from, flavored mayonnaise or butters to use. There is good reason to bring out everything in the refrigerator when you first try these, for you can use all sorts of odds and ends to good advantage. To be truly Danish, each sandwich must be as beautiful as it is delicious.

BREADS

White and whole-grain rye slices are fine, but so are the small slices of icebox rye with the seeds in it. Whole-wheat and French bread, too, and Italian whole-wheat loaves with the flaky crust. Never trim crusts off for Danish sandwiches. You might try the delicious rye bread on page 335.

BUTTERS AND MAYONNAISE

Flavor softened butter or Lemon Mayonnaise with any herbs, spices, or chopped greens which will associate palatably with the food in your bowls. This includes—for a starter—thyme or rosemary, orégano or mustard in either butter or mayonnaise to be used with seafood. Tarragon or curry flavor for chicken. A touch of marjoram is a good idea too. Go easy in using these, for ⅛ to ¼ teaspoon may be enough. Or just serve the butters plain and get variety through the tops.

FOR TOPS

• Cole slaw or red cabbage, sliced or chopped pickled beets, nippy potato salad (and occasionally have it *hot*), sliced crisp raw vegetables, or fruit slices which are good with meat.

• Seafood, pickled, or seasoned and cooked and cooled. Chop it, slice it, or serve it whole to become part of the assembly.

• Cold meat and fowl—small bits of many things are more interesting and colorful than a lot of two things. The slices should be thin, small in size, for combining neatly. A colorful jelly or two can accompany the fowl.

• Marinate cold cooked vegetables in French Dressing. Drain and serve for building sandwiches.

• Cheese, of course. Have every cheese you like, with mustard in the butter foundation. Slice sweet pickles to go on top.

• Garnish sandwiches with capers, chopped chives, grated horseradish, chopped onion or parsley.

CHAPTER 15

SALADS

TOSSED GREEN SALADS . . . . CRISP AND FRESH

A remarkable variety of flavor and color combinations can appear day after day on the table of any woman interested in creating her salads according to whim rather than from recipe. All greens go together in a salad. The choice available in this country is a constant delight. Select whatever is in the market. Crisp them by washing, draining the last drop of water from them, chilling while retaining the last drop of water in them (let none of it evaporate, for it takes flavor as it goes), then break or pull the greens into bite-sized pieces. Add salad dressing of your choice, toss until each piece is shiny with oil (but never dripping), and you have a new salad every day.

GREENS WITH FROZEN VEGETABLES FOR SALADS

Or add to the greens from your hydrator drawer (or plastic bag or glass jar in the refrigerator where the greens stay fresh) a package of frozen peas, green beans julienne, or turnip greens. Chop the frozen vegetables into inch blocks, or break them into pieces. Add to the salad bowl on a hot day; allow them to chill it as they thaw, and the whole thing will be ready to be tossed in dressing at the table 20 minutes after you assembled the greens in the bowl.

MIXED VEGETABLES TOSSED SALAD

A Green Salad, I'm sure you know already, is an assembly of greens, or merely lettuce leaves or wedges. It can be any green alone, or a dozen thrown together for nature's variety in shades of green with different textures to make the salad bowl more exciting. But add tomato wedges, slivers of cold cucumber, slivers of peeled chilled raw turnip, sliced and drained water chestnuts from a can (these are wonderful and may be new to your family or friends), or add slivers or curls or slices of chilled raw carrots.

Make the vegetable juices you like into solids by adding gelatin to the juice, chilling as for any aspic, cutting into inch cubes. After tossing a green or mixed vegetable salad, add a few of the aspic cubes. Delicious surprise.

MOLDED SALADS . . . . . . FOR FANCY EFFECT

GINGER ALE SALAD

Makes 8 to 12 servings:

2 envelopes unflavored gelatin
½ cup grapefruit juice
½ cup syrup
¼ cup orange juice
1 teaspoon lemon juice
2 cups ginger ale
⅛ teaspoon salt
⅓ cup halved, drained maraschino cherries
1 cup drained grapefruit sections
1 cup drained orange sections
salad greens

Soften gelatin in cold grapefruit juice. Place over boiling water and stir until dissolved. Remove from heat. Add syrup, orange juice, lemon juice, ginger ale, and salt. Mix well. Chill until slightly thickened. Add maraschino cherries and drained grapefruit and orange sections. Turn into mold which has been lightly oiled with salad oil. A 6 x 9 x 2-inch loaf pan, an 8½-inch ring mold, or 8 individual molds may be used. Chill until firm. Unmold. Arrange on crisp salad greens. Serve topped with Banana Salad Dressing, Maple Fluff Dressing, or mayonnaise.

CRANBERRY ORANGE CELERY MOLD

Makes 8 to 10 servings:

4 cups (1 quart) cranberries
2¼ cups water
2 envelopes unflavored gelatin
½ cup water
1¼ cups sugar
grated peel of 1 orange
grated peel and juice 1 lemon
2 oranges, peeled and cut into chunks
½ cup diced celery

Wash cranberries; cook in 2¼ cups water until soft; strain. Soften gelatin in ½ cup water. Thoroughly mix sugar and softened gelatin with strained cranberries. Add orange peel, lemon peel and juice. Cool until gelatin mixture is almost set. Fold in orange chunks and celery. Turn into 1-quart mold and chill until firm. Unmold and serve as a salad with greens or as a meat accompaniment.

FROZEN FRUIT SALAD

Makes 6 servings:

1 orange
1 medium banana, diced
½ cup drained crushed pineapple
¼ cup diced maraschino cherries
2 tablespoons chopped celery
¼ cup sliced toasted almonds
½ cup mayonnaise
½ cup cream, whipped

Peel and section orange; cut in small pieces. Combine fruits, celery, and nuts. Mix mayonnaise and whipped cream; carefully fold into fruit mixture. Turn into shallow refrigerator freezing tray and freeze at coldest setting until firm, about 1½ hours. Cut into squares and serve on crisp lettuce.

MELON SALADS . . . . BOTH SALAD AND DESSERT

BIG PARTY SALAD

Fill a watermelon "bowl," with an assortment of melon balls and cubes—cantaloupe, honeydew, watermelon, Persian, cranshaw, or casaba. Add fresh berries in season. . . . Guests can serve their own salads on lettuce-lined salad plates. This is stunning and decorates any table.

RAINBOW SALADS

Arrange a combination of chilled melon rings, wedges, balls, and cubes on a bed of crisp western iceberg lettuce. Add other fresh fruits and berries in season. Serve with peaks of frosty sherbet—or with this:

FLUFFY FRUIT SALAD DRESSING

Makes 3¾ cups:

1 cup sugar
2 tablespoons all-purpose flour
½ teaspoon dry mustard
¼ teaspoon salt
4 egg yolks or 2 eggs, beaten
½ cup pineapple juice
¼ cup orange juice
¼ cup lemon juice
whipped cream

In a saucepan combine sugar, flour, mustard, salt, and egg yolks or whole eggs. Stir until blended. Gradually stir in fruit juices. Place over medium heat and cook until thickened, about 10 minutes, stirring constantly. Remove from heat and pour into pint jar. Cool. When ready to use, fold in an equal amount of whipped cream.

SALAD TALK . . . . . MIX ACCORDING TO WHIM

KIDNEY AND BACON SALAD

Makes 6 servings:

5 cups canned kidney beans
8 slices bacon, diced
1 cucumber
⅓ cup French dressing made with basil wine vinegar

Drain the beans, crisp the bacon, and chop the cucumber. Combine and mix with dressing. Arrange on crisp romaine and serve with additional French dressing.

MARINATED VEGETABLE SALAD

cooked green lima beans, chilled
slivers of Chinese cabbage
strips of any cold meat or fowl
thin slices red Spanish onions
few canned artichoke hearts, drained and chilled

Combine and marinate in French dressing at least 3 hours. Lift out of the dressing. Arrange on a mound of lettuce leaves. Serve with a bowl of yogurt which has been sprinkled with nutmeg and chopped mint.

This is one assortment, but you can make up your own.

GARLIC DRESSING FOR MARINATING:

Makes ½ cup:

1 teaspoon salt
1 teaspoon sugar
⅛ teaspoon freshly ground pepper
¼ teaspoon paprika
5 tablespoons oil
3 tablespoons garlic wine vinegar

Mix dry ingredients; moisten with a little oil; add vinegar and remaining oil and beat vigorously.

RED AND WHITE COLE SLAW

Makes 8 to 10 servings:

Shred rather finely 1 small firm head of red cabbage and 1 of white. Cover the shredded cabbage and crisp by chilling thoroughly in refrigerator 1 hour. Drain well and pat with paper towel. Put in bowl and serve with French dressing. Toss and return to refrigerator for another hour of chilling. When ready to serve, drain off excess dressing and sprinkle with 3 tablespoons celery seed, 3 tablespoons herb-flavored mustard sauce, 3 tablespoons cream, and enough mayonnaise to make the slaw the right consistency.

MEAT AND VEGETABLE WONDERS

Cans of meat can be the backbone of wonderful salads and can be prepared on the spur of the moment. A 5-ounce can of boned turkey or chicken meat, chilled and popped into a bowl, can grow into something marvelous with:

4 big tomatoes, peeled and chilled
1 cup chopped celery
½ teaspoon curry powder
1 tablespoon chopped onion
¼ cup French dressing

Remove tomato skins and tomato pulp. Combine turkey meat with celery, curry, and onion. Mix well. Fill hollowed-out tomatoes with this mixture, and serve on lettuce leaves.

Chicken will do just as well as turkey for these salads. Another mixture is:

1 5-ounce can chicken or turkey meat
½ cup diced celery
1 tablespoon chopped green pepper
1 tablespoon chopped onion
¼ teaspoon freshly ground nutmeg
½ teaspoon finely chopped garlic
½ cup mayonnaise
1 cup corn chips

Combine all ingredients except corn chips. Toss and chill. When ready to serve, stir in 1 cup crushed corn chips. Serve immediately on crisp greens.

Another time, add ½ cup chopped nuts, instead of the corn chips.

Garnish for this can be colorful slices of melon. Both watermelon and canteloupe—or the salad can be surrounded with red globs of crisp radishes, salted thin slices of cucumber, peeled and chilled tomato wedges, or avocado slices.

MEAT AND POTATO RING MOLD

Something new in potato salads, definitely fine-looking and fine-flavored. Nonetheless, its chief claim to fame is that it uses what you have to make something you'll be proud to put on the table. It is made in two layers.

To fill 8-cup ring mold:

FIRST LAYER:

¾ cup ground meat
2 tablespoons chopped onion
⅛ cup mayonnaise
1 tablespoon lemon juice
½ cup chili sauce
dash tabasco
1 teaspoon prepared horseradish
1 teaspoon dry mustard
1 envelope unflavored gelatin
¼ cup cold water
1 cup boiling water

The meat used with this can be anything you have left over—spiced ham, chicken, beef, pork, or some of each. It should be put through the grinder twice so that it will be very fine. Combine it with all ingredients except gelatin and water. Soften the gelatin in cold water, and stir in the boiling water until gelatin has dissolved. Combine with meat mixture and turn into ring mold (of course you can use a loaf pan for this too). Place in refrigerator to chill until firm, while you make:

SECOND LAYER:

1 envelope unflavored gelatin
½ cup cold water
1 cup hot water
1 cup sliced celery
2 tablespoons chopped onion
1 tablespoon chopped green pepper
1 tablespoon chopped parsley
2 cups sliced cooked potatoes
½ cup salad dressing
1 teaspoon salt
sprinkling of freshly ground pepper

Soften gelatin in cold water. Add to hot water and stir until blended. Combine all other ingredients and add to gelatin. When first layer in mold is firm, add this mixture. Return to refrigerator and chill until firm.

• If pork is used, omit the chili sauce and use ½ teaspoon ground ginger, 1 tablespoon brown sugar, and ¼ cup applesauce.

SHRIMP SALAD

Makes 6 servings:

¾ pounds cooked shrimp
¼ cup diced celery
3 tablespoons salad oil
2 tablespoons lemon juice
1 tablespoon rich prepared mustard
1 tablespoon minced onion
¼ teaspoon salt
⅛ teaspoon pepper
⅛ teaspoon garlic powder
lettuce cups

Remove veins from shrimp and, if large, cut into pieces. Mix together celery, salad oil, lemon juice, mustard, onion, salt, pepper, and garlic powder. Pour over shrimp. Cover; marinate 2 to 3 hours in refrigerator. Drain and serve in lettuce cups. Top with mayonnaise or with a tablespoon of chili sauce.

SALMON MOUSSE MOLDS

Makes 8 ¾-cup molds:

2 envelopes unflavored gelatin
¼ cup cold water
2 cups boiling water
¼ cup cider vinegar
1 teaspoon Worcestershire sauce
2 teaspoons grated onion
½ teaspoon salt
¼ cup catsup
¼ cup heavy cream, whipped
¾ cup mayonnaise
½ cup sliced celery
2 cups flaked salmon
½ cup sliced stuffed olives

Soften gelatin in cold water; dissolve in boiling water. Add vinegar, Worcestershire sauce, onion, salt, and catsup; mix well. Chill until slightly thickened. Blend in whipped cream and mayonnaise with rotary beater. Fold in remaining ingredients. Pour into large mold or individual molds. Chill until firm. Unmold and garnish with salad greens. Serve Caper Sauce to spoon over this.

TUNA SALAD

Makes 12 servings:

1 cup Lemon Mayonnaise
1 tablespoon rich prepared mustard
3 cups cubed canned tuna
2 cups well-drained pineapple cubes
½ cup chopped celery
salad greens
½ cup ripe olives
3 tomatoes, peeled and cut into wedges

To make this thing of beauty, blend mayonnaise and mustard. Add to tuna, pineapple, and celery and mix lightly. Arrange on crisp salad greens. Garnish with shining black olives and red ripe tomato wedges.

CHAPTER 16
MAIN COURSE DISHES

CHICKEN . . . . BUT DIFFERENT

CHICKEN SOUTH SEAS

Makes 4 servings:

1⅓ cups (5-ounce package) precooked rice
½ teaspoon salt
1½ cups boiling water
3 tablespoons butter or margarine
1 cup chopped celery
¾ cup sliced green pepper
¾ cup drained canned pineapple chunks
2 tablespoons flour
1 cup chicken broth
½ cup pineapple juice
2 teaspoons soy sauce
⅛ teaspoon pepper
½ teaspoon salt
2 cups diced cooked chicken or turkey
1 tablespoon lemon juice
1½ cups cut, shredded coconut

Add rice and ½ teaspoon salt to boiling water in saucepan. Mix first to moisten all rice. Cover and remove from heat. Let stand 13 minutes. Meanwhile, melt butter in saucepan. Add celery, green pepper, and pineapple chunks. Sauté about 5 minutes. Stir in flour. Add chicken broth, pineapple juice, soy sauce, pepper, and salt. Cook, stirring constantly, until mixture is slightly thickened. Add chicken and lemon juice; heat. Arrange on rice; sprinkle with coconut.

CHICKEN LUAU

Makes 4 to 6 servings:

2½-pound chicken, cut for frying
seasoned flour
½ cup butter or margarine
1 teaspoon salt
1 cup water
1 cup milk
1½ cups shredded coconut
2 pounds fresh spinach
2 tablespoons finely chopped onion
½ teaspoon salt
¼ cup water

Roll chicken in seasoned flour. Melt butter in heavy skillet; fry chicken in butter until lightly browned. Add 1 teaspoon salt and 1 cup water. Cover and simmer until chicken is tender, about 30 minutes. Meanwhile, combine milk and coconut in a saucepan; bring to a boil. Remove from heat and let stand 5 minutes. Drain well; then simmer the milk 10 minutes. Wash spinach and remove stems. Place spinach in a saucepan with onion, ½ teaspoon salt, and ¼ cup water. Simmer 2 to 3 minutes. Drain. Add spinach and hot milk to chicken. Simmer 3 minutes longer. Serve chicken on a bed of spinach and sprinkle with ½ to ¾ cup drained coconut. Remaining coconut may be discarded, since most of the flavor has already been absorbed by the milk.

If frozen chicken is used, thaw before cooking.

3 PORK RECIPES . . . . FROM FARAWAY PLACES

SWISS PORK CHOPS

Makes 8 servings:

⅓ cup flour
2 teaspoons salt
½ teaspoon pepper
8 thick loin pork chops
3 cups evaporated milk, undiluted
1 cup whole milk
8 strips bacon

Grease a 2-quart casserole or flat baking dish. Combine flour and seasonings. Blend. Dredge pork chops with seasoned flour. Arrange the chops in the bottom of the baking dish. Cover with thick milk mixture. Cut the bacon slices in half so that there are 16 short pieces, and arrange them over the top of the chops. Cover tightly with cover of the baking dish or aluminum foil. Bake in preheated oven (325 F.) 1½ hours, until chops are very tender.

SWEET AND PUNGENT PORK

Makes 8 servings:

2 pounds lean pork cut in small pieces
salt and pepper
1 cup brown sugar
4 tablespoons cornstarch
1 teaspoon salt
1 cup vinegar
1 tablespoon soy sauce
2 No. 2 cans pineapple chunks
2 green peppers cut in strips
3 medium onions cut in rings

Sprinkle meat with salt and pepper. Cook thoroughly in large frying pan, turning to brown evenly. Mix together in saucepan brown sugar, cornstarch, salt, vinegar, and soy sauce. Drain syrup from canned pineapple chunks and measure. Add enough water to make 2 cups. Pour into brown sugar mixture and mix well. Cook until slightly thick, stirring constantly. Add green pepper, onion, and pineapple chunks. Cook 3 minutes. Remove from heat. Add pork and let stand at least 10 minutes. Just before serving, bring to boil, stirring constantly. Serve with hot fluffy rice.

SHRIMP AND PORK PHILIPPINE

Makes 8 servings:

1⅓ cups sliced radishes
2¼ teaspoons salt
2⅔ cups precooked rice
1 teaspoon salt
3 cups boiling water
¼ cup butter or other shortening
2 cups cooked pork cut in ½-inch cubes
2 cups sliced onions
2 cloves garlic
2 cups peeled tomatoes
2 cups halved cooked shrimp
1 teaspoon salt
¼ teaspoon pepper
3 cups shrimp liquid
3½ tablespoons vinegar
3 cups shredded coconut

Sprinkle radish slices with 2¼ teaspoons salt. Let stand about ½ hour; then rinse and drain. Add rice and 1 teaspoon salt to boiling water in saucepan. Mix just enough to moisten all rice. Cover and remove from heat. Let stand 13 minutes. Melt butter in large skillet. Fry pork until well browned. Remove meat from pan and set aside. Sauté onion slices, garlic, and tomatoes in same skillet until tender, about 5 minutes. Add shrimp, ½ teaspoon salt, pepper, and drained radish slices. Cook 3 to 5 minutes longer. Add cooked pork, shrimp liquid, and vinegar. Simmer, covered, 15 minutes. Remove garlic. Arrange rice on platter; pour shrimp and pork mixture over rice. Sprinkle with shredded coconut.

2 GOOD DISHES . . . . REMEMBER DURING LENT

WESTERN FISH AND AVOCADO STRIPS

Makes 6 servings:

2 pounds fish fillets (flounder, cod, haddock)
2 cups milk
1 teaspoon salt
¼ cup butter or margarine
¼ cup flour
2 tablespoons rich prepared mustard
1 small avocado, sliced

Place fish in saucepan. Add milk and salt. Cover and cook over low heat until tender, 15 to 20 minutes. Remove fish to a 1½-quart casserole. Melt butter or margarine; blend in flour and mustard. Stir into milk and cook until thickened. Pour over fish in casserole. Top with avocado slices. Place under preheated broiler until lightly browned, about 5 minutes.

CRANBERRY RELISH TO ACCOMPANY FISH

Makes 2 cups:

Combine 2 tablespoons lemon juice and ½ cup sliced celery with one 16-ounce can of whole cranberry sauce. Blend and chill for at least 30 minutes before serving.

EGGS BENEDICT

Makes 6 servings:

3 tablespoons cornstarch
1 teaspoon salt
¼ teaspoon pepper
2 cups milk
2 egg yolks
4½ tablespoons lemon juice
6 tablespoons butter
6 toast rounds
6 thin ham slices, broiled or fried
6 poached eggs

Mix cornstarch, salt, and pepper in a small amount of milk until smooth. Add remaining milk. Cook over low heat, stirring constantly until mixture thickens and comes to a boil. Boil 1 minute, stirring constantly. Remove from heat; gradually add to egg yolks. Cook 2 minutes longer, stirring constantly. Remove from heat; gradually beat in lemon juice. Add butter, beating until smooth. Place toast rounds on serving dish. Place a slice of ham on each; cover ham with hot poached eggs; pour sauce over top. Sprinkle with paprika and serve immediately. If desired, place under broiler a few minutes until sauce is lightly browned.

CHEESE DISHES . . YOU WILL CLAIM AS YOUR OWN

HAM ROLLS

Makes 4 servings:

2 cups Medium White Sauce
2 egg yolks, beaten
4 ounces (1 cup) grated Swiss cheese
4 ounces (1 cup) diced Swiss cheese
1 cup seasoned tomato sauce
8 thick slices smoked boiled ham
¼ cup heavy cream, whipped

Heat White Sauce in top of double boiler and stir in the egg yolks and grated cheese. Stir until cheese is melted. Allow to cool and blend in the diced cheese. Butter a baking dish large enough to hold 8 ham rolls. Cover the bottom with tomato sauce. Now spread ½ the cheese sauce mixture over the ham slices, rolling each one and placing it in the baking dish. Combine the remaining sauce with the whipped cream and pour over the ham rolls. Bake in moderately hot oven (375 F.) until brown, about 15 minutes.

CHEESE SALAD IN TOMATO CUPS

Makes 4 servings:

2 tablespoons mayonnaise
1 clove garlic, minced
2 tablespoons horseradish
¾ pounds (1½ cups) cubed Swiss cheese
2 red apples, cored and cubed
¼ teaspoon salt
½ cup heavy cream, whipped
⅓ cup chopped nuts
4 whole tomatoes, uniform in size

Combine first three ingredients with cheese cubes; cover and let stand about 1 hour at room temperature. Add salt to cream and whip until it holds peaks. Combine the cubed apples, chopped nuts, and ¼ cup whipped cream; stir lightly. Mix in with the cheese mixture. Fill the tomato cups and top with remaining whipped cream.

Make 4 tomato cups by slicing the tops off the tomatoes and scooping out the centers. Fill with cheese mixture and serve.

SWISS CHEESE OMELET

Makes 2 servings:

4 to 6 eggs
½ teaspoon salt
dash of pepper
½ tablespoon butter
3 to 4 ounces (1¼ cups) diced Swiss cheese
1 ounce (4 tablespoons) grated Swiss cheese
1 cup White Sauce
2 tablespoons heavy cream, whipped

Beat eggs. Add seasonings. Heat butter in skillet but do not let it brown. Add eggs and stir vigorously with a fork over low heat until eggs have started to thicken evenly. Now spread diced cheese over eggs, then roll up into an omelet. Place omelet in baking dish; cover with White Sauce which has been heated and combined with grated cheese and the whipped cream. Brown quickly under broiler.

CHEESE RABBIT À LA SUISSE

Makes 2 servings:

1 teaspoon caraway seeds (optional)
1 tablespoon butter
2 tablespoons flour
2 cups milk
½ pound (2½ cups) shredded Swiss cheese
1 teaspoon salt
1 pinch nutmeg

Soak caraway seeds in hot water for 15 minutes. Melt butter in saucepan; add flour and stir over low fire until well blended. Dissolve gradually with the milk; add the strained caraway seeds and bring almost to the boiling point. Blend in cheese gradually, stirring until it has completely dissolved and rabbit starts bubbling. Season with salt and nutmeg. Serve on hot toast. Keep balance of rabbit hot, but not boiling.

In the Valais district of Switzerland this dish is served bubbling at the table, with each guest spearing bread on a fork and "dunking" it in the cheese mixture for each hot bite.

CHEESE SOUFFLÉ

If you had the idea that soufflés and omelets were not for you—let this convert you!

Makes 2 servings:

2 tablespoons butter
2 tablespoons flour
1 cup milk, boiling
1 teaspoon salt
¼ teaspoon nutmeg or cayenne
3 eggs, separated
4 ounces (1¼ cups) grated Swiss cheese
½ teaspoon cornstarch

Melt butter in saucepan; add flour and blend. Dissolve with boiling milk; add salt and nutmeg. Stir and simmer until smooth. Remove from heat; cool slightly. Beat in egg yolks one at a time. Dredge cheese with cornstarch; blend in with mixture. Fold in the stiffly beaten egg whites. Fill buttered, flour-dusted baking dish. Bake in moderate oven (350 F.) 25 to 30 minutes, or until knife inserted remains clean. Serve at once.

DOROTHY'S CURRIED LAMB

Makes 6 to 8 servings:

3 pounds lamb, cubed
2 teaspoons salt
¼ teaspoon pepper
4 tablespoons butter
1 teaspoon celery salt
⅛ teaspoon cayenne
1 cup coarsely chopped apple
1½ cups stock or water
¾ cup onions, sliced
2 tablespoons butter
⅓ cup flour
¾ cup chopped onions
4 teaspoons curry powder
½ teaspoon ginger
4 cups stock
½ cup shredded coconut

Perhaps I should not tell you, but a curry sauce is wonderful or ordinary, depending upon how much care is taken in securing good stock.

Stock to make this superb curry begins with boiling a few cracked beef bones with a little meat sticking to them. Put in water to cover, along with an onion, celery, and a little salt, and 6 peppercorns. Cover; simmer slowly 3 hours. It doesn't require watching, and if it cooks gently 4 hours, so much the better. Strain off the liquid; boil it rapidly if you need to reduce it to approximately the 5½ cups liquid needed for this recipe, or add water if more is needed to make the 5½ cups.

To prepare the curry, sprinkle lamb cubes with salt and pepper and place in a heavy pot in which 4 tablespoons butter have been melted. Add celery salt, cayenne, and apple. Stir until lightly browned. Add 1½ cups water (or use some of that stock you made); cover; simmer over low heat 1 hour. In a small skillet melt 2 tablespoons butter and sauté the onions until translucent. Add flour, curry powder, ginger, and blend. Gradually stir in the 4 cups stock. Cook until thickened. Combine with the meat and stir in the coconut. Cool; cover and let stand until ready to reheat for serving, preferably overnight.

Curry dishes are best the day after they are made.

• This same procedure can be used for veal or beef.

• Dorothy, who has children in the family, always divides the sauce, adding curry to only part of it, making uncurried sauce for the children. Sometimes a guest can't eat curry either, and this comes in handy.

• All curry dishes are served with rice and a variety of condiments.

Condiments that can be served with curry:

Serve 2 or 3 of these—or all of them if you like—each in a separate bowl on a tray that can be passed.

Chopped white of egg, hard-cooked egg yolks put through a sieve, ground peanuts, chopped coconut, crushed French-fried onions (these can be bought in cans, heated, and crushed), crisp bacon which has been cooked and crushed, chutney, tiny sautéed bread cubes, chopped parsley, and ground coffee.

CHICKEN CURRY

You can make superb Chicken Curry by replacing stock in first first part of the Curry recipe with chicken broth. Replace 4 cups of stock in last part of Curried Lamb recipe with 2 cups cream and 2 cups chicken broth thickened with 3 beaten egg yolks.

When ready to serve, surround the dish with condiments as for the lamb, beef, or veal curries.

VEAL CUTLETS "CORDON BLEU"

Makes 2 servings:

4 thin veal cutlets
salt
pepper
2 thick slices Swiss cheese
2 thin slices smoked, boiled ham
1 tablespoon flour
1 egg, beaten
½ cup bread crumbs
4 tablespoons butter

Have your butcher cut and flatten 4 thin veal cutlets of equal size and shape. Season them lightly. Place 1 slice of cheese and 1 slice of ham of somewhat smaller size than the meat on 1 slice of veal. Cover with another slice of veal, then seal the edges by pressing or beating them together. Coat with flour, then dip in egg and cover with bread crumbs. Heat the butter on the grill or in frying pan and fry cutlets 4 to 5 minutes on each side.

CHAPTER 17
SEAFOOD CELEBRITIES

MARVELS FROM THE SEA . . . COOKING SEAFOOD

Did you ever hear that in Alaska there is a place where the admission price to the movies is one fish? Well, it's the truth. Fish are the main food of much more than half the world, no doubt. The only place seafood isn't used often and with great variation is in the center of our country.

"What is a fillet?" a woman asked last summer as she picked up a package of frozen flounder fillets. She is from Kansas, where fish are not from. Since there are a good many people who have had no reason to meet a fish fillet (or filets), let me announce that these are the sorts of fish you want if you thought fish were dreadful things you had to clean. Fillets are strips of pure-white wonderful meat taken off the bones and ready to cook in a few minutes, or to bake in some of the ways suggested here.

There are so many ways—each one good—to prepare seafood that a book the size of a mail-order catalogue could be written about them. Less space than that cramps my style, but now that everyone has access to seafood frozen and canned so skillfully it is almost as good as fresh-caught (and far less trouble), here are a few recipes you may like.

Let's begin with a few oysters you will broil on the rotisserie or in the oven or on the barbecue grill, over and over again the year round. How many skewers this recipe fills depends upon the size of the oysters, a thing that varies considerably. Anyhow, these are something special.

OYSTERS EN BROCHETTE

1 pint oysters, drained
1/3 cup chili sauce
1 teaspoon horseradish
1/4 cup canned or frozen lemon juice
1/4 teaspoon Worcestershire sauce
1/8 teaspoon salt
2/3 cup (6-ounce can) mushroom crowns

You are going to like these. Drain oysters. Combine chili sauce, horseradish, lemon juice, Worcestershire sauce, and salt. Dip oysters in mixture. Place oysters and mushrooms alternately on skewers. Be firm about this. They may not want to go on! Season with additional salt and pepper and cover with remaining sauce. Broil about 3 minutes, then turn and broil 3 minutes longer, or until the little mushrooms are tender.

SHRIMP TEMPURA

Makes 6 servings:

2 pounds jumbo shrimp, cooked
1 cup flour
1/2 teaspoon salt
2 eggs
1 cup milk—more if necessary

The Japanese, with their eye for beauty, prepare shrimp this way. Peel the shrimp without removing tails. Dry and slit shrimp (don't cut through) down the back without separating the halves, so that they can be pressed flat to look like butterflies. Combine the other ingredients and be sure the batter is very thin. Dip the shrimp and deep-fry in 375 F. until brown and tender, 2 to 3 minutes.

SHRIMP SALAD

The color of cooked shrimp is so attractive that they are beautiful when served alone. Add slivers of avocado, pickled beets; arrange on crisp lettuce leaves. Drench with French dressing made with lemon juice. Or serve them as a fine first-course cocktail nestled into lettuce cups and topped with a spoonful of chili sauce.

SEAFOOD SALAD

Makes 6 servings:

This salad can be made as a combination of any seafood you have left over. It can be both fish, shrimp, scallops—anything that is cooked, seasoned, and chilled. Flake or dice the seafood and put into a mixing bowl, making the pieces generous so that it will not appear to be something made from leftovers. With this combine ½ cup thinly sliced celery, 1 cup cooked green peas (undercooked rather than overcooked), 1 tablespoon chopped onion, ¼ cup chopped sweet pickles, ¼ teaspoon curry. To blend with this combine:

½ cup mayonnaise
¼ cup cream
2 tablespoons lemon juice

Combine and mix lightly with a fork. Add seafood mixture, mixing lightly to avoid breaking up the pieces of seafood. Add 2 cups crushed potato chips, either sprinkling over the top or folding them into the mixture. Serve on greens immediately.

BROILED FILET OF FLOUNDER

Nothing could be simpler to prepare than the frozen filet of flounder; each package is enough to serve 4. Thaw it and broil or pan-fry it as directed on the package for a delicious and quickly prepared fish dish.

BOILED FROZEN FILET OF FLOUNDER

Remembering that 1 package serves 4, put thawed filets from either 1 or 2 frozen packages of filet of flounder in a large saucepan. Add enough water to about half cover. Add ¼ teaspoon salt for each package of fish used and ⅛ teaspoon each of marjoram, basil, thyme, and rosemary. Cover and cook over medium heat 8 to 15 minutes, or until the fish is cooked through and tender. Pour into a ring mold or other pan to shape it as it congeals. Chill in refrigerator, unmold, and serve with Lemon Mayonnaise or any fish dressing you like.

TUNA SHORTCAKE ALMOST ANY FISH OR OTHER SEAFOOD IS GOOD THIS WAY

Makes 6 servings:

2-cup recipe biscuit mix
½ teaspoon orégano
evaporated milk, undiluted
3 tablespoons butter or margarine
¼ cup chopped onion
1 can cream of mushroom soup
1 7-ounce can tuna fish
½ teaspoon salt
¼ teaspoon pepper
⅛ teaspoon basil

Mix biscuit mix as directed on the package for shortcakes, omitting the sugar and adding orégano. Use evaporated milk for liquid and bake as directed.

Melt butter or margarine in saucepan. Add onion and cook until translucent, about 4 minutes. Add soup, diluted as directed on can, and stir in tuna and seasonings. Mix gently until heated through. Cover until biscuits are ready.

• If you double this recipe, try using one can of cream of pea soup and one of mushroom.

• If you like using herbs, combine ⅛ teaspoon each of basil, thyme, rosemary, and marjoram. Use in place of orégano. Do not be fooled by the small amounts; herbs brew like tea and send up a cloud of aroma along with their flavor. Too much spoils the dish you use them in.

TUNA TAMALE PIE

Makes 6 servings:

1½ teaspoons salt
3 cups boiling water
1 cup corn meal
1½ tablespoons oil drained from tuna fish
7-ounce can tuna fish
½ cup chopped onion
½ cup chopped green pepper
2 cups (No. 303 can) tomatoes
½ cup sliced ripe olives
¼ teaspoon pepper
¼ teaspoon orégano
2 teaspoons salt
2 teaspoons chili powder
1 clove garlic, chopped

Add salt to boiling water in top of double boiler. Add corn meal gradually, stirring constantly. Cook over hot water 30 minutes, stirring occasionally. Spread a thin layer of mush over the bottom and halfway up the sides of a greased 9 x 9 x 2-inch baking dish. Drain oil from tuna fish into a skillet and heat. Crumble tuna fish over the bottom of corn-meal-mush-lined baking dish. Sauté onion and green pepper in hot tuna fish oil. Add tomatoes and sliced ripe olives and seasonings. Pour over tuna fish and cover with remaining corn meal mush. (If the mush becomes too stiff to spread easily, flatten spoonfuls between palms of hand and place over the tomato mixture.) Bake in moderately hot oven (375 F.) 1 hour, or until done.

CURRIED EEL

Eels come out of the streams in parts of the country where there are almost no other fresh fish. As anyone knows who has eaten them, the meat is tender and delicious and well worth preparing. In Denmark anglers regard eels so highly that they sometimes congregate to enjoy fried eels and do not consider the evening well spent unless the discarded backbones form a ring around each plate.

Remember that 1 large eel or 2 small ones is sufficient for 4 persons. Skin the eel and cut into pieces 3 or 4 inches long. Boil in rapidly boiling salted water with a bunch of parsley in it. The water should only cover the fish about halfway. Boil until the eel is tender, and then make a sauce by adding Thick White Sauce to the strained fish stock (if the stock has not been sufficiently reduced to be strong, boil it a little before straining). Add ½ cup chopped onion and 1 teaspoon curry powder for each 2 cups of sauce.

Pour this over the eel and serve a side dish of hot fluffy rice.

HOW TO EAT A LOBSTER . . . WHEN YOU CATCH ONE

No one who has met a lobster fresh from the sea would imagine it could be a social asset. Dark and murky-colored on top, too fierce in appearance for anyone the least bit timid to turn him over to see its lovely coral color underneath, these wiggly big fellows offer one of the most beautiful and delicious of all edible pleasures from the ocean's depths. After steaming 15 minutes in sea water, or water resembling it through a generous addition of salt, the gorgeous coral shade is complete, and it is your turn to bite the lobster which may have threatened to bite you.

HOW TO EAT A TWO-CLAW LOBSTER

Most of everything inside the brilliant coral shells is good eating. But how to approach the problem? It is not difficult. Is anything, when you know exactly what to do? Your pursuit of the sweet meat is aided by a pair of lobster shears. Those that ensure your winning this battle to eat him *all* up are heavy steel shears with pointed blades. Lacking the shears, the heavy kitchen scissors will help, or a pair of nutcrackers will do too. The perfection of these implements are in the order mentioned, the pointed steel lobster shears being best. These instructions, straight from a Maine citizen whose business is everything from clambakes shipped to your door to canning various seafood and selling bibs, plates, and lobster shears to seafood addicts, are explicit and the real McCoy.

Before telling you about the eight pointers he gives for eating a lobster, once it is cooked, you may like to know that a lady lobster is wider through the derrière than is the gentleman lobster. You may think you do not care about such things, but you will when you learn that, although both the male and female lobsters have grown large claws where nice big lumps of lobster meat await you, the lady lobster has a collection of "coral" inside the body. These bright red lumps are delicate morsels to be enjoyed along with a generous helping of pale sea-green liver. The male has no such treat to offer, but the lobster meat is the same in both. Everything inside a lobster is edible and good for you except the brain, a small portion about the size of a quarter that you can easily avoid. Now to eat the *cooked* lobster. (We shall follow with how to cook them.)

To Eat a Lobster Do This . . . and This . . . and This:

Pick up the biggest one, or take the wider-bodied one, knowing very well, you sly devil, that there is coral inside the one you select.

• Twist off the claws, then twist to separate each knuckle from the big claw, for there is meat in both.

• Crack each claw with scissors or nutcracker. Or if you are lucky enough to have those pointed lobster shears, insert the scissors in the open end of the claw and cut up each "seam," the thin edge of the lobster claw. Presto! It is open and there lies your nugget of meat. Scrape the inside of the shell to put all this soft curd into the melted butter you are using to dunk your lobster meat.

• Now pick up the body with both hands, give a gentle twist to separate it midway. This separates the tail portion from the body.

• Snap the small red flippers off the tail and dredge for meat by pulling each one gently between your teeth, pressing out the meat and juice.

• Push the meat out of the tail shell with a small fork or with your finger. And once more scrape the "curd" or fat off the shell into your plate or into the butter.

• Pull the body portion from the covering shell to discover the green liver and hope for the bright red dots of coral which are the lady lobster's eggs. This is delicious. You eat every portion of the meat you can get from this part of the lobster except the small brain part referred to before.

• End by extracting each drop of juice and meat from the eight coral legs. These are slender, can be cut with the scissors or pressed with the teeth to give up their bounty.

Note: To make this whole thing a meal or a picnic of importance, spread the table, floor, or ground with newspaper. Toss empty shells on the paper for easy disposal. And while busy emptying the shells, all you need is access to the scissors, a bowl of melted butter, plus a bib tucked around your neck and plenty of paper napkins.

HOW TO STEAM OR BOIL A LOBSTER

Whether you steam or boil a lobster depends upon your school of thought. The methods vary only in the amount of water, and therefore salt, used in the cooking. Pad the bottom of a very large pot—one that can be tightly covered—with rockweed to about one inch depth, or with a wire cooling rack. For either steaming or boiling, sea water is preferred, but if you have none use ⅓ cup salt to each quart of water used in cooking. No other seasoning is necessary.

For Steaming, place the lobster in the rockweed, or on the rack, pour in one quart of sea or salt water, cover snugly, and place over high heat. When steam begins to emerge from the pot, reduce to medium heat without removing cover and cook 15 minutes. Remove from heat and serve immediately.

To Boil lobsters, arrange the rack or the rockweed in the bottom of the pot. Fill about half full with sea water or the salt water made by adding ⅓ cup salt to each quart water used. Cover and bring to a rolling boil. Drop the lobsters into the boiling water one at a time, allowing the water to boil before adding the next, until the lobsters are all in the pot. Cover and boil 15 minutes.

Either steamed or boiled lobsters can be served hot or cold, and if you want them cold it is best to cool them quickly by plunging them into the sea or in any cold water that is handy.

TROPICAL LOBSTER WITH CURRY SAUCE

Makes 6 servings:

6 bananas, firm but not too ripe
2 tablespoons melted butter
2 cups Curry Sauce
3 cups fresh or frozen lobster meat
2 cups rice
2 cups chicken broth
1 teaspoon salt

Peel the bananas. Place in lightly greased baking dish. Coat bananas with melted butter. Place in moderately hot oven (375 F.) 15 to 20 minutes, or until bananas are tender when pierced with a fork.

Combine lobster meat and Curry Sauce in the top of a double boiler. Stir until heated thoroughly.

Meanwhile, cook rice in chicken broth until rice is tender and has absorbed all the liquid.

To serve: Make a ring of rice on your hot serving platter. Fill with the curried lobster and arrange the curved bananas on top.

Curry Sauce

Make the 2 cups Curry Sauce by adding ½ cup chicken broth to

1½ cups Thick White Sauce, and stir in 1½ teaspoons curry powder. Heat in top of double boiler, stirring until blended.

DE LUXE LOBSTER NEWBURG

Makes 6 servings:

2½ cups cubed cooked or canned lobster
2 cans condensed cream of mushroom soup, undiluted
¼ teaspoon thyme (optional)
⅛ teaspoon marjoram (optional)
2 tablespoons lemon juice
2 tablespoons wine vinegar
¼ cup butter
1 cup soft bread crumbs

Combine the lobster, soup, spices if used, lemon juice, and vinegar. Stir until well mixed. Melt the butter in a skillet and add the bread crumbs. Sauté, stirring constantly until the butter has all been absorbed. Pour the lobster mixture into a baking dish. Sprinkle the buttered crumbs over the top and bake about 20 minutes in oven preheated to 325 F. Be sure the oven is turned on to heat before beginning to mix this.

ROCK LOBSTER TAILS . . . .

The South African rock lobster tails that have come into the market, either frozen or canned, bring lobster right to the table the year round clear across the country. These are sweet and wonderful, with the meat in one large piece. They are, as with all seafood, quickly cooked. Boil and cool them and cut the meat into chunks for Lobster Newburg, Seafood Salad with mayonnaise, or to add to any seafood chowder or bisque or jambalaya. Broil or bake them to eat as a main course with butter sauce. Eat them boiled or broiled without sauce or with one made from non-fat dry milk if you want low-calorie dishes. You will serve them many ways. Allow at least one 6-ounce lobster tail for each serving.

BOILED ROCK LOBSTER TAILS

Place tails, either thawed or frozen, into large kettle boiling salted water (1 teaspoon salt for each quart water). When water reboils, lower heat so water boils gently and begin counting time. Keep covered. Boil tails 1 minute longer than their individual weight in ounces. For instance, boil a 4-ounce tail 5 minutes. Add 2 minutes to all boiling times when tails are cooked frozen. To remove meat easily from shell, drain off hot water, drench with cold water. Using scissors, cut lengthwise through center of membrane covering flesh and insert fingers under meat at open end and pull meat out.

BROILED ROCK LOBSTER TAILS

Thaw the lobster tails. Preheat broiler. Now use scissors to cut lengthwise down sides of membrane covering flesh. Remove membrane. Grasp tail in both hands and bend it backward toward shell side to crack and prevent curling. Arrange tails, shell side up, on rack of preheated broiler. Turn heat to medium and broil 5 minutes, 5 inches from heat. Turn flesh side up, spread with butter, and broil 6 minutes if tails are under 10 ounces. For larger tails, broil 9 minutes on flesh side. Seasoning is not necessary. Serve with cups of melted butter and lemon wedges.

BAKED-IN-FOIL ROCK LOBSTER TAILS

Thaw the lobster tails. Using scissors, cut lengthwise down sides of membrane covering flesh. Remove membrane. Cut foil into pieces 4 inches longer than lobster tails. Place each tail on piece of foil. Fold foil lengthwise over tails, then fold ends toward center. Place on baking pan and bake in hot oven (450 F.). Bake small tails (4 to 8 ounces) 25 minutes; medium tails (9 to 12 ounces) 30 minutes; large tails (13 to 16 ounces) 35 minutes. Serve in foil to be opened at the table. Serve with a pitcher of melted butter and wedges of lemon.

If you like, minced chives or minced parsley can be sprinkled over the flesh side before wrapping in foil. No other seasoning is necessary.

4 HANDY RECIPES . . . . FOR BAKING FISH

FISH IN LEMON SAUCE

Flounder or cod fillets, halibut or salmon steaks are good in this recipe. Use fresh or frozen.

Makes 4 to 6 servings:

1 tablespoon butter or margarine
½ pound mushrooms, sliced
3 tablespoons corn meal
1 teaspoon salt
¼ teaspoon white pepper
½ teaspoon paprika
1 pound fish fillets
½ medium onion, thinly sliced
½ bay leaf
4 peppercorns
¼ cup lemon juice
1¼ cups light cream

Place butter and mushrooms in casserole. Put in hot oven (400 F.) 15 minutes. Meanwhile combine corn meal and seasonings. Dip pieces of fish in mixture and coat thoroughly; place over mushrooms. Separate onion into rings and place over fish. Add bay leaf and peppercorns. Pour lemon juice and cream over. Bake in hot oven (400 F.) 30 minutes, basting occasionally.

FISH FILLETS BAKED WITH HERBED BREAD

Makes 6½ cups:

1½ pounds fish fillets
dash of salt
6 slices margarine or butter, ¼ inch thick
3 cups soft bread crumbs
¾ to 1 teaspoon salt
⅛ teaspoon pepper
¼ teaspoon orégano
¼ teaspoon marjoram
⅓ cup melted margarine or butter

Cut fish into 6 serving pieces; place in greased 9-inch baking pan. Over each serving sprinkle a dash of salt and place a slice of margarine or butter. Combine remaining ingredients and cover each piece with ½ cup of the mixture. Bake in moderately hot oven (375 F.) 25 to 30 minutes, or until crumbs are brown.

SEAFOOD SUPREME

Fish used in the Fish in Lemon Sauce can be used in this, but it is especially good made with crabmeat or lobster, fresh or canned.

Makes 6 to 8 servings:

2 cups fish flakes
½ cup grated cheese
2 eggs
1 cup evaporated milk diluted with
1 cup water
3 rolled crackers
2 tablespoons melted butter
juice of 1 lemon
paprika

Combine fish flakes and cheese; add beaten eggs and diluted milk and pour into buttered casserole. Cover with cracker crumbs mixed with melted butter. Pour lemon juice over all. Cover; set casserole in a pan of warm water. Bake in a moderate oven (350 to 375 F.) about 30 minutes. Sprinkle with paprika and serve.

CREAMED SALMON DE LUXE

Makes 8 servings:

2 8-ounce cans red salmon
½ cup margarine or butter
½ cup flour
⅛ teaspoon pepper
3½ cups milk (use all or part undiluted evaporated milk to make rich dish)
2 tablespoons chopped anchovies
2 cups cooked or canned peas, drained
1 tablespoon chopped parsley
8 slices toast

Canned salmon is as good as fresh in many people's opinion. Drain salmon, reserving liquor; remove skin and bones and flake the red meat. Melt margarine in a saucepan. Add flour, pepper, and blend. Combine salmon liquor with milk to make 4 cups liquid and gradually add this to flour mixture. Cook until smooth and thick, stirring constantly. Add salmon flakes, anchovies, peas, and parsley. Heat thoroughly and serve on toast.

TROUT . . . . QUEEN OF THE WATERS

Trout, small ones, are so delicious and delicate—and so beloved for their not having scales—that they are easily the favorites from crisp-fried in butter and served with bacon for breakfast, to the fine lunch they provide when steamed and served with Brown Butter Sauce. Trout, as you probably know, are always served with their heads on. Slit open; steam over boiling water (but not in it) until tender, 10 to 12 minutes per pound.

Big trout are more manageable baked than sautéed. Put them in the oven on a bed of lettuce leaves in a roomy roasting pan. Sprinkle them with lemon juice and Worcestershire sauce after rubbing with salt inside and out. Cover with sliced lemon if you have enough, cover with more lettuce, and bake. Then serve with Brown Butter Sauce or Lemon Mayonnaise.

"Bake" means until done, which is about 30 minutes in a preheated 325 F. oven for a trout 2½ inches thick.

Little boiled potatoes, with their jackets on, or peeled if you must, and asparagus are the perfect accompaniment for the trout, big or little ones. Let each person help himself to a whole one and pass the:

BROWN BUTTER SAUCE

Melt butter in a skillet and watch carefully, stirring of course, allowing it to turn lightly brown but not burned-brown. Add a dash of Angostura bitters if you like, or serve as it is to spoon over the flakes of trout as they are peeled off the bones.

7 WHOLE-MEAL "SOUPS" . . . FISH AND SEAFOOD

Offer any one of these 7 steaming pots and everyone is happy. You can serve your choice of these whole-meal "soups" any time of day or night you like. Good company for them is crisp crackers or hot buttered biscuits along with cole slaw or a green salad. Or just stick to plenty in the pot and biscuits. Then a Fruit Float for dessert. Melons are perfect endings for these dinners, too, and so are berry-laden shortcakes.

CRABMEAT BISQUE

Makes 4 cups:

1½ tablespoons quick-cooking tapioca
1 teaspoon salt
⅛ teaspoon pepper
⅛ teaspoon paprika
1 teaspoon dry mustard
1 tablespoon minced onion
3 cups milk
1 cup (6½-ounce can) crabmeat, drained and flaked
2 tablespoons butter
1 tablespoon chopped parsley

Combine tapioca, salt, pepper, paprika, dry mustard, onion, and milk in top of double boiler. Place over rapidly boiling water and cook 10 to 12 minutes, stirring frequently. Add crabmeat, butter, and parsley; mix. Keep over hot water 15 to 20 minutes to heat thoroughly and blend flavors. Serve in cups or bowls.

Given here for the small family supper, this is an easy-to-increase recipe. Make it with fresh crabmeat when you have it, canned crabmeat when you don't—but serve it winter and summer.

POTATO FISH CHOWDER

Makes generous 12 cups:

2 pounds haddock or cod in 1 piece
⅓ teaspoon thyme
¼ pound fat salt pork
¾ cup sliced onions
4 cups diced potatoes
¼ cup diced green pepper
¼ cup diced celery
2 cups boiling water
4 cups milk, scalded
1 cup thin cream, scalded
1 teaspoon salt
⅛ teaspoon pepper
6 crackers, split
2 tablespoons butter

Wash the fish and put it on to cook in cold, salted water to cover. Add thyme. Bring slowly to boiling point, then simmer 5 minutes. Take from water and remove bones and skin and cut in pieces. Reserve the stock. Cut salt pork in small pieces and fry in kettle. Remove to drain and crisp on paper towels, for you are going to serve these with the chowder. Add onion to fat and fry 4 to 5 minutes. Add potatoes, green pepper, celery, and water; bring to a boil and cook 5 minutes.

Add fish and stock; cover and simmer 10 to 15 minutes. Add milk, cream, seasonings. Butter split crackers and place in the bowls as you serve the chowder or in bottom of tureen.

To make this with frozen fillets of fish, proceed the same and skip over the bone and skin business—since there won't be bones and skin, just beautiful strips of meat to cook.

NEW ENGLAND CLAM CHOWDER

Makes 5 cups:

¼ cup diced salt pork
¼ cup chopped onion
1½ tablespoons rich prepared mustard
¾ cup cubed potatoes
2 cups milk
2 tablespoons butter or margarine
2 tablespoons flour
1 teaspoon salt
¼ teaspoon pepper
1 (10½-ounce) can minced clams

Place salt pork in a 2-quart saucepan over medium heat until lightly browned. Add onion; sauté until golden and tender. Drain clams and set aside, reserving liquor. Blend rich prepared mustard into clam liquor and add to onions. Add potatoes and simmer until tender, about 15 minutes. Stir in milk. Melt butter; blend in flour. Stir into milk mixture and cook until thickened. Add clams, salt, and pepper. Cook about 3 minutes longer.

SEAFOOD STEW

Makes 12 cups:

1 12-ounce package frozen oysters
1 can minced clams
1 can lobster meat
¾ cup butter
4 cups milk
3 cups undiluted evaporated milk
1 teaspoon salt (or more)
1 tablespoon Worcestershire sauce
paprika
½ teaspoon pepper

Remove frozen brick of oysters from package. Place in bowl; cover and leave in refrigerator for several hours to thaw. About 20 minutes before you want to serve the stew, place the butter in an iron skillet over low heat until melted. In a 4-quart saucepan combine whole milk and evaporated milk and place over medium heat until it begins to simmer. Meanwhile, drain juice from minced clams and the oysters, stirring it into the milk which is heating. Place drained and canned seafood—from which cartilage has been carefully removed—into skillet with melted butter. Add seasonings. Cover and cook 5 minutes. Remove from heat and combine with the milk and seafood liquor. Serve immediately with a sprinkling of paprika on each bowl.

OYSTER STEW

Makes 8 cups:

6 cups rich milk or half milk and half cream
¼ teaspoon ground cloves
⅛ teaspoon cayenne
½ teaspoon tabasco sauce
½ cup butter or margarine
1 Bermuda onion, sliced
oysters, 3 to 6 per person
1 cup oyster liquor
salt to taste

Put milk in saucepan, add seasonings, and cook over moderate heat until hot, not boiling. Melt butter in a skillet. Add onion slices and cook until slices are translucent. Remove onions and add to the milk. Add flour to skillet and stir until blended; add oysters and oyster liquor. Cook about 5 minutes, only until edges of oysters begin to curl. Add to hot seasoned milk and onion mixture. Salt to taste. Serve immediately with sprinkling of paprika on top.

CHICKEN-OYSTER GUMBO

Makes 6 to 8 servings:

1 tender chicken, 3 or 4 pounds
¼ cup flour
3 tablespoons bacon fat
1 pound okra, sliced, or 1 package frozen
1 onion, chopped
salt and pepper to taste
2 quarts boiling water
1 small bay leaf
3 or 4 dozen oysters
1 quart oyster liquor

Cut chicken in pieces, dredge with flour, and fry until brown. Remove chicken to stewing pot. Put okra and onion in skillet and stir until cooked and onion is slightly browned. Add to the chicken pot; salt and pepper to taste. Cover with boiling water and add seasoning. Cover and cook over low heat until chicken is tender. Add oysters and liquor; cover and cook no more than 5 minutes, until oyster edges curl. Test for seasoning, adding salt if necessary.

JAMBALAYA

Makes 12 cups:

½ cup butter or margarine
3 cups rice
½ teaspoon saffron
1 cup cubed cooked ham
3 cups cubed or shredded chicken
4 cups chicken broth
1 cup cooked shrimp
3 dozen oysters
2 cups oyster liquor or clam broth
salt and pepper to taste

Melt the butter in a skillet and add rice, stirring gently until rice is nicely browned. Add saffron. Pour into 4-quart saucepan. Put bacon drippings or lard in skillet and fry ham until tender. Add the ham, chicken, and chicken broth to the pot. Cover and cook slowly about 30 minutes, until rice is tender. Combine shrimp, oysters, and oyster liquor in the skillet for a few minutes until the edges of the oysters begin to curl. Add them to the Jambalaya pot and serve.

CHAPTER 18
PIES AND CASSEROLES

6 FABULOUS PIES . . . . SAVORY MAIN COURSES

For a small fireside supper at home . . . for a big church supper . . . for a work party . . . certainly for a square-dance crowd . . . there is nothing better than one—or several—of these meat pies . . . English pies . . . American pies . . . hot and wonderful. Each recipe fills an 8-cup casserole.

PORK SAUSAGE TAMALE PIE

Makes 8 cups:

SAUSAGE BASE:

1 pound pork sausage links	*1 cup whole kernel corn*
½ cup chopped onion	*1 cup cooked lima beans, drained*
¼ cup chopped green pepper	*½ cup chili sauce*
2⅓ cups (No. 2 can) tomatoes	*1 teaspoon salt*

For sausage base, brown sausage links in frying pan. Remove links and drain all but a few tablespoons of fat from the pan. Add onion and green pepper and cook until golden brown. Cut sausages into 1-inch pieces. Add with remaining ingredients for Sausage Base. Cover and simmer gently 30 minutes. (May be cooled, covered, and refrigerated for a day. Heat mixture to boiling.) Leave in frying pan or pour in a 2-quart casserole. Cover with:

CORN BREAD TOPPING:

¾ cup enriched corn meal
1 tablespoon flour
½ teaspoon salt
1½ teaspoons baking powder
1 egg
⅓ cup milk
1 tablespoon shortening

Sift dry ingredients together into medium-sized bowl. Add egg, milk, and shortening. Beat with rotary beater until blended. Do not overbeat. Pour over the bubbling hot sausage mixture. Bake in hot oven (425 F.) 20 to 25 minutes, until corn bread is browned.

• You can use a corn-bread mix for this if you like. If you do, try adding an extra 2 tablespoons of melted butter. Otherwise follow directions on the package.

SHEPHERD'S PIE

Makes 8 cups:

12 slices Bermuda onion
⅓ cup butter
3 cups chopped and seasoned mixed vegetables
1 cup fresh celery leaves
3 cups diced cold cooked meat
3 tablespoons flour
2 cups beef bouillon
4 cups mashed potatoes, hot
butter

The secret of making a good Shepherd's Pie is to use leftover vegetables (which have already been cooked and seasoned) in a variety of yellow, green, and white combinations when that is possible. The meat can be all of one kind or a combination of beef, lamb, pork, and veal which has been cooked and was seasoned in cooking. Brown the onion slices in half the butter. Combine vegetables, celery leaves, and meat in a 2-quart or larger casserole and cover with the sautéed onion. Add flour to butter remaining in skillet and brown lightly. Add beef bouillon and stir until thickened. Pour over the vegetables and top with the fluffy hot mashed potatoes. Brush with remaining butter which has been melted. Bake in hot oven (425 F.) until potatoes are browned, about 25 minutes.

CHICKEN PECAN PIE

Makes 8 cups:

8 thin slices day-old white bread, generously buttered
½ cup chopped pecans
3 tablespoons butter
3 tablespoons flour
1¼ cups strong, full-flavored chicken broth
1¼ cups heavy cream or undiluted evaporated milk
1 teaspoon Worcestershire sauce
3½ to 4 cups cubed cooked chicken
1 cup sliced mushrooms
2 tablespoons chopped parsley
⅓ cup chopped onion
salt and pepper
1 2-cup recipe biscuit mix with 1 teaspoon sage

Sprinkle 4 buttered pieces of bread with the pecans and cover with the other buttered slices to form 4 sandwiches. Line the bottom of a 2-quart or larger casserole with these, pressing them down to fit closely together. Melt the butter in a skillet; stir in the flour but do not brown. Add chicken broth, stirring constantly. Add the cream and Worcestershire. Stir until thickened. Combine with the chicken, mushrooms, parsley, and onion. Test for seasoning. Pour over the pecan sandwiches. Top with Sage Biscuits and bake in a preheated oven (450 F.) 15 minutes, or until biscuits are done.

STEAK AND KIDNEY PIE

Makes 8 cups:

¼ cup bacon drippings
1 cup coarsely chopped onion
2½ pounds beef (round or chuck) cut into 2-inch cubes
1 pound beef kidneys, cleaned and cubed
⅓ cup sliced mushrooms
1 cup beef bouillon
⅛ teaspoon cayenne
1 teaspoon Worcestershire sauce
2½ teaspoons salt
¼ teaspoon pepper
2 tablespoons Bovril
3 tablespoons flour
water
1 (2-cup) recipe drop biscuit mix

As you will know if you have a pressure saucepan, the meat for this pie can be prepared very quickly. However, this recipe is for cooking in a Dutch oven or in any big iron pot. Melt bacon fat in it; add onion and brown lightly, stirring constantly. Add beef and kidneys; stir until lightly browned. Add mushrooms and stock and all the seasonings. Cover and simmer over low heat until meat is tender, about 1 hour. Drain the liquid off and measure. Transfer contents from the Dutch oven to an 8-cup casserole. Add enough water to the broth to make a total of 2 cups. Blend 3 tablespoons flour with this and stir over low heat until thickened. Test for seasoning and pour into casserole. Cover with the Dropped Biscuit dough which has been pushed out roughly on aluminum foil to fit the top of the dish. With a fork make it attractively rough on top. Cut 4 slits in the dough to allow steam to escape and bake in a hot oven (450 F.) 15 minutes, or until brown.

CRABMEAT PIE

Makes 8 cups:

1 recipe for 2-crust pastry
4 cups (4 6½-ounce cans) crabmeat
1⅓ cups chili sauce
1 cup chopped green pepper sautéed in butter
1 cup chopped cooked celery
1 tablespoon grated lemon peel
½ teaspoon salt
1 tablespoon chopped onion
2 cups Cheese Sauce

Roll out the pastry to fill a deep 2-quart or larger casserole. Bake in hot oven (450 F.) 10 minutes. Combine crabmeat with all the other ingredients except the Cheese Sauce. Stir and pour into the partially baked pastry shell. Bake in hot oven (400 F.) 30 to 40 minutes. Cover with Cheese Sauce after first 20 minutes of baking. Sprinkle with paprika and serve steaming hot.

PORK AND POTATO PIE

Makes 8 cups:

2 tablespoons butter
2 tablespoons bacon fat
4 cups (2 pounds) ground pork
2 cups diced cooked potatoes
3 teaspoons salt
1 teaspoon ginger
½ teaspoon cinnamon
½ teaspoon cloves
½ teaspoon pepper
1 cup pineapple tidbits
1 cup water
1 recipe for 2-crust pastry

Melt butter and fat in a large skillet and add the pork, stirring constantly until cooked and browned. Drain off excess fat and combine the meat with the potatoes, seasonings, pineapple, and water. Mix thoroughly and pour into a 2-quart or larger casserole and cover with pastry top in which a design has been cut. Bake in hot oven (450 F.) 50 to 60 minutes.

SUSAN'S 15-MINUTE DINNERS

SUSAN'S BEEF CASSEROLE

Makes 6 servings:

½ box (8 ounces) egg noodles
2 quarts boiling salted water
¼ cup butter
1 can corned beef hash
1 cup canned beef stew
1 teaspoon Worcestershire sauce
1 teaspoon French mustard
salt and pepper to taste

Drop noodles into the boiling salted water; cook until tender and drain. Melt the butter in a large skillet. Add the cooked noodles and all other ingredients. Stir over low heat until thoroughly heated, 8 to 10 minutes, and serve.

CHILI NOODLE CASSEROLE

Makes 8 servings:

1½ to 2 quarts water
2 teaspoons salt
1 box (8 ounces) egg noodles, unsalted
No. 2 can tomatoes
No. 2 can string beans
3 tablespoons chopped onion
½ green pepper, chopped
1 teaspoon celery salt
½ teaspoon garlic salt
1 teaspoon sugar
2 tablespoons butter
¼ cup heavy cream
1 can (15½ ounces) chile con carne
1 can chicken noodle soup
2½-inch slices canned luncheon meat

Add salt to water; when water is boiling add noodles and cook until tender. Drain and put in a 2-quart casserole. Add the next 7 ingredients and stir. Melt butter in a skillet; add heavy cream, chile, and chicken noodle soup. Stir in luncheon-meat slices. When thoroughly heated, stir into the casserole and serve.

CHAPTER 19
VEGETABLES

VEGETABLES . . . . BUT DO YOU KNOW THESE?

Nothing new about vegetables . . . except! When did you last have these extraordinary greens in your kitchen? And what did you do with them? If you will just take a look at these, next will come the everyday vegetables, with some seasonings you may not have tried.

ENDIVE

Endive chicory and endive Whitloof, along with escarole and Hanover salad are greens which should not be neglected when you make a tossed salad. Chicory is available the year round, but its peak season is in the autumn, as is the endive whitloof, which comes into the market in October and is gone by April. There is a year-round supply of escarole, and Hanover salad appears in December and by May disappears entirely. This should make it popular in the winter when some of the summer greens to be mixed into green salads are missing. And while talking about green salads, do you use velvety green spinach leaves in yours?

Another bright idea when combining greens in a crisp salad is to prepare all the fresh ones in your salad bowl, then add a block of frozen green beans julienne. Break them up with a fork, and they will mix quite nicely and help keep the salad cold until serving time.

ARTICHOKES

Artichokes are in the market from November to May. There are many ways to serve them once they have been boiled to tenderness. Wash, remove any sad-looking leaves, cut stems off to about ½ inch, and plop them upside down into boiling salted water to which 1 tablespoon lemon juice or vinegar has been added. If you like garlic, add a clove of garlic too. About 45 minutes later they will be tender enough to put a fork through. Drain upside down, serve right side up, pushing the petals out to expose the center. This, on a salad plate, resembles a large green flower. Douse it with French Dressing. Eat hot or cold.

JERUSALEM ARTICHOKES

These have practically no calories and somewhat resemble a potato. Despite its name, which suggests a resemblance to the green artichoke, it doesn't. Best way to include these is peeled, sliced, and salted. Eat them raw and crisp for fun and fatless food.

KOHLRABI

Kohlrabi season is from June right through October, and to eat this you will want to boil it. First cut off the leaves and wash and peel and cube it; then cook in the smallest amount possible of salted boiling water until tender, about 30 minutes. Keep it covered through the cooking, then drain and serve with heated Lemon Mayonnaise or with plain melted butter perked up with a few grains of tarragon.

CELERY ROOT

This round vegetable with the roots still clinging to it and giving it the appearance of having tentacles is something not to be missed. Scrub and pare it, slice or cube it, and cook until tender in chicken broth. Add salt to taste and serve in the remaining broth which has been rapidly boiled over high heat until reduced to a small enough amount to pour over the celery root like a sauce.

LEEKS

Leeks look like giant scallions and taste much as onion and scallions do. During the depression one friend of mine existed on braised leeks with toasted bread crumbs and melted butter served over them for days on end. She had never seen a leek before but bought them the first time because they were the cheapest thing in the market. A leek added to a pot in which meat or fowl is being simmered is a must if you can get one. Leeks are even better than onions in potato soup, or you might cook them this way: To serve as my friend did for the main course at mealtime, you will need 5 or 6 leeks per person. Cut off the ragged part of the green tops and cook in a large flat pan in a small amount of boiling salted water. A skillet is really best for this so that the leeks can lie flat. Cover, place over heat, and in about 15 minutes the leeks will be tender. When they are, drain, cover with melted butter to which you have added ¼ teaspoon ground cloves, ½ teaspoon salt, and ⅛ teaspoon cayenne to each ⅓ cup melted butter. Sprinkle with toasted bread crumbs and serve.

ZUCCHINI

Zucchini is a delicate Italian squash which looks very much as if it were a striped cucumber. It is very good boiled in salted water until tender, then served with melted butter, or you can sauté the slices. You never peel zucchini, and you want at least ½ zucchini for each person.

Zucchini are so attractive when made into fans. Slice lengthwise to within ½ inch of the end to make 3 or 4 slices in each zucchini. Do not bother to separate. Put in boiling salted water, cover, and cook until tender. Now spread the zucchini fanwise on each person's plate or on a serving platter, drench with melted butter, and enjoy looking at it before you eat it.

JUST VEGETABLES

. . . . BUT HAVE YOU COOKED THEM THIS WAY?

ASPARAGUS WITH BLACK WALNUT SAUCE

Makes 6 servings:

2 packages cooked frozen asparagus, or 4 cups cooked fresh asparagus
3 cups Thick White Sauce
1 cup cream
4 tablespoons butter
1 cup chopped black walnuts

Serve asparagus as you would ordinarily—cooked, seasoned, and without the sauce, which is served separately. In the top of a double boiler combine the White Sauce and cream and stir until heated through. Meanwhile place the butter and the nuts in a small pan and put them in a hot oven (400 F.) about 5 minutes, stirring a couple of times to crisp and season them. If the pan in which this is done is the pan in which the sauce can be passed, so much the better. Add the sauce to the nuts, stir well, and pass with the asparagus.

GREEN STRING BEANS

You serve these with butter, and they are so good they appear to need little else. For variety sprinkle crisped, crushed bacon over the top of the beans just before serving. For a real company dish sprinkle them with slivered, toasted almonds, or toasted, slivered Brazil nuts.

Another time combine one package of julienne green beans with one package of frozen lima beans after cooking them separately. Combine in the serving bowl, stir gently to blend, and dot with butter.

This combination or almost any vegetable you can think of is wonderful when you serve a smörgåsbord. Every little bit of leftover vegetable can be attractively used as a relish by marinating for several hours in French Dressing. Drain and serve each little bit of marinated vegetable in a lettuce cup or in a small bowl. Sprinkle some with finely chopped parsley or mint. These have no leftover look and are good as a family salad with 3 or 4 lettuce cups holding yesterday's uneaten vegetables on tonight's salad plate. As anyone would agree, these are nice enough for company salad plates, so don't snub them.

STRING BEANS WITH HERB SAUCE

Makes 8 servings:

8 cups green string beans (4 pounds)
salt and pepper to taste

Cook slowly in covered pan with very little water until tender, or follow directions on package for cooking frozen beans.

Make 2 cups Herb Sauce:

⅓ cup olive oil or salad oil
2 tablespoons butter
2 cloves garlic, chopped
3 tablespoons chopped onion
2 tablespoons finely chopped celery
4 fresh or 1½ cups canned tomatoes
2 tablespoons finely chopped parsley
½ teaspoon rosemary
2 tablespoons mixed herb-wine vinegar
½ teaspoon sugar
½ teaspoon salt

Combine oil and butter in saucepan, and when blended add the garlic, onion, and celery. Cook over low heat 5 minutes. Add cut-up peeled tomatoes, rosemary, parsley and vinegar. Test seasoning, adding salt if necessary, and cook over low heat about 10 minutes. Pour over the cooked beans and serve.

GREEN BEANS WITH PEPPERS

Makes 8 servings:

2 packages frozen green beans
½ teaspoon basil
1 pimiento, shredded
2 green peppers, shredded
½ cup butter or margarine
salt and pepper to taste

Add basil to green beans and cook as directed on the package. Garnish with shredded pimiento and peppers which have been cooked in the butter until tender, but not browned.

GREEN BEANS WITH TARRAGON SAUCE

Makes 8 servings:

1 teaspoon salt
1 cup water
4 cups green beans (2 packages frozen)
¼ cup olive oil or salad oil
2 cloves garlic, finely chopped
⅓ cup finely chopped onion
2 small tomatoes
1 teaspoon sugar
¼ cup best wine vinegar
¼ teaspoon tarragon
¼ teaspoon freshly ground black pepper

Add salt to water and cook beans about 10 minutes over low heat. Meanwhile prepare a sauce by combining all the remaining ingredients and cook together over low heat 10 minutes, stirring occasionally. Add the beans and liquid to the sauce in the skillet. Cover tightly and cook over low heat about 20 minutes, or until beans are tender.

BEETS

Did you every try buying cans of small, whole, round beets, draining them and letting them stand overnight in wine vinegar? This gives them a very nice tart flavor, and you can then combine 2 cups of beets with ¾ cups of Hungarian cream; add 1 tablespoon lemon juice and 1 tablespoon of poppy seeds. Stir. Chill and serve them this way either as a vegetable or as a salad.

Makes 8 servings:

2 No. 2 can (2½ cups) sliced beets
2 medium-sized tart apples
1 teaspoon salt
¼ cup brown sugar
1½ tablespoons cornstarch
2 tablespoons wine vinegar

Drain beets, reserving the liquor. Dice apples. Mix salt, sugar, and cornstarch in a saucepan and stir in the beet liquor and vinegar until smooth. Add beets and apples. Cook over low heat about 25 minutes, until pieces of apple are soft but still hold their shape. Do not overcook, because the apples, when tender but still in fine form, add to the decorative appearance of this dish.

BROCCOLI WITH HERB SAUCE

Makes ½ cup sauce for 6 servings:

½ cup melted butter or heated olive oil
2 tablespoons wine vinegar
1 teaspoon dry mustard
¼ teaspoon garlic powder
¼ teaspoon orégano
salt and freshly ground pepper to taste

Combine all ingredients in small saucepan and cover. Let stand in warm place for 10 minutes, or put the covered pan in the oven to keep warm. Pour over 3 cups cooked broccoli.

RED CABBAGE

Makes 8 servings:

1 red cabbage
4 tart apples, pared and sliced
½ cup brown sugar
1 tablespoon basil wine vinegar
¼ cup red wine vinegar
¾ cup water

Shred cabbage very fine and put in heavy kettle with all the other ingredients except vinegar and water. Cover tightly and simmer about 1½ hours. Add vinegar and continue to cook slowly ¾ hour longer.

CARROTS WITH HERBS

Makes 6 servings:

3 bunches young carrots
¼ cup butter
4 large lettuce leaves
¼ cup boiling water
2 teaspoons sugar
½ teaspoon chopped parsley
¼ teaspoon tarragon
¼ cup heavy cream
1 teaspoon salt
¼ teaspoon freshly ground black pepper

Wash carrots. Cut off tops and split each carrot lengthwise. Melt butter in a skillet; add carrots, lettuce leaves, boiling water, and sugar. Sauté by shaking the pan and stirring a little. Add parsley, tarragon, and cream along with salt and pepper when carrots are almost cooked.

CARROTS WITH MUSTARD

Makes 6 servings:

2 tablespoons bacon fat
2 tablespoons butter or margarine
1 teaspoon dry mustard
1 tablespoon brown sugar
3 cups sliced carrots

Combine all ingredients except carrot slices in a skillet and place over low heat, stirring constantly until well blended. Add carrot slices; increase the heat slightly. Watch carrots carefully as they sauté and become almost caramelized with this mustard sauce in the pan.

CAULIFLOWER DUNDEE

Makes 8 servings:

1 large or 2 medium-sized cauliflower
1 cup finely cut green beans
4 cups hot milk
¼ cup butter, margarine, or bacon drippings
¼ cup flour
1 teaspoon vegetable herb blend or basil
1½ cups bread crumbs

Cut leaves and tough stem from cauliflower and break head into flowerets. Soak in salted water 15 minutes; drain and cook in rapidly boiling salted water until tender. Drain. Cook beans in milk until tender. Melt fat, blend in flour, and add beans and milk. Add vegetable herb blend. Cook over low heat until thickened. Put cauliflower in baking dish and add beans and cream sauce. Cover with crumbs and brown in hot oven (400 F.) 20 minutes.

CORN CASSEROLE

Makes 8 to 10 servings:

4 eggs, beaten
1 cup milk
1 teaspoon salt
⅛ teaspoon cayenne
2 cans (No. 2) cream-style corn
1 cup cracker crumbs
3 tablespoons butter

Combine eggs, milk, salt, cayenne, and corn. Put in greased 2-quart casserole; top with crumbs and dot with butter. Bake in moderate oven (350 F.) 30 minutes.

BAKED KIDNEY BEANS—RANCH STYLE

Makes 6 servings:

2 cans (No. 2 size) red kidney beans
1 can (10½ ounces) condensed tomato soup
¼ cup salad oil
1 cup chopped onion
1 tablespoon Worcestershire sauce
½ cup chopped celery
2 sweet pickles, chopped
1½ teaspoons salt
⅛ teaspoon pepper

Drain kidney beans and reserve the liquid. Add enough of the liquid to the tomato soup to make 1½ cups. Combine with remaining ingredients. Add beans and mix thoroughly. Pour into 2-quart casserole or bean pot. Bake in moderate oven (350 F.) about 1 hour.

BAKED LIMA BEANS

Makes 12 servings:

2 pounds dried lima beans
1 teaspoon salt
¾ cup cubed salt pork
½ teaspoon savory
2 teaspoons dry mustard
¼ teaspoon cayenne
½ cup molasses
1 large red onion, sliced

Wash the beans and soak 6 hours before cooking. Place over high heat until boiling; add salt. Reduce heat and simmer 45 minutes. Drain, saving the liquid. Combine beans and pork cubes in a large casserole or bean pot. Combine seasonings and molasses with the bean liquor; blend well and pour over the beans. Add water if necessary to cover. Top with onion rings; cover and bake in moderate oven (350 F.) 1½ hours. Uncover, stir gently, and bake 30 minutes longer, or until brown.

ONION SOUFFLÉ

Makes 6 servings:

4 medium-sized onions, chopped (1½ cups)
⅔ cup Thick White Sauce
1 teaspoon salt
⅛ teaspoon pepper
3 egg yolks, beaten
¼ teaspoon cream of tartar
3 egg whites, stiffly beaten

Chop onions very fine or put them through a food mill. Combine with White Sauce, salt, and pepper. If the sauce was freshly made, cool before blending with the egg yolks beaten until thick and lemon-colored. Add cream of tartar to egg white, beat until stiff peaks are formed, and fold into the onion mixture. Pour into a greased 1½-quart casserole. Set in shallow pan of water. Bake in moderate oven (350 F.) 1 hour, or until a knife thrust in the center comes out clean. The nice thing about this soufflé is that the mixture can be prepared ahead of time and stored in the refrigerator until ready for the final baking, to come out of the oven hot at the moment it is wanted on the table.

PEAS

There is nothing new about peas. You have eaten them all your life. Of course you have. But have you had them with ¼ teaspoon marjoram or rosemary and tarragon dropped into the pan as the peas are cooking?

Or have you had them this way:

Makes 6 servings:

¼ head lettuce, cubed
3 cups green peas
1 cup boiling water
⅛ teaspoon thyme
½ cup fresh mushroom slices, or 1 4-ounce can sliced mushrooms
2 tablespoons bacon drippings
several slivers pimiento for garnish

Combine lettuce and peas; cover with the boiling water. Cover. Cook until peas are just tender. Drain the liquid. Add thyme to liquid and boil rapidly until it is reduced to about ¾ cup. Sauté mushroom slices in bacon drippings until slightly brown, about 5 minutes. Add mushrooms and peas to the liquor. Reheat thoroughly and serve in hot serving dish with a garnish of strips of pimiento.

PEAS WITH LETTUCE

Makes 8 servings:

½ teaspoon marjoram
2 packages frozen peas
2 small solid heads of lettuce, or 4 hearts, chopped into small pieces
¾ cup cooked tiny white onions
1 teaspoon brown sugar
¼ cup butter or margarine

Add marjoram to peas and cook according to directions on package. About 5 minutes before they are done add the lettuce, small onions, sugar, and butter. Cover tightly and continue cooking until peas are tender.

NEW POTATOES IN MUSTARD-WATERCRESS SAUCE

Makes 8 servings:

16 new potatoes
4 tablespoons butter
4 tablespoons flour
2 cups milk
2 tablespoons rich prepared mustard
1 cup chopped watercress

Scrub potatoes. Put them in a saucepan with a small amount of salted water. Cover and simmer 30 minutes, or until tender. Peel. Melt butter; add flour; blend. Stir in milk gradually and cook until mixture is smooth and thick. Add mustard and watercress. Heat thoroughly and pour over potatoes.

CARAMELIZED POTATOES

This is a Danish trick, and you may be glad to learn it. Cook small round potatoes or drained canned potato balls. Be sure they are very dry. Roll them in sugar, then brown in a skillet in which butter has been melted, turning to brown on all sides.

Carrots and onions can be browned in this same way. These are to be served with meat, of course, and are particularly nice with cold meat, although the Danes serve theirs with hot pork or with goose at Christmas time.

BAKED SPICED SWEET POTATOES

Makes 8 servings:

2 cans (No. 2½) sweet potatoes in syrup
1 tablespoon butter
3 tablespoons brown sugar
½ teaspoon cinnamon
½ teaspoon salt

Drain sweet potatoes, reserving ½ cup of the syrup. Arrange potatoes in shallow, greased baking dish and dot with butter. Combine the brown sugar, cinnamon, and salt and sprinkle over the top. Pour the ½ cup of syrup over the top and bake in moderate oven (350 F.) 30 minutes. Baste several times with the syrup to make a thick glaze.

SPINACH WITH HERBS

Makes 8 servings:

2 packages frozen chopped spinach
½ teaspoon MSG (monosodium glutamate)
½ teaspoon rosemary
¼ cup bacon drippings or butter
½ cup cream or undiluted evaporated milk
½ cup strong chicken broth
¼ teaspoon freshly ground black pepper
½ teaspoon salt

Cook spinach according to directions on package, adding MSG to the spinach before cooking. Add rosemary to the cream and let stand while the fat is melted in a saucepan. Add chicken broth to the fat; stir. Add the liquid from the spinach and boil until it has been reduced to about the amount of liquid in the saucepan before it was added. Add the spinach, cream, rosemary, pepper, and salt. Stir until heated thoroughly and test seasoning, adding more salt if desired.

HERB TOMATOES

Makes 8 servings:

2 cans (No. 2½) tomatoes
¼ cup butter or margarine
2 tablespoons chopped onion
1 teaspoon salt
2 teaspoons sugar
dash of freshly ground black pepper
whichever one of the herbs mentioned that you want to try out today
2 tablespoons cornstarch

Drain tomatoes. Melt butter or margarine in a saucepan. Add onion and sauté until golden brown. Add salt, sugar, seasonings—did you know that sugar improves the flavor of almost anything when added in such small quantities that you don't taste it at all?

Stir in the cornstarch with about ¼ cup of the tomato juice until it forms a smooth paste. Add the cornstarch mixture to the rest of the juice and stir until blended. Add to the onions and cook over low heat, stirring constantly until thick enough to make an attractive sauce. Add the tomatoes and heat thoroughly. Garnish with strips of green pepper if you like, and there you are.

TOMATOES WITH SPINACH

Makes 8 servings:

8 tomatoes
2 cups chopped cooked spinach
½ teaspoon basil
½ cup Thick White Sauce
2 tablespoons bread crumbs
4 tablespoons grated cheese
2 tablespoons butter

Cut a thin slice from each tomato, hollow out part of the center, sprinkle with salt, and invert. This chef trick not only seasons the tomato but draws out excess water. After ½ hour turn hollow side up and fill with spinach cooked with basil and mixed with the White Sauce. Sprinkle with crumbs and cheese; dot with butter. Bake in hot oven (400 F.) about 15 minutes.

Now you know, don't you, that this should be served piping hot, and it wouldn't hurt at all to have the serving plate warmed a bit too.

TOMATO SOUP

Canned tomatoes make fine soup when simply heated in a saucepan with a little fresh pepper added and no nonsense about breaking up the big hunk of tomato in the pot.

However, for variety try adding ⅛ to ¼ teaspoon basil, orégano, or sage when heating tomatoes straight from the can. Serve them with this additional flavoring for variety, not because you can improve upon them. One or the other of these is sure to appeal to your family and make tomatoes an even greater favorite than they already are.

By the way, you knew that tomatoes were called love apples, at one time, didn't you? The addition of herbs, not to mention their delightful, appetizing red coloring, makes them beloved apples even in our day.

RICE . . . SIDE DISH . . MAIN DISH . . DESSERT

SAVORY RICE

Makes 8 servings:

½ cup salad oil or butter
2 cups uncooked rice
2 teaspoons salt
5 cups beef or chicken broth

Heat salad oil in heavy skillet. Add rice and cook, stirring constantly, about 5 minutes, or until golden brown. Add salt and meat stock. Cover and bring to a boil. Cook over low heat 45 to 50 minutes, or until done, stirring occasionally. Add water if necessary.

RICE RING

The one time rice is dreadful is when it has been forced too tightly into a ring mold or other form, which removes the attractive, fluffy whole-grain appearance of the rice. If you are going to mold it, don't be hard on it. Allow it to stay flaky and show that each grain is separate and beautifully cooked.

Cook 1½ cups rice in boiling salted water until tender. Drain but do not rinse. Add ¼ cup melted butter and pack firmly but not tightly into a greased 9-inch ring mold. Let this stand 10 minutes and turn out on a warm platter.

SPANISH RICE

Makes 6 servings:

⅓ cup salad oil
1 cup chopped onion
¾ cup chopped green pepper
⅔ cup uncooked rice
2 teaspoons salt
½ teaspoon pepper
3½ cups (No. 2½ can) tomatoes
1 small bay leaf

Mix ingredients and pour into 2-quart casserole or individual casseroles. Cover and bake in moderate oven (350 F.) 1¼ hours, stirring occasionally.

FRIED RICE

This is a good company dish made from leftovers. One of the advantages of Fried Rice is that it can be made with what you have in your refrigerator or something you have on the shelf. For best results, select vegetables that will not break up when stirred while cooking.

Makes 8 servings:

¼ cup peanut oil
2 tablespoons diced bell pepper, or 1 fresh bell pepper, chopped
2 scallions, sliced
4 cups boiled rice (day or two old)
1 teaspoon garlic salt
⅛ teaspoon cayenne
½ teaspoon pepper
½ teaspoon cornstarch
1 tablespoon sugar
4 slices cooked ham, diced
2 slices bacon, diced
8 paper-thin slices of beef
½ cup coarsely chopped parsley
6 eggs
2 tablespoons soya sauce
parsley leaves for garnish

Heat peanut oil in a large skillet and sauté pepper and scallions about 1 minute, stirring constantly. Add the rice and break it up with a fork.

When it is well separated and heated through, make a hole in the center and toss in the seasonings which have been combined and mixed. Stir well. Make a hole in the center of the rice and add the ham, bacon, and beef. Allow meat to cook 1 minute before stirring it in with the rice mixture. Make another hole in the center and add parsley. Now make a larger hole in the center and drop in eggs. Allow them to cook only slightly and then once more stir until contents of the skillet are well mixed and the eggs blended with the rice. Finish by sprinkling with soya sauce and garnish with parsley leaves.

This is a recipe that can be altered at will without losing its delightful flavor unless the contents are overcooked. The secret is to see that nothing is overcooked and that all ingredients are blended without being mashed together. For this reason a fork is best for stirring. Almost anything you can think of can be added instead of the ingredients above, keeping in mind that the eggs, rice, and seasonings are the necessary ingredients. Vegetables and meats can be varied, depending upon what you have on hand. Chicken and tuna are very good in Fried Rice, but vegetables such as cauliflower and asparagus become mushy when stirred and for that reason are not the best. Taste at the end for seasoning and add salt if necessary.

BANANA RICE

Makes 8 servings:

3 cups boiled rice
2 cups hot Savory Cheese Sauce
2 firm bananas, not too ripe
melted butter
salt
paprika

Mix together rice and ½ cup Cheese Sauce. Spread over bottom of 10 x 6 x 2-inch baking dish. Peel bananas. Cut crosswise into halves, and then cut each half lengthwise. Arrange pieces cut side down on top of rice. Brush bananas with butter and sprinkle with salt. Bake in a moderately hot oven (375 F.) 10 to 15 minutes, until bananas are tender. Pour remaining Cheese Sauce over bananas and sprinkle with paprika. Serve hot.

LANI LAIKI "HEAVENLY RICE"

Makes 6 servings:

1 cup cold cooked rice
½ cup heavy cream whipped with 1 tablespoon sugar
1 cup (14-ounce can) drained pineapple tidbits
½ cup coarsely chopped, pitted dates
½ cup seedless grapes

Mix all ingredients together and chill before serving in your prettiest dessert dishes.

CHAPTER 20

DRINKS FOR 5 OR 50

GORGEOUS TO LOOK AT . . . . . . AND TO DRINK

HONOLULU PUNCH

Makes 10 punch cups:

1 6-ounce can frozen pineapple juice
1 6-ounce can cold water
1 28-ounce bottle ginger ale, chilled
1 cup maraschino cherry juice
whole strawberries

Combine juice and water. Blend and add to ginger ale. Tint a delicate pink with maraschino cherry juice or grenadine if you feel like it, and float perfect whole strawberries (just before serving) for a party effect.

HAWAIIAN FRUIT PUNCH FOR 50

Makes over 6 quarts or 50 punch cups:

3 6-ounce cans frozen pineapple juice
1 6-ounce can frozen orange juice
1 6-ounce can frozen lemonade
3 quarts cold water
1 cup strong tea
2 1-quart bottles ginger ale, chilled

This punch is so quickly prepared that you can make it just before serving. Combine frozen concentrates, water, and tea in a large punch bowl, stirring well. Add chilled ginger ale and ice and serve immediately. For a Hawaiian touch, float a fresh flower or two on the punch and surround the bowl with a "lei" of green garden leaves.

RHUBARB PUNCH

Makes 24 punch cups:

4 cups rhubarb cut into small pieces
4 cups water
1 cup white sugar
½ cup brown sugar
½ can undiluted frozen orange juice
⅔ cup lemon juice
¼ teaspoon salt
1 quart ginger ale

Combine rhubarb and water in a saucepan and place over low heat. Cook until rhubarb is soft enough to put through a fine strainer. Return to saucepan; add white and brown sugar. Heat, stirring constantly until sugar is dissolved. Add fruit juices and salt. Remove from heat; place in electric blender and beat 1 minute, or beat with rotary beater until thoroughly blended, about 3 minutes. Cool and chill. When ready to serve, combine with cold ginger ale and serve with ice cubes in each cup.

LEMONADE

Makes 40 measuring cups:

10 cups fresh lemon juice
7½ cups sugar
10 cups water
10 cups warm water
2 cups mint leaves
2 cups maraschino cherries

Combine lemon juice, sugar, and water. Stir until sugar is dissolved. Pour into ice trays with cube dividers or into 5 or 6 pans with no dividers. Freeze until firm.

When ready to serve, chop up the frozen lemon mixture; place in a large container. Add warm water; stir. Serve immediately.

A clever idea is to freeze ⅓ of the lemon mixture in cube trays, placing a cherry and a mint leaf in each square. Reserve these when mixing the lemonade in the big container; add 1 for each serving as the lemonade is passed around.

STRAWBERRY FESTIVAL PUNCH

*Makes 40 cups
or 80 punch cups:*

2 cups sugar
1 cup water
1½ cups strong hot tea
1 can frozen lemon juice
2 cans frozen orange juice
2 cans frozen grapefruit juice
2 quarts iced water
2½ cups (No. 2 can) pineapple chunks
4 quarts soda water, icy cold
2 packages frozen strawberries

Combine sugar and water in saucepan. Place over low heat and bring to a boil. Boil 5 minutes. Pour into a large container with tea, fruit juices, iced water, pineapple chunks and juice from the can. Let stand until ready to serve. Combine with the soda water and pour over a large chunk of ice. Break up the frozen strawberries and allow them to float about in the punch while still slightly icy.

RELATIVES . . . . HOT AND COLD

FRUIT PUNCH FOR A CROWD

Makes 30 punch cups:

1½ cups sugar
2 cups hot tea
1 cup lemon juice
5 cups orange juice
2 quarts iced water
citrus slices

Dissolve sugar in hot tea and let cool. Pour into gallon jar with fresh lemon and orange juice. Add iced water and keep cold until ready to use. Pour over ice in punch bowl. Garnish with fresh orange and lemon slices.

To make 15 punch cups:

¾ cup sugar
1 cup hot tea
½ cup lemon juice
2½ cups orange juice
1 quart ice water
citrus slices

CITRUS COOLER

Makes 30 punch cups:

1½ cups grape juice
2 cups fresh lemon juice
3 cups fresh orange juice
1½ cups sugar
2 quarts water

Mix ingredients and cover. Chill 4 to 8 hours to ripen flavors. Pour over block of ice in punch bowl. Garnish with orange and lemon slices.

To make 15 punch cups:

¾ cup grape juice
1 cup fresh lemon juice
1½ cups fresh orange juice
¾ cup sugar
1 quart water

LEMON-GRAPE ADE

Makes 12 punch cups:

8 cups boiling water
1¼ cups sugar
2 cups fresh lemon juice
2 cups grape juice

Combine boiling water and sugar; stir until sugar dissolves. Add lemon juice and grape juice and heat to boiling point. Serve hot.

To make 50 punch cups:

2 gallons boiling water
5 cups sugar
2 quarts fresh lemon juice
2 quarts grape juice

Combine as above.

CHOCOLATE CALYPSO

For 1 serving:

1 banana, very ripe
¾ cup cold milk
1 scoop chocolate ice cream
1 tablespoon chocolate syrup
½ teaspoon Angostura bitters

Peel and mash banana. Beat with rotary beater, adding milk gradually. Add ice cream, syrup and Angostura and beat until creamy. Enjoy this on a lonely afternoon or multiply to make up. . . .

Makes 16 to 18 measuring cups:

12 bananas, very ripe, mashed
9 cups cold milk
3 pints (6 cups) chocolate ice cream
¼ teaspoon ground nutmeg
¼ teaspoon salt
¾ cup chocolate syrup
1½ tablespoons Angostura bitters

Blend and chill until ready to serve in very cold glasses.

HOT CHOCOLATE

Makes 12 measuring cups:

4 squares unsweetened chocolate
3 large cans sweetened condensed milk
7½ cups water
¼ teaspoon salt
1 teaspoon vanilla

Melt chocolate in saucepan with a little water, stirring constantly. Add other ingredients except vanilla. Stir until blended and heated through. Remove from heat. Add vanilla and serve.

ICED CHOCOLATE

Reduce water in Hot Chocolate recipe to 4½ cups. Add 3 cups chopped ice before serving.

HOT MULLED CIDER

Makes 12 cups
or 24 punch cups:

10 cups (2½ quarts) cider
6 cloves
2 sticks cinnamon
½ teaspoon allspice
1 cup brown sugar
⅓ cup melted butter
½ cup water

Place cider in a large saucepan and add the spices. Bring to a boil and cook 3 to 4 minutes. Add brown sugar and allow to boil 5 minutes more. This should be heated just before serving, or else kept hot until ready to serve in mugs, glasses, or cups, as hot as it can be drunk. Combine butter and water; add to hot cider when ready to pour.

HOT SPICED CRANBERRY PUNCH

Makes 20 cups
or 40 punch cups:

4 cups cranberries
8 cups water
½ cup sugar
2 quarts Mulled Cider (omit butter)

Combine cranberries, water, and sugar in a saucepan. Bring to a boil and cook until the berries are soft. Drain twice by forcing through a fine strainer or cheesecloth. Combine with hot mulled cider and test for sweetness, adding more sugar if necessary.

SPICED HOT TOMATO "CIDER"

Makes 6 quarts
or 24 cups:

1 cup brown sugar
1 teaspoon cloves
1 teaspoon cinnamon
½ teaspoon nutmeg
16 cups (1 gallon) tomato juice
4 tablespoons vinegar or lemon juice
2 quarts carbonated water
1 tablespoon Angostura bitters
salt to taste

Combine sugar and spices with 2 cups tomato juice in 8-quart pot. Place over low heat; simmer until sugar is dissolved. When ready to serve, add remaining tomato juice. Stir over moderate heat until hot but not boiling. Add vinegar or lemon juice, carbonated water, Angostura. Stir. Season. Remove from heat and serve immediately.

NOGS . . . . FOR WINTER PARTIES

COFFEE EGG NOG

Makes 16 to 18 cups or 36 punch cups:

12 eggs, separated
⅓ cup sugar
6 cups strong coffee, cold
6 cups cream or milk

Combine egg yolks and sugar and beat until blended. Beat the whites until stiff, add yolk mixture, and fold until blended. Combine the coffee and cream; mix well. Combine with egg mixture, stirring gently. Chill thoroughly and serve.

APRICOT EGG NOG

Makes 8 cups or 16 punch cups:

6 eggs
⅓ cup sugar
¼ teaspoon salt
½ teaspoon vanilla
4 cups cream or milk
¾ teaspoon ground nutmeg
1 small jar puréed apricots (baby food)

Beat eggs until blended and fluffy. Add sugar and salt. Blend thoroughly. Add vanilla and gradually stir in milk, nutmeg, and apricots. Unless this has been mixed in an electric mixer or blender, strain through a fine sieve. Chill thoroughly and serve in cold glasses. Sprinkle a little nutmeg on top of each.

part five

COOK AT THE TABLE OR UNDER THE OLD SHADE TREE

CHAPTER 21

THE ART OF MOVABLE COOKERY

The cook is where you find her these days, and it may not be in the kitchen. The infra-red broiling and roasting done on rotisseries; the crisp delicacies brought from the depths of the cook-and-fry deep-fat cookers in 2 minutes; the charcoal cooking done on grills which are as easily used in the fireplace or in the patio as at the beach (and which will also set up a kitchen under the shady tree in your back yard) are beguiling inventions that take the kitchen to the cook. They have not only moved cooking to where you want to cook but have ensnared the men of the house. On week ends or summer evenings, these contraptions become a challenge to their skill. This gives the wife a rest and brings a share-the-cooking to any home where the movable cookers are used. The pleasure of preparing a meal as well as eating it is enjoyed by everybody.

Since every appliance comes accompanied by a booklet of instructions, be sure to put it where you can find it. Paste the cooking-time section on the inside of a kitchen cabinet where you will be able to find it. Almost everything except a roast requires less than 20 minutes on a rotisserie infra-red. Most deep-fat cooking is done in 5 minutes or less. Charcoal grilling is leisurely, drawn out.

SEASONING

The quick or slow cooking produces very tender fine-flavored meat. If meat for kebabs is prepared by marinating overnight covered, to inhale its own mixture, the seasoning will almost always be improved. When that is not possible, prepare the meat in the morning, marinating it a few hours for noon or evening cooking.

TENDERNESS

The best cuts of the best meat are everyone's choice but fit few pocketbooks. Tender meat is secured by low heat rather than high in charcoal and stove cooking, by infra-red cooking, and by sprinkling meat with a meat tenderizer about 30 minutes before cooking. Since all grades of beef are equally nutritious, buy the least expensive grade and use the low-heat cooking or tenderizer if you would afford meat frequently.

LET'S BEGIN . . . . WITH KEBABS

A good supply of metal skewers make kebabs easy to do, fun to eat. Fancy as they are, they use up what is around to very good advantage. Everyone likes kebabs as an appetizer. Several kebabs make a meal. Marinate the meat in barbecue sauce, in French Dressing, or simply in cooking oil well seasoned with salt and pepper and a bit of lemon juice. Add herbs to your liking. Two hours or more in this solution, then drain on paper towels and put on skewers! Broil. Uhmm . . . so good.

Ground meat, seasoned, shaped for cooking, and "blended" through a few hours' standing, produces the finest flavor. And for finest texture have the meat put through the grinder twice.

Each person has his own notion about handling steaks for broiling. But try brushing them with olive oil which has had garlic cloves to keep it company for 24 hours to a week. Give the steaks several hours to assimilate the flavor, then broil. Or bring out of the refrigerator in time to sprinkle with tenderizer and stand at room temperature the necessary tenderizing time before grilling.

SWISS LIVER AND BACON EN BROCHETTE

Makes 6 servings:

2 pounds beef liver in 1-inch-thick slices
meat tenderizer
12 slices bacon
salt
pepper

Cut beef liver into squares; sprinkle lightly with unseasoned meat tenderizer, being careful to reach all the portions of the liver and sprinkling on each side. This should be done 30 minutes before you are ready to cook them. Cut the bacon slices in half. Wrap the liver squares in the bacon and fill 6 skewers. Sprinkle lightly with salt and pepper and broil.

PORK LIVER EN BROCHETTE

Pork liver is usually not used for delicate morsels such as kebabs, but if you prepare it exactly as described above for beef liver, being sure to tenderize as instructed, it will be delicious. When seasoning the pork liver on the skewers, sprinkle lightly with ½ teaspoon powdered ginger which has been mixed with ½ teaspoon brown sugar.

CHICKEN-LIVER KEBABS

Makes 6 servings:

24 chicken livers
12 slices bacon
12 mushrooms
6 skewers
1 tablespoon melted butter
1 tablespoon finely chopped onion
¼ teaspoon salt
¼ teaspoon pepper
½ teaspoon Angostura bitters

Cut bacon strips in half and wrap each half around a chicken liver. Clean the mushrooms, remove stems but do not peel. Arrange alternately with chicken livers on skewers, allowing 2 mushrooms and 4 chicken livers for each skewer. Mix remaining ingredients until blended, and with a pastry brush be sure that the kebabs are all coated. If there is time for these to stand before broiling, ½ teaspoon thyme or ½ teaspoon tarragon can be added to the basting mixture.

CHICKEN KEBABS

Use cold chicken cubed and marinated in French Dressing to which ½ teaspoon tarragon has been added. Alternate on skewers with the vegetables suggested for lamb.

KEBABS WITH TOMATOES

Makes 6 servings:

2 pounds ground beef
1 cup prepared bread stuffing
1 egg, slightly beaten
¼ teaspoon cinnamon
⅛ teaspoon cloves
1 tablespoon orange juice
⅓ cup brown sugar
½ cup wine vinegar
12 small yellow tomatoes
1 teaspoon salt

Combine meat, bread stuffing, egg, and spices. Mix thoroughly and shape into 18 small meat balls. Cover and let stand a little while, in or out of the refrigerator. Combine brown sugar, orange juice, and vinegar in a small saucepan and place over low heat. Cook until sugar is melted. Arrange meat balls and the yellow tomatoes on 6 skewers, allowing 3 meat balls and 2 tomatoes for each. Brush with the sugar mixture and broil the time necessary for the equipment you are using.

MEAT BALL TRIO WITH ONIONS EN BROCHETTE

Makes 6 servings:

1 pound ground beef
1 pound ground veal
1 pound ground pork
½ cup bread crumbs
¼ cup milk
1 teaspoon salt
½ teaspoon pepper
½ teaspoon thyme
⅛ teaspoon cayenne
1 teaspoon dry mustard
12 small whole onions or 12 halves of 2-inch onions

Combine all ingredients except the onions. Blend well and form into balls. Arrange on skewers, alternating so that there are 3 fairly large meat balls and 2 onions on each skewer. Brush with olive oil or melted butter; cover and chill 30 minutes before broiling.

LAMB KEBABS

Marinate 1½-inch cubes of lamb in French Dressing to which a little chopped mint has been added and a little chopped garlic—about 1 tablespoon fresh mint and 1 clove garlic per ¾ cup dressing. Alternate these with canned artichoke hearts, canned potato balls, little red or yellow ripe tomatoes to fill the skewers, and broil. Try sprinkling very lightly with curry powder before broiling.

SEAFOOD KEBABS

These are best when made with cooked lobster meat or shrimp which were seasoned as they cooked. Arrange a selection of black ripe olives which have been pitted, mushroom caps, drained pineapple chunks, and 1-inch chunks of peeled banana. Alternate these on skewers to please your eye. Drench with melted butter and heat in the broiler.

FRUIT KEBABS

Make these up from what you have, or what is ripe, or what you like to serve side by side with meat or Seafood Kebabs.

Fruit Kebabs are wonderful to accompany your roast, and if you have prepared a roast in the oven or have roasted a fowl which is to be served cold, skewer the fruit on the long spears of the rotisserie and have hot fruit with the cold meat. Or serve these with a cold meat platter.

Apricot halves, drained and alternated with cooked prunes which have been stuffed with peanut butter, pineapple wedges, ripe bing cherries which have been pitted, cubes of unpeeled red apple, ¼-inch slices from a whole orange, and an occasional square of watermelon pickle along with logs cut from peeled banana or pineapple chunks and drained canned or fresh peach halves are a few to remember. Brush them with melted butter; sprinkle with confectioners' sugar. You will never forget these!

You can cook everything from soup to dessert in the electric deep-fat fryers we have now. Sometimes I think it is more fun to cook in these than with any of the new gadgets I am grateful for, because food browns so quickly. And did you know that less fat is absorbed by the food when deep-fried in a controlled electric cooker than when you fry things in a skillet?

Mine cooks stewed chicken with dumplings and makes popcorn as well as it crisps fritters or doughnuts or French-fried potatoes. However, everyone has recipes for those things, so let's concentrate on cooking seafood in only 2 or 3 minutes and in making desserts in no more than 5. You can, by the way, just set your dial for 375 and forget it for all these things. All of these recipes produce appetizers, which also turn into a luncheon dish or an accompaniment for a meat course when you cook them either in larger quantities or in larger sizes. For appetizers, keep each thing very small, bite-size if possible.

DEEP FRYING

DEEP FRYING WITHOUT AUTOMATIC DIAL

Deep-fat frying without an automatic dial or thermometer can be done with a heavy flat-bottomed kettle, a wire frying basket, and cubes of stale bread for testing heat of fat. Fill kettle two-thirds full (if fuller, it may boil over—which is dangerous). Heat fat slowly, using salad or other cooking oil, lard, or homogenized fats. When hot but not smoking, test this way:

Fat is right for cooked food . .	if cube browns in 40 seconds
other uncooked food . .	if cube browns in 60 seconds
Fat is right for French-frying potatoes . .	if cube browns in 20 seconds

POTATO PUFFS

2 cups mashed potatoes
1 egg
1 tablespoon finely chopped chives
½ cup grated cheese
½ teaspoon salt
⅛ teaspoon pepper
¼ teaspoon paprika

Combine all ingredients and blend. Form into balls and chill if you have prepared these well in advance of the time you want to serve them piping hot from the cooker. Roll in fine bread crumbs until thoroughly coated. Drop into preheated fat (375 F.) and fry until brown, about 3 minutes. Drain on paper towels and serve immediately.

BUSTIN' BISCUITS

These are made from "the hole in the doughnuts" or from biscuit dough. The biscuit dough lends great variety to these because after mixing a 2-cup recipe of biscuit mix it can be divided into several portions, with herbs or flavorings or marmalades added to each one to make a great assortment. Cut into tiny rounds about the size of the dough that would come from the inside of the doughnut. Drop the small rounds into fat (375 F.) and fry until brown.

These can be made of plain biscuit mix and rolled in powdered sugar while hot or sprinkled with a mixture of half granulated sugar and cinnamon.

FRIED SHRIMP OR SCALLOPS

To fry frozen, breaded shrimp or scallops which have been precooked, it is not necessary to defrost them. Place contents from one package of the frozen seafood into the fry basket. Separate carefully with a fork without breaking the shrimp or scallops. Since the seafood is very cold, lower the basket slowly into the preheated fat (375 F.) and cook until both thawed and tender, 2 to 3 minutes. Drain on paper towel, sprinkle with salt, and serve with or without a sauce. Chile sauce, Lemon Mayonnaise with chopped parsley added, Russian dressing, or tartar sauce is good with these.

To cook fresh shrimp, wash them, drop into boiling salted water—¼ cup salt for 1 quart water—cover, reduce heat, simmer 5 minutes. Drain, peel off the shell, and cut down the back to remove the black vein. Rinse. Then chill or dip in an egg batter made by beating 2 eggs with ½ cup milk and ¼ teaspoon orégano. When the shrimp are coated dip into fine cracker crumbs, shake to remove excess crumbs and fry in hot fat (375 F.) until golden brown. Drain on paper towel and sprinkle with salt.

To fry uncooked scallops, dip them in this egg batter or into the fritter batter and fry until golden brown, about 5 minutes.

FRILLY VEGETABLE FRITTERS

To make the batter:

1 cup sifted all-purpose flour
½ teaspoon salt
1 teaspoon baking powder
2 eggs, beaten
1 tablespoon melted butter
½ cup milk

Sift flour before measuring the necessary 1 cup. Add salt and baking powder and sift again. Stir in well-beaten eggs, melted shortening, and milk.

Now dip the green-leaved ends of hearts of celery into the batter so that they are lightly coated. Drop into the fat (375 F.) and fry until delicately brown, about 5 minutes. Drain on paper towel and serve, either as an appetizer or as an accompaniment for meat.

Almost any kind of fruit in slices or chunks, drained, dipped in batter, and fried a delicate brown, is good with meat or on the appetizer tray.

If you have several things ready to dip in batter and fry, such as a variety of fruit and vegetable chunks, fry a few of each at a time and pass them on a long-handled griddle.

FRENCH-FRIED ONION RINGS

Clean and slice big sweet Bermuda onions into ¼-inch slices. Separate the rings as you dip them into the egg batter suggested for shrimp. Dip into fine cracker crumbs. Shake off the excess crumbs and drop into the hot fat until brown, about 3 minutes. Drain on paper towel, sprinkle with salt, and serve.

It is a good idea to fry only a few onion rings at a time. They should not cling together.

PETITE CORN FRITTERS

1 cup cream-style canned corn, drained
1 egg yolk
½ cup plus 2 tablespoons flour
⅛ teaspoon marjoram or
¼ teaspoon rosemary
½ teaspoon salt
⅛ teaspoon paprika
1 egg white
½ teaspoon baking powder

If you have an electric blender, combine the drained corn and egg yolk and blend 1 minute. Otherwise chop corn, beat egg yolk until thick, and mix together. Combine dry ingredients, sift together, and add to the corn mixture. Beat egg white until very stiff and fold into the corn batter. Drop small spoonfuls into the hot fat (375 F.) and fry until brown, 3 to 5 minutes. Drain and serve.

FISH FRITTERS

Use Petite Corn recipe, replacing 1 cup corn with 1 cup white, cooked fish which has been mashed to a purée. When these have been deep-fried for 3 to 5 minutes and drained, they are fluffy and delicious. Add ⅛ teaspoon orégano or 1 teaspoon finely chopped parsley to the Fish Fritters if you like.

FRUIT COCKTAIL FRITTERS

Makes 15 fritters:

1½ cups sifted flour
1½ teaspoons baking powder
1 teaspoon salt
1 tablespoon sugar
2 eggs
½ cup milk
1 cup well-drained canned fruit cocktail

Sift together dry ingredients. Combine eggs and milk and beat well; add to flour mixture all at once and stir only until all flour is moistened. Fold in fruit cocktail. Heat fat to 375 F. Drop batter from a tablespoon into fat and fry 5 minutes, or until golden brown on all sides. Remove from fat and drain on paper towels. Serve hot with maple syrup or sprinkled with confectioners' sugar.

PANCAKE MEALS . DEFINITELY FUN AND DELICIOUS

You have had pancakes, but have you had these? Cook them on a table broiler, on a griddle over barbecue coals, on the infra-red roaster if yours has a griddle top. Cook them at the table on your plugged-in grills, or cook them in the kitchen and eat them there.

BLUEBERRY GRIDDLE CAKES

Add ½ cup blueberries to your favorite pancake mix or recipe. These cakes should not be too thin and can be served 1 or 2 at a time as they come off the griddle, with plenty of butter and good maple syrup.

CHEESE PANCAKES

Makes 4 servings:

½ pound (2½ cups) grated Swiss cheese
1 cup undiluted evaporated milk
1 tablespoon lemon juice
4 egg yolks, or 2 whole eggs
3 tablespoons flour
1 teaspoon salt
2 teaspoons mustard, or ¼ teaspoon curry powder
1 teaspoon thyme
2 or 3 tablespoons butter (for frying)

Mix all ingredients except butter, and stir until blended. Melt the butter a little at a time as needed for frying the batter dropped by spoonfuls onto the hot griddle. Brown on both sides.

Dollar-sized Cheese Pancakes make such good appetizers too. At the beginning, for lunch, or for dessert with a bunch of grapes or slivers of unpeeled red apple—once you make them, Cheese Pancakes are here to stay!

BUCKWHEAT CAKE STACKS WITH SAUSAGE

These are so good and so beautiful that once you have had them you will serve them often. Use a buckwheat pancake mix, making the batter a little thinner than is required for the usual pancakes, so that it will spread quickly to make thin cakes about 4 inches across. Pile these on hot plates as they are cooked, putting butter between each layer, until 6 cakes are stacked on top of each other. Pour melted butter over the stack and surround it with 4 to 6 broiled sausages, depending on how big a meal you want to make of this. Pass maple syrup.

These can be stacked and cut like a cake into wedges, serving each person a wedge as the stack is completed, or each person can wait until his own stack is completed.

These can also be cooked in advance with a paper towel put between each cake as it is finished. When served, drench with hot melted butter and heat the maple syrup which is to go over them.

POTATO PANCAKES

Makes 10 pancakes:

2 cups fluffy mashed potatoes
2 cups finely chopped stewed cabbage
½ cup chopped onions
2 eggs, lightly beaten with 1 tablespoon water
salt and pepper to taste

Combine all ingredients. Shape into balls, then flatten with a pancake turner and arrange in a greased baking pan. Brush the tops with butter and bake until brown in a moderate oven (350 F.). Serve with coarsely chopped nuts on top and a sprinkling of cinnamon. These can be passed separately if being done at a party.

MEXICAN CORN-MEAL STACKS

Makes 4 stacks of 3 corn cakes each:

1 egg, unbeaten
1 cup milk
1 tablespoon melted butter or margarine
1 12-ounce package corn muffin mix
½ package (½-pound size) processed American cheese
⅓ cup evaporated milk
2 teaspoons prepared mustard
⅛ teaspoon cayenne pepper
½ cup chopped onions
½ cup chopped parsley
4 slices bacon, halved and fried crisply

Add egg, milk, and melted butter to the corn muffin mix. Stir only until mixed but not smooth. Bake 12 cakes 4 inches in diameter (about 2 tablespoons each) on a hot ungreased griddle until browned on both sides. Melt cheese with evaporated milk. Season with rich prepared mustard and cayenne pepper. Serve griddle cakes in stacks of three. Between the first two corn cakes place 2 tablespoons of the onions. Use the parsley for the second filling. Top with the third cake. Spoon on the hot cheese sauce. Decorate with crisp bacon.

WAFFLED FRENCH TOAST

Makes 10 slices:

2 eggs
1 cup milk
¼ teaspoon salt
2 tablespoons salad oil
10 slices of bread

Beat eggs slightly; add milk, salt, and salad oil. Pour into a shallow dish. Dip bread slices into egg mixture, coating both sides well. Bake in preheated waffle iron according to manufacturer's directions, or until steam no longer appears and bread is golden brown. Serve hot with Honey Butter.

Honey Butter

You can buy honey-butter spread, but you can also make it this way: Combine ⅔ cup honey with ½ cup butter or margarine which has been softened. Blend well.

PECAN WAFFLES

Makes 6 waffles:

2 cups sifted all-purpose flour
3 teaspoons baking powder
1½ teaspoons salt
2 tablespoons sugar
2 eggs, slightly beaten
1½ cups milk
½ cup salad oil
½ cup coarsely chopped pecan meats

Mix and sift dry ingredients. Combine slightly beaten eggs, milk, and salad oil; add to the dry ingredients; blend well. Stir in pecans. Bake in hot waffle iron about 3 minutes, or until steaming ceases. Serve hot with butter and syrup.

SAUCES FOR PANCAKES

Try any of the sauces suggested for Ice Cream Sundaes on pancakes or waffles. The thickened fruit sauces are especially good. Serve them hot.

CHAPTER 22

—OR UNDER THE OLD SHADE TREE

BARBECUE . . . . IT'S A MAN'S WORLD

Men fancy the barbecue as their special talent and are as good at it as they think they are. Nice thing about barbecues is that everybody who is going to eat shares in preparing the food. Many a woman has learned it is more fun to watch, or to be watched, cooking dinner than to prepare it alone in the kitchen.

Barbecue used to refer to the elevated frame on which oxen or other large animals were roasted whole for a feast. Long ago this was especially the custom for wedding feasts. In our country it was used by early-day politicians to rally their followers in each town before a speech.

Eventually barbecue referred to the flavoring. Any meat, fowl, or fish marinated or basted in highly seasoned sauce was "barbecued," whether cooked in the oven or out of doors. Now we barbecue any old place from dusk until midnight. It may be over a bed of coals in a big outdoor barbecue, on a portable one which accommodates itself to any location in or out of the house, including the fireplace. We barbecue in the oven and lately in rotisseries with their infra-red heat.

"Barbecuing" starts with flavoring whatever is to be cooked, and this begins with a sauce in which the meat is basted or in which it stands for several hours to acquire distinctive flavor. Some like the sauce very hot, others like more lemon-seasoning taste. The tomato flavor attracts others, herbs only for others, and mustard or tart fruit sauces have votes too. Begin with these and improve for your own taste. These can be made, cooled, tightly sealed, and stored a week or two.

ABOUT BARBECUES . . . . . KEEP THEM SIMPLE

If barbecuing is being done over coals, you know—probably—that the fire must be built and your meat taken out of the refrigerator at about the same time—*an hour before you intend to cook.* This results in the good deep bed of coals you need for cooking, and meat with no chill in it. Besides, this is the time to sprinkle the meat with salt and pepper.

Steak being the first choice for barbecuing, let's suggest you have *thick* ones. Two inches or more, and use tenderizer if you've economized and bought beef that needs it. (As I've said before somewhere, the price you pay for beef does not buy nutritious quality but tenderness. Supply the tenderness for yourself when there is need.)

Use any sauce you like. Buy a bottled barbecue sauce or several of them to try different flavors, until you learn to make your own, or marinate in herb-flavored vinegar and oil before cooking. *Always keep barbecued food moist during cooking by frequent basting.*

I don't know why steaks should be first choice. Spareribs are as good as anything can get, and a leg or shoulder of lamb, boned and barbecued open in butterfly position, is excellent, and so are slow-toasted steaming frankfurters, which aren't very good any other way. Barbecued, they are marvelous. And don't forget the hickory salt, which can put a flavor into meat if the fire you use does not.

Serve melted butter, or some of the heated sauce, or half and half when the meat is ready to eat.

Choose your meat, your sauce, and your fire, and proceed as your equipment recommends. In the event that your "fire" is an oven, here are recipes for kitchen barbecuing, recipes that can readily be used elsewhere.

SPARERIB BARBECUE SAUCE

This is good for basting pork chops or chicken too. It is very hot but loses some of its "fire" in cooking.

Makes 6 cups:

1 cup wine vinegar
½ cup water
1¼ cups brown sugar
1¼ cups ketchup
1 teaspoon tabasco
2½ tablespoons Worcestershire sauce
¼ teaspoon cayenne
½ can frozen lemon juice, undiluted
2 tablespoons grated lemon peel
⅔ cup melted butter
½ cup chopped onion
2 cloves garlic, chopped

Combine all except last three ingredients in saucepan over low heat. In another pan melt the butter and add the chopped onion and garlic, stirring until lightly browned. When the sugar has thoroughly dissolved in the vinegar mixture, add browned onions and garlic. Blend thoroughly.

Try this on short ribs of beef. For lamb roast omit ketchup; increase garlic to 4 cloves.

TARRAGON BARBECUE SAUCE

Excellent for seafood, chicken, turkey, fish, and fine for duck, squab, or pheasant.

Makes 4 cups:

6 strips bacon
6 cloves garlic, chopped
1 tablespoon chopped onion
1 cup water
1 cup sugar
2¼ cups tomato ketchup
2½ tablespoons Worcestershire sauce
¾ teaspoon red pepper
¾ teaspoon chili powder
½ cup tarragon vinegar

Cook bacon in saucepan until crisp; remove from fat and add garlic and onion. Brown lightly. Add water and sugar. Stir until sugar dissolves. Add all other ingredients and stir, continuing to cook until heated thoroughly. Cool; use or seal and store.

KATJONG SAUCE

Makes 1½ cups:

4 almonds, blanched and chopped (optional)
2 teaspoons minced onions
½ teaspoon salt
⅛ teaspoon cayenne
1 cup peanut butter
½ cup heavy cream or undiluted evaporated milk

Make this sauce to serve over veal chops. Combine all ingredients and blend, adding a little cream if necessary for spreading consistency. Broil veal chops on one side; turn and cover with the sauce. Broil until done, and serve with more sauce spooned over the meat. The veal may be better if a tenderizer is sprinkled over the meat 30 minutes before broiling.

FRANKFURTER SAUCE

Use either of the sauces suggested for spareribs. Or try heated chili con carne poured over the toasted frankfurter as it is nestled into a split bun.

HOT MUSTARD BARBECUE FOR HAMBURGERS OR FISH

2 teaspoons dry mustard
1 cup mayonnaise
½ cup undiluted evaporated milk
salt to taste

Add mustard to the mayonnaise. Put in top of double boiler and add the milk slowly, stirring constantly until heated through and blended, about 5 minutes. Add salt to taste and a few grains of cayenne pepper. Remove from heat and serve at once over hamburgers or fish.

SPARERIBS ANGOSTURA SAUCE

Makes 1⅔ cups:

1 cup water
1 tablespoon Angostura bitters
1 teaspoon dry mustard
¼ tablespoon Worcestershire sauce
1½ teaspoons salt
½ cup ketchup

Combine; blend well without cooking. Use as basting sauce or pour over each layer of spareribs which have been covered with sliced onions (2 medium onions). Place a layer of the spareribs (3 pounds) in the bottom of a Dutch oven. Cover with a layer of onion slices. Sprinkle with part of the sauce, and continue until the spareribs and all ingredients have been used.

CRANBERRY BARBECUE RELISH

1 pound can jellied cranberry sauce
½ cup sliced stuffed olives
½ cup chopped pecans
2 teaspoons lemon juice
1 teaspoon grated onion

Crush jellied cranberry sauce with a fork. Stir in all other ingredients. Chill for several hours before serving. An excellent sauce for hamburgers or fried chicken or with venison.

BAY LEAF STEAK

For each steak measure out 1 tablespoon garlic wine vinegar and soak a bay leaf in it for an hour. Then, just before you pop your steaks under the broiler, brush the vinegar onto both sides of each steak. See what that does for your great reputation.

BASIL OR GARLIC STEAKS AND CHOPS

Tenderize steaks or chops by marinating them in a good wine vinegar before broiling. Flavor at the same time by adding ½ teaspoon basil or 2 chopped cloves of garlic to ⅓ cup wine vinegar. Combine with ½ cup olive or salad oil. Put meat in a deep platter, cover with the liquid, and let stand 2 hours or 12, turning it a time or two.

ROAST LAMB AND KEBABS . . . A SIGN OF SPRING

Lamb has been as traditional on the Easter table as an Easter bonnet on Easter Sunday. This time let's have Roast Lamb and Gravy! Begin with buying an 8-pound leg of lamb and have steaks cut off. Freeze these wrapped in heavy paper for a meal weeks or days later. Now is the time to have 2 pounds of the lamb cut off to make 16 2-inch squares for kebabs. Prepare the rest for roasting. Next remove the parchment-like skin so that carving the lamb will be easier after it is roasted. Coat with prepared mustard and insert 2 or 3 slivers of garlic between meat and bone at each end if you would have a fine flavor. Place fat side up on a rack in an open pan; no water is necessary. Bake in moderately slow oven (325 F.) until a meat roasting thermometer registers 175 F. for medium and 182 F. for a well-done roast, about 3½ hours.

Now we get to the lamb kebabs:

LAMB KEBABS AND RICE

Makes 2 servings:

16 (1½ x 2 inches) squares tender lamb, without bone, cut cross-grain
8 tiny whole onions, peeled
8 2-inch squares green pepper
8 tiny tomatoes or wedges
½ cup olive oil
⅓ cup vinegar (tarragon preferably)
1 teaspoon orégano
1 teaspoon salt
3 teaspoons rich prepared mustard
¼ teaspoon pepper
1 clove garlic, finely chopped
⅔ cup quick-cooking rice

Wipe lamb cubes with damp cloth. Place in a large bowl with vegetables. Mix remaining ingredients, except rice, and add to bowl. Let stand 2 hours in refrigerator; stir several times. Arrange lamb and vegetables on 4 long or 6 short skewers (metal nut picks are good substitutes). For well-done lamb, leave space between pieces on skewers; for rare, place close together. Broil under medium heat 10 to 12 minutes, turning until well browned.

Serve with quick Turkish rice made by adding ice cubes to ½ cup lamb drippings to make ¾ cup cold liquid. Add to instant rice and cook according to package directions.

SPRING LAMB SHANKS—MUSTARD BARBECUE

Try shoulder lamb shanks, cut off the first joint, for this recipe. Each should weigh about ¾ of a pound. If the breast is purchased with it, at considerable saving per pound, freeze the balance (in the ice tray of your refrigerator) for another recipe many days later.

Makes 6 servings:

6 small shoulder lamb shanks, ¾ pound each, or 4 pounds breast of lamb cut in 2-inch squares
6 tablespoons rich prepared mustard
4 teaspoons salt
¾ teaspoon pepper
3 tablespoons melted fat
¾ cup chopped onion
1½ cups tomato sauce
¼ cup Worcestershire sauce
1½ cups water
⅜ teaspoon red pepper

Wipe lamb shanks with a damp cloth. With pastry brush or knife spread on rich prepared mustard, covering the entire shank generously. Season with salt and pepper. Brown all over in melted fat in a frying pan over medium heat. Remove shanks to a roaster which has a tight-fitting cover. Brown onions in remaining fat in the same frying pan over medium heat. Add remaining ingredients. Combine well and bring this barbecue sauce to a boil. Pour over lamb shanks. Cover tightly. Cook in preheated moderate to moderately hot oven (350 to 375 F.) about 1½ hours, or until tender.

• If you have barbecue sauce for lamb in the refrigerator, it can be used instead of this sauce.

STUFFED LAMB CHOPS

6 double rib chops
1 pound good sausage
2 tablespoons lemon juice
1 teaspoon Worcestershire sauce
1 teaspoon dry mustard
⅔ cup mayonnaise
2 tablespoons bacon fat
1 cup hot water
1 teaspoon Angostura bitters

Remove bones; split chops through ¾ of the width and stuff with the sausage. Roll and secure with a skewer. Combine the lemon juice, Worcestershire sauce, and mustard with the mayonnaise and spread on each side of the chop, coating thickly. Add bacon fat and Angostura to the hot water for basting while these roast at the barbecue, or bake in a moderately hot oven (375 F.) about ½ hour, basting twice.

A GOOD PORK BUY . . . . . . 3 MEALS FOR TWO

The family of two could follow these directions; the larger family multiplies the original purchase and the recipes to fit—then follows:

Buy a 3-pound loin roast and ask your butcher to cut out the tenderloin and to cut off 2 chops. Wrap the chops in aluminum foil and freeze in your freezing compartment to use about a week later. Then prepare the guest-meal Pork Loin Roast of about 6 or 8 medium-sized servings this way:

ROAST LOIN OF PORK WITH PRUNES

Wipe the meat with a clean damp cloth. Sprinkle heavily with salt and lightly with black pepper. Spread all sides with a rich prepared mustard. If you are roasting this in the oven, it would go into an open roasting pan with fat side up to bake in a moderately slow oven (325 F.) about 40 minutes for each pound, until the pork is very well done.

For rotisserie roasting, pierce the roast, put into place, and roast 1¾ to 2 hours, or until very tender. Baste with the drippings from the pork several times during roasting.

Another way to roast in the rotisserie is to marinate the tenderloin in barbecue sauce for at least 2 hours before cooking. Drain. Place on the spit, sprinkle with salt and pepper, and baste with more of the barbecue sauce while roasting.

During the roasting let cooked, pitted prunes which have been drained heat in the pan below and be seasoned with the drippings from the pork.

BARBECUED SPARERIBS

Makes 6 servings:

3 pounds meaty spareribs
fat for browning

SAUCE:

3 cups tomato juice
¼ cup mixed herb wine vinegar
¼ teaspoon garlic
1½ tablespoons brown sugar
1 tablespoon olive or salad oil
½ cup finely chopped onion
1½ teaspoons celery seed
½ teaspoon freshly ground pepper
¼ teaspoon hot paprika
1 bay leaf
¼ teaspoon rosemary
¼ teaspoon marjoram

Combine ingredients for sauce and cook over low heat 20 minutes. Cut the ribs to make 6 portions. Brown on all sides in a little fat and place in a baking pan. Cover with the sauce and bake 1¼ hours in moderate oven (350 F.), basting frequently with the sauce.

BEEF . . . . MANY WAYS TO COOK IT

2 BEEF DINNERS

Buy less tender cuts of beef—flank, chuck, plate, brisket, or heel—then make them tender by tender cooking. Long, slow moist heat does the trick. Prepare these 2 recipes from round or from the cuts just mentioned.

BARBECUED BEEF STEAK STRIPS

Makes 4 servings:

2 pounds round steak ½ inch thick
3 tablespoons rich prepared mustard
flour
4 tablespoons fat
1 piece garlic, minced
½ cup finely chopped onion
½ cup diced green pepper
¼ cup finely cut celery leaves
¼ cup finely cut parsley, or 2 tablespoons dried flakes
1 cup (8-ounce can) tomato sauce
¼ cup vinegar, cider or tarragon
1½ cups water
2 tablespoons brown sugar
½ teaspoon salt
¼ teaspoon cayenne pepper

Wipe meat with damp cloth and cut into strips about 1½ inches wide by 3 inches long. Toss in bowl until well-coated with mustard. Roll well in flour. Brown both sides in hot fat or oil, adding more fat as necessary. Remove steak strips to 6- to 8-cup casserole. To fat in frying pan add garlic and onion. Sauté until brown. Stir in remaining ingredients. Bring to a boil, then simmer about 10 minutes. Pour over steak strips. Cover tightly.

If prepared ahead, cool quickly and store in refrigerator until ready to bake in slow oven (300 F.) 2 to 2½ hours, or until tender. Add more water if necessary. This may also be simmered over low heat on top of stove in tightly covered kettle.

BROWNED SHORT RIBS

Makes 4 servings:

Use 3 pounds short ribs of beef cut into 3-inch serving pieces. Cut off extra fat. Put in a hot skillet and cook until the fat is rendered, and use to brown the ribs evenly on all sides. Coat the pieces of beef with 4 tablespoons of prepared mustard and proceed as for Barbecued Steak Strips.

• Short ribs can be prepared for barbecuing in any quantity you like, allowing from ½ to 1 pound per person. Brown the ribs well after marinating in your favorite barbecue sauce for at least 1 hour before cooking.

BEEF MEAT CAKES

Makes 12 cakes:

2 pounds ground steak, put through the grinder twice
1 pound ground pork
1 teaspoon freshly ground black pepper
2 tablespoons chopped onion
2 eggs
1 teaspoon Worcestershire sauce
2 tablespoons chopped parsley garnish

Combine all ingredients except parsley. Form into balls and flatten. Broil about 10 minutes for well done and less to secure rare or medium. Sprinkle with chopped parsley and serve.

BARBECUED ROUND STEAK

Makes 4 servings:

½ cup flour
½ teaspoon salt
¼ teaspoon pepper
1½ pounds beef round cut 1 inch thick
2 tablespoons fat or salad oil
½ cup chili sauce
⅓ cup vinegar
1 tablespoon sugar
1 clove garlic, mashed
1 teaspoon chopped onion
1 tablespoon rich prepared mustard

Combine flour, salt, and pepper. Cut steak into 1½-inch crosswise slices and dredge in seasoned flour. Heat fat in skillet; brown steak on all sides. Remove meat to 1½-quart casserole. Pour off fat and place chili sauce, vinegar, sugar, garlic, and onion in skillet and simmer 3 minutes, scraping any flour sticking to skillet into the sauce. Stir in mustard and pour sauce over steak. Bake covered in a moderate oven (350 F.) 1 hour. Uncover and bake an additional ½ hour, or until meat is tender.

SWISS STEAK

Makes 6 servings:

1 cup flour seasoned with ¼ teaspoon pepper and ½ teaspoon thyme
3 pounds prime round steak, 1½ inches thick
4 tablespoons butter
3 cups sliced onions
2 cloves garlic, minced fine
1½ cups beef bouillon
⅓ teaspoon thyme

Mix seasoned flour well and pound generously into steak. Melt 3 tablespoons of butter in an iron pan. Brown sliced onions and garlic lightly and remove from pan. Add 1 tablespoon of butter to pan; increase heat and brown the steak well and quickly on both sides. Reduce heat; add browned onions and garlic and enough broth to cover the onions. Sprinkle with ⅓ teaspoon thyme. Cover tightly. Simmer over low heat 50 minutes, or until meat is tender. Salt and pepper to taste. Remove cover and let cook down a few minutes while you check seasonings.

DON'T MISS THESE . . . . FOR SUMMER COOKING

BARBECUED TURKEY OR CHICKEN

Makes 6 servings:

1 turkey, 7 pounds
or
1 chicken, 4 to 6 pounds, fresh or frozen
or
3 frying chickens, 2 to 2½ pounds
1 lemon
2 teaspoons salt
½ teaspoon pepper
1 cup barbecue sauce

When buying the broilers or the turkey, have the butcher split them in half. Soak in cold water to cover, to which you have added 2 tablespoons salt, for about 1 hour or overnight. Drain and wipe dry. Rub inside and out with lemon wedges. Sprinkle with freshly ground pepper and very lightly with salt.

If these are to be done in the oven, they should be placed in a flat pan, skin side up. Cover with 1 cup of barbecue sauce recommended for chicken and bake at (325 F.) 2 to 3½ hours, or until tender, adding more sauce once or twice during the baking. Spoon a little more sauce over the top. Place under the broiler about 4 inches from heat and leave under high heat until crusty brown.

BARBECUED FROGS' LEGS

Makes 6 servings:

24 large frogs' legs
2 tablespoons salt
1½ cups barbecue sauce (any sauce you would use on chicken)
salt and pepper
½ cup flour
½ teaspoon pepper

Cover the cleaned, white frogs' legs with water. Add salt and let stand 6 hours. Drain; marinate in barbecue sauce 30 minutes. Roll in flour and broil or pan-fry in half bacon fat and half butter until crisp and brown.

THESE MEAT PATTIES . . MAKE ANY MEAL A PARTY

VENISON PATTIES

Makes 18 2-inch patties:

3 pounds ground venison
1½ teaspoons salt
½ teaspoon monosodium glutamate (MSG)
¼ teaspoon pepper
1 egg, lightly beaten
1 tablespoon orange juice
¼ cup French dressing

Combine all ingredients except French dressing. Mix and form into patties, brush with French dressing, and broil.

DANISH VEAL PATTIES

Makes 12 small patties:

3 pounds veal, put through grinder twice
1½ teaspoons salt
¼ teaspoon pepper
3 tablespoons butter
½ teaspoon brown sugar
2 tablespoons flour
1½ cups water

Mix veal, salt, and pepper. Shape into thin patties and brown in butter over low heat. Remove to hot platter. Add brown sugar and flour to skillet. Stir until browned. Add water and stir until gravy is thickened. Pour over cakes and serve.

SAUERBRATEN CAKES WITH GINGERSNAP SAUCE

Makes 6 servings:

3 pounds ground beef
2 teaspoons salt
¼ teaspoon pepper
⅓ cup chopped onion
¼ cup wine vinegar
¼ cup flour
3 tablespoons bacon fat
2 tablespoons butter or margarine
3 tablespoons flour
6 gingersnaps, crushed
1½ tablespoons molasses
2 teaspoons brown sugar
¼ cup seedless raisins
2 cups cold water

Mix beef with the seasonings and vinegar and form into 12 flat meat cakes. Pat them into the flour until lightly coated. Melt the bacon fat in a skillet and fry the cakes until done as you like them, being sure they are browned on both sides. Remove to a hot serving platter. Add butter and flour to the skillet and cook until lightly browned, stirring constantly. Add the gingersnaps, molasses, brown sugar, and raisins. Slowly add the water, stirring until the gravy is thickened. Serve the gravy over the meat cakes.

MEXICAN MEAT CAKES

Make regular hamburgers—big 3- or 4-inch ones—seasoned as you like best. Open canned chile con carne and heat to boiling point while the hamburgers brown. Pour about ½ cup over each hamburger as served.

STUFFED HAMBURGERS

Makes 8 servings:

2 pounds hamburger
1 teaspoon salt
¼ teaspoon pepper
1 egg

Mix thoroughly and press half the meat mixture into greased custard cups. Spread stuffing and cover with the remaining meat mixture. Dot with butter or margarine. Set custard cups into a pan of water and bake in moderate oven (350 F.) 45 minutes.

Make the stuffing by combining 2 cups prepared bread stuffing for poultry, 2 tablespoons chopped onion, ¼ cup melted butter or margarine, ½ teaspoon thyme, 1 teaspoon salt, and 2 tablespoons hot bouillon. Combine ingredients in order given and blend.

CRISP SEAFOOD MEALS . . . . FOR FUN COOKING

When it is hot you want something crisp to contrast with your wilted feeling. Crisp fried chicken you know about. Why not try crisp seafood now that freezing, canning, and shipping fresh seafood have made enjoying these treasures nation-wide?

Keep the menu crisp and salty. French-fried potatoes, potato chips, or potatoes pan-fried to crusty brown in half butter and half bacon fat, oven-toasted bread. Serve these with shimmering molded gelatin salads made in the cool of the morning. These are good company for the crisp seafood recipes to follow.

For dessert, a Fruit Float or any melon. A deep-dish pie is marvelous after seafood dinners, and so is ice cream and cake. Choose your favorite, or the one you have the time to prepare, and then enjoy these:

SEAFOOD CAKES

2 cups cooked seafood (cooked lobster, crabmeat, or white fish)
2 tablespoons chopped parsley
2 tablespoons chopped onion
½ teaspoon celery salt
⅛ teaspoon mace
⅛ teaspoon cayenne
1 pimiento, chopped
¼ cup Thick White Sauce
2 tablespoons lemon juice
1 cup buttered crumbs

Combine all ingredients except crumbs. Form into balls and flatten with a fork. Roll in bread crumbs and chill so that they will "set" and not fall apart when browned. Broil or fry, browning each side.

To prepare buttered crumbs, melt 2 or 3 tablespoons butter and stir the fine crumbs in the butter until all are coated. The well-buttered crumbs ensure well-browned cakes.

CRABMEAT PATTIES

Makes 6 servings:

2 tablespoons butter
½ cup onion
2 cups crabmeat, canned or fresh
1 teaspoon celery salt
¼ teaspoon mace
¼ teaspoon cayenne
1 teaspoon dry mustard
1 cup milk, or replace cream and milk with 2 cups undiluted evaporated milk
1 cup cream
1½ tablespoons cornstarch
2 eggs, well beaten
⅔ cup buttered crumbs
2 tablespoons lemon juice

Melt 2 tablespoons butter in saucepan, add onion and stir until brown. Add crabmeat and seasonings; stir about 1 minute. Combine milk, cream, cornstarch, and beaten eggs and stir into the crabmeat mixture. Cook over low heat about 15 minutes, stirring constantly. Fill clam shells and sprinkle with buttered bread crumbs. Sprinkle with the lemon juice and place under broiler until browned.

DE LUXE CRAB CAKES

When crabmeat is fresh and you aren't trying to "stretch" it, this is the recipe you want, for there is nothing better in the world than crabmeat unadorned, huddled together in a crisp outside.

Makes 6 cakes:

2 cups fresh, cooked crabmeat, flaked
½ teaspoon salt
⅛ teaspoon pepper
1 teaspoon Worcestershire sauce
2 teaspoons lemon juice
1 egg, beaten
flour

Mix all ingredients except flour and shape into cakes. Dredge lightly with flour. Chill 10 minutes to ½ hour before cooking in hot deep fat (375 F.) 3 to 4 minutes until golden brown.

TUNA FISH CAKES

Makes 8 cakes:

2 cans tuna fish, flaked
1 cup cold mashed potatoes
½ teaspoon orégano
⅛ teaspoon marjoram
½ teaspoon salt
1 egg
1 cup buttered crumbs

Combine all ingredients except buttered crumbs. Form into cakes and roll in the crumbs. For easy browning, chill for a little while before cooking.

SYDNEY FISH CAKES

This fish cake recipe comes from Australia.

Makes 8 small cakes:

2 cups boiled fish, flaked
2 tablespoons melted butter
1 cup soft bread crumbs
½ tablespoon chopped parsley
salt and pepper to taste
2 eggs

Mash the fish and butter together with ¼ cup of the bread crumbs. Add parsley and seasonings and the beaten yolk of 1 egg. Shape into round or flat cakes, then dip into remaining egg which has been well beaten, and then into more of the crumbs. Fry in deep fat (375 F.).

SPANISH SHRIMP IN HOT SAUCE

In Spain big spider crabs and shrimp are cooked in boiling sea water with no other flavoring except a bay leaf. If you live near the sea you might do the same, allowing ½ pound shrimp for each person. Drop the uncooked shrimp in boiling salted water and cook 15 to 20 minutes until they turn coral pink. Do this immediately before you want to eat them, and serve them hot with this sauce.

HOT SAUCE:

Makes 2 cups:

1 cup melted butter
½ cup lemon juice
½ cup ketchup
1 teaspoon paprika
1 tablespoon Worcestershire sauce
1 tablespoon brown sugar

Combine all ingredients in a saucepan and place over moderate heat, stirring constantly until sugar is dissolved. Serve 2 bowls, one at each end of the table, with the hot shrimp in their shells piled on a platter in the middle so that each person can shell his shrimp and dip them in the sauce.

OYSTER PATTIES

Makes 8 servings:

1 quart oysters
⅓ cup chopped celery
1 cup chopped mushrooms
¼ cup butter
⅓ cup chopped onion
1 teaspoon mace
1 tablespoon chopped parsley
1 tablespoon Worcestershire sauce
1 teaspoon celery salt
1 cup Thick White Sauce
1 cup bread crumbs
2 tablespoons butter

Drain oysters, reserving the liquid; chop into fairly small pieces. Combine with celery and oyster liquor in a saucepan and boil about 3 minutes. Melt butter in a skillet, add onion. When slightly brown, add mushrooms, mace, parsley, Worcestershire sauce, celery salt, and pour in the cooked oysters and celery and White Sauce and cook over low heat. When thick and smooth, spoon into clam shells. Cover with bread crumbs and dot with butter. Place under broiler until browned.

part six

BIG DOIN'S—
FOOD FOR 12 OR 50

CHAPTER 23

FOOD FOR A CROWD

It's food for 12 . . . or 24 or 50 . . . when there is a crowd to feed.

Here are tips on preparing for the big gathering, beginning with the recipes for 12 you will often feed your family, then make again to feed your friends on occasions such as these:

CHURCH SUPPERS
PIE SUPPERS
FIRESIDE SUPPERS
SQUARE DANCES
AFTER SKATING
WORK PARTIES or
BARN RAISING

or when it's

FOOD IN A HURRY

before the card game which ends at midnight.

THINK . . . . BEFORE YOU START COOKING

Did you ever try having 4 people make recipes for 8 or 12 when you want food for 40 or 50 people? Recipes for 12 turn out well; quantity recipes may not. Large pots of food have different cooking times, less even cooking than the contents of smaller ones.

Successfully feeding a large crowd and keeping them happy can be done more easily with one menu than when a half dozen pies or cakes or other desserts or when several main courses are there to choose from. Then everyone is inclined to want some of everything and the food does not "go round."

Soup is a good starter for a hungry crowd. Soup, unlike most food, can be prepared in a large pot without difficulty, stirred to heat evenly, served from the pot in which it is cooked, and kept hot by covering between dipping up portions.

Make soup with canned cream soups diluted with a gallon of chicken broth made at home. Don't forget frozen mashed potatoes, shrimp, canned seafood when mixing large quantities of soup. It is difficult to go wrong so long as everything that goes into the pot is good and not too much thinning with too much water, and so long as there is no risk of curdle, such as combining tomatoes with milk. Use evaporated milk to make the pot richer, Worcestershire and cayenne to "pick up" the flavor, French-fried onion slices for garnish on the soup for a crowd.

Try serving fluffy butter, easy to spread and goes farther, when feeding a crowd.

Desserts do not have to be difficult to make in order to be marvelous meal finales. Why bake pies and cakes for big group desserts, when cake or biscuit-topped Cobblers are so wonderful, so easy to make? Fruit Floats are still easier and as good as they are gorgeous, with almost no work involved except chilling and opening cans!

For pie suppers, or making the pies for any big gathering, the baking can be streamlined. Ask the women who make the tenderest pie shells to bake a dozen or so each. Let someone else prepare the fillings. Goes faster, too, and it's pleasant working together. Makes two parties instead of one.

Recipes here given for 12 are good for 6, you know. But these and the ones given for 6 or 8 may turn out to be the ones you can multiply for a crowd. Also—when you cook these dishes for 12 to feed the family, the part left over is still good, better maybe, next day.

PICNIC IDEAS . . . . . . TIPS FOR THE TIMID

Ever try 2 cans, a can opener, a loaf of bread and thou type of picnic? You can have a good one with a can of chicken, a can of cranberry sauce, and a loaf of crusty bread, with butter for spreading at sandwich time. Add a blunt knife for spreading and slicing, and a can opener for the cans. Fill buttered bread with chicken and a layer of cranberry sauce. And of course you brought paper napkins, a thermos of coffee or lemonade, and are all set. Plenty to eat. No trouble.

Having a picnic over the Fourth of July? Prepare for it the day before by frying chicken, placing cantaloupes to chill. Pack the chicken in waxed paper, the bread-and-butter sandwiches in more waxed paper, and wrap the melons in waxed paper, then in newspaper, and secure in a brown paper bag. This way they keep cold and do not extend their flavor to the fried chicken.

Chill a fruit punch (see the punch recipes and select the one you prefer), carry in a large thermos, adding a few ice cubes to keep it cold. If ginger ale or any sparkling waters are to be added, add them to the cold fruit juice when ready to drink so the soda won't lose its sparkle.

If you have one of those bags that keep everything cold, chilled cans of fruit juice can be packed straight out of the refrigerator, opened and combined in a container when you picnic. The thermos bucket container will carry the big whole-wheat bread and corned beef sandwiches, (canned corned beef mixed with lemon mayonnaise) and goose-liver sandwiches on thin buttered rye bread. Pack these with the chilled cans of juice to keep everything cold. Save the egg cartons to pack deviled eggs, each 2 halves put together after deviling and wrapped in waxed paper. Fine picnic. No utensils except paper napkins, paper cups or plastic glasses, and a can opener for the cans.

Cover the peanut butter in your picnic sandwiches with slices of ripe bananas. These and a good cold fruit punch are the most successful and simple of all picnic fare.

CHURCH SUPPERS . . . . . . EASY AND GOOD

Chicken South Seas
Buttered Green Peas—Pickled Beets
Savory Biscuit Blossoms
Blueberry Deep-Dish Pie
Coffee—Tea

Spanish Pork Chops
Buttered Hot Crusty Rolls
Orange Wedges on Lettuce with tart French Dressing
Banana Refrigerator Cake
Tea

Rock Lobster Tails (Broiled or Baked)
Melted Butter Sauce
Fresh Fruit Salad with Lemon Mayonnaise
Ginger Applesauce Refrigerator Cake
Iced Tea—Hot Coffee

WELCOME-NEIGHBOR . . . . PARTY MENUS

Chiffon Cake with Orange Chocolate Frosting
Apricot Egg Nog

Basketful of Fresh Fruit
Basketful of Rolls or Bread (buttered)
Two or Three Cheeses
Thermos of Coffee

An Assortment of Pies
Thermos of Coffee
Cookies and Cold Milk for the Children

Chocolate Senegalese Cake
(Lemon-Filled, Nutmeg Frosting)
Café au Lait

Hot Gingerbread—Ice-Cold Milk

Strawberry Festival Punch
Banana-Oatmeal Cookies

Fill up the Salad Bowl with One of These:

Big Party Salad
Caesar Salad
Ginger Ale Salad
Melon Salad
Crisp Greens (with French Dressing to add "on location")

Add Any Filling Main Course You Like or One of These:

Tropical Lobster with Curry Sauce
Spiced Ham Loaf
Pork Sausage Tamale Pie
Crabmeat Pie
Shepherd's Pie
Veal Brunswick Stew

Or One of These Assortments to Cook on a Totable Grill:

Kebabs . . . an assortment prepared for "on-location" broiling and eating
Meat or Seafood Patties . . . to broil "on location"

With One of These for Dessert with Coffee:

Deep-Dish Cherry Pie
Blueberry Biscuit Cobbler
Your Favorite Fruit Float
Melon Ice Cream Compote
Chocolate Malted Ice Cream
Orange Velvet Cream Cake

And select a biscuit, roll, or muffin or a flavored-butter loaf to take along.

Juicy Hamburgers on Charcoal Grill
Garlic-Buttered Corn Muffins (toasted on grill)
Casserole of Curry—Scalloped Potatoes
(add curry powder to canned mushroom soup for this)
Pineapple Upside-Down Cake (warmed on the grill)
Hot Coffee

Lamb Hot Pot
Salad Greens with Tomato Wedges
Cranberry Pie
Coffee

Tamale Pie
Hot Corn Sticks
Apple Deep-Dish Pie
Cheese Wedges
Coffee

Steak and Kidney Pie
Baked Potatoes—Zucchini
Fruit Gems

De Luxe Lobster Newburg
Banana Bran Muffins
Lemonade
Lemon Refrigerator Cake
Coffee

Black-Eyed Peas and Spareribs
Rice
Chilled Fruit Compote
Coffee

Indian Hot Pot
Peanut-Buttered Loaf
Ice Cream Cones
Coffee

Hot Mulled Cider
Western Beef Stew
Irish Biscuit Pie
Chilled Melons

Chile Con Carne
Corn Bread (cut into squares, toasted, buttered)
Chilled Grapefruit and Orange Juice
Chocolate-Chip Mint Ice Cream
Unfrosted Angel Cake

Hot Clam Juice
Baked Lima Beans
Spinach with Herb Sauce
Kadota Figs
Hungarian Cream

SHARE-THE-DINNER FEASTS . . EVERYBODY PITCH IN

The high cost of food and families, not to mention the work involved, encouraged a meal with three or four people supplying the food, which has grown in popularity because it is fun.

In a large group, hostesses can rotate so that three or four provide the food for one feast, passing the privilege along until it comes their turn again. The food can be carried to one meeting place, one person's home, or several homes can be visited for a "progressive" party, with nothing moved except your friends, who enjoy canapés and punch at one home, a hot dish and salad at another, and dessert and coffee in the home where everyone intends to spend the evening. Do it as you like. Take a look at the totable Chuck-Wagon Fare Menus, or serve one of these:

Fruit Cocktail Fritters
Cold Grape Ade
Dorothy's Curried Lamb with condiments
Heavenly Rice—Green Salad
Strawberry Shortcakes
Coffee

Curried Eel or Tuna Shortcakes
Crisp Brown Country-Fried Potatoes
Green Beans with Peppers
Garlic Parmesan Bread
Melon Fruit Bowl
Hot Coffee

Hawaiian Fruit Punch
Fish Fillets Baked with Herbed Bread
Artichokes with Butter
New Potatoes in Mustard Watercress Sauce
Assorted Cookies
Mocha Java

Iced Grape Juice
Cheese Pancakes
Barbecued Beef Steak Strips
Buttered Peas
Grapefruit Sections
Chocolate Ladyfinger Icebox Cake

FOOD . . . . FOR THE SQUARE DANCE

Think about the Cooking at the Table Menus, the Chuck-Wagon Fare "Totable" Menus, or one of these:

Cheese Board and Cheese Spreads
Steak and Kidney Pie
Green Salad with French Dressing
Strawberry Float
Coffee

Strawberry Festival Punch
Pecan Chicken Pie
Sage Biscuits
Open Apple Pie

Crisp Cauliflowerets, Celery, Carrot Sticks, Radishes
Lemon Mayonnaise Dip
Susan's Casserole
Chocolate-Orange Soufflé Pie
or
De Luxe Peach Chiffon Pie

SERVE AS HORS D'OEUVRES . . OR A SMÖRGÅSBORD

SOFT-CENTER CHEESE BALLS

Makes 12 to 14 balls:

4 ounces (1¼ cups) grated Swiss cheese
1 tablespoon flour
¼ teaspoon salt
½ teaspoon Worcestershire sauce
3 egg whites, stiffly beaten
bread crumbs

Mix cheese with flour and seasonings. Add stiffly beaten egg whites. Shape mixture into walnut-sized balls. Roll in bread crumbs and fry in deep fat until golden brown. Drain on paper towel. Serve hot or reheated. These can be prepared several hours in advance of serving.

CARAWAY CHEESE DIP

Makes about 3 cups:

½ pound Swiss cheese, finely grated
¾ pound sharp soft Cheddar
2 teaspoons caraway seeds
1 teaspoon dry mustard
⅓ cup cream
salt to taste

Combine all ingredients in a mixing bowl and beat with an electric or rotary beater until blended. Arrange in serving bowl, cover with foil, and chill until ready to serve. Place cheese bowl in center of large plate and surround it with crisp crackers or crisps for dipping up the cheese.

CHEESE SPREADS

Add 1½ teaspoon caraway seeds to 1 pound soft Cheddar. Stir and let stand at room temperature ½ hour before serving.

Make a supply of Swiss cheese spread, which can be used in small portions with various flavorings. This basic cheese spread is made by combining 8 ounces of Swiss cheese, which has been finely chopped or put through the meat chopper, with ⅓ cup heavy cream, ½ pound butter, ¼ cup water, and ⅛ teaspoon cayenne and salt to taste. If you have an electric blender, combining all this is no problem, and the meat-chopper part is not necessary for the cheese. Put everything in the blender, increase the water to ⅓ cup, and let it mix until light and fluffy. Then chill, or immediately divide and flavor with these or any other combinations you wish to try:

- dry mustard, chopped ham, tongue, or hard-cooked egg
- caraway seeds or a little anchovy paste
- drained, chopped pineapple tidbits with a few black walnuts added
- chopped chives or parsley, chervil, dill, thyme, or marjoram
- or try horseradish with a little mustard and some chopped dill pickle.

Fill scooped-out hard rolls with any of these mixtures, chill them, and then slice in thin slices as you would a sausage. These are very pretty if colored with a few drops of vegetable coloring.

GUACAMOLE

It may be that everyone has already made and kept a recipe for this avocado spread. If not, and you want a good one, here it is:

2 avocados, velvety, soft, and ripe
⅓ cup peeled, chopped tomato
2 tablespoons finely chopped onion
1 tablespoon lemon juice
1 teaspoon Worcestershire sauce
salt and pepper to taste

Mash avocados and blend all the ingredients. If it has to be stirred, sprinkle with more lemon juice to keep it from losing its delicate green shade until you are ready to serve it as a delicious dip for small crackers or potato chips, which is my way of introducing a new idea. Guacamole is a beautiful and delicious dressing on red ripe tomato slices served on lettuce leaves.

SHRIMP BUTTER

Blend 1 cup butter, which has been softened, with 1 cup finely chopped cooked shrimp. Add ¼ cup lemon juice, ¼ teaspoon paprika, and salt to taste. Use this either as a dip or to make delicious whole-wheat sandwiches.

MAYONNAISE DIP

Perk up 1 cup of Lemon Mayonnaise by adding 4 tablespoons chopped watercress and 2 tablespoons prepared horseradish. Stir well and surround with potato chips for dipping.

MAYONNAISE PUFFS

Makes 24 puffs:

1 egg white, stiffly beaten
½ cup mayonnaise
2 dozen assorted, salted crackers

Beat egg white until stiff but not dry. Gradually fold in mayonnaise. Pile lightly on crackers. Place on baking sheet and bake in very hot oven (500 F.) 2 to 3 minutes, or until puffed and lightly browned. Serve immediately.

SALAD DREAMS

Put filling of deviled ham, cheese spread, or peanut butter and chili sauce between slices of unbuttered bread. Cut into circles or triangles. Sauté in small amount of salad oil, turning until golden brown on both sides. Serve immediately.

PEANUT-STUFFED CELERY

Makes 24 4-inch lengths:

4 ounces cream cheese
1 tablespoon onion juice
½ teaspoon curry
2 tablespoons heavy cream
12 stalks celery cut in 24 4-inch lengths
½ cup chopped peanuts

Mix cheese with onion juice and curry and cream until thin enough to spread easily when filling the celery. Dip each filled top into the chopped nuts and arrange on a platter. Cover with aluminum foil and chill.

TOMATO TANTALIZERS

Hollow out small yellow or red tomatoes which have been chilled. Fill the tomato cups with any seafood cocktail you like, or a mixture of cooked, chopped seafood held together with a little mayonnaise. Chill and serve as bite-sized appetizers.

CLEMA'S SQUARE-DANCE APPETIZERS . MEN LIKE THESE

LIVERWURST SPREAD

Makes 1 generous cup:

½ pound liverwurst
1 teaspoon lemon juice
½ teaspoon Worcestershire sauce
¼ teaspoon sage
¼ teaspoon paprika

Combine all ingredients and mix until softened.

SARDINE MIX

Makes 1 cup:

10 sardines, mashed
1 teaspoon onion juice
1 teaspoon prepared mustard
1 teaspoon vinegar
½ teaspoon salt
1 teaspoon lemon juice

Combine all ingredients and blend.

CHEESE TRIO

Combine equal parts of cream cheese and bleu cheese with 6 chopped olives and 1 tablespoon chopped chives for each cup of cheese mixture. Add a little thick cream if necessary to mix to a light, fluffy consistency.

CHAPTER 24

CHUCK-WAGON FARE

SPICED HAM LOAF

Makes 26 1-inch-thick slices:

1 quart soft bread crumbs
1 No. 2 can pineapple tidbits
2 eggs
2 pounds ground smoked ham
1 pound ground veal
1 medium onion, chopped
1 tablespoon prepared mustard
¼ teaspoon pepper

Mix all ingredients in large mixing bowl. Pack into well-greased 9-inch tube pan or 2½-quart pan. Bake in moderate oven (350 F.) 2 hours. Pour off drippings and turn loaf onto plate. Serve hot or cold. Garnish with pineapple slices and serve with Hot Mustard Sauce.

HOT MUSTARD SAUCE

Makes 24 servings:

2½ cups (No. 2 can) sliced pineapple
½ cup butter
½ cup flour
1 teaspoon salt
½ teaspoon white pepper
¼ cup prepared mustard

Drain syrup from can of pineapple. (Use pineapple slices for garnishing loaf.) Melt butter in saucepan. Remove pan from heat and stir in flour until smooth. Gradually add ¾ cup pineapple syrup drained from can. Return to heat and cook, stirring constantly, until thick, about 2 minutes. Stir in salt, pepper, and mustard.

WESTERN BEEF STEW

Makes 8 cups:

3 pounds beef
3 teaspoons salt
¾ cup flour
pepper
paprika
½ cup wine vinegar
boiling water
1 tablespoon chili powder
2 cups cut-up carrots
2 cups cut-up celery
1 cup sliced onion
4 cups cut-up potatoes
2 tablespoons minced parsley

Use less tender cuts of beef and cut in uniform pieces, 1- to 2-inch cubes. Dredge in a paper bag containing a mixture of flour, salt, pepper, and paprika. Brown in 3 tablespoons hot fat in heavy kettle, turning to brown on all sides. Add the vinegar and enough boiling water almost to cover. Stir in chili powder. Cover kettle tightly and simmer meat about 2 hours, or until almost tender. *Do not boil.* Add vegetables and continue cooking until tender. To thicken gravy, slowly stir in a paste made by blending flour and water (1½ tablespoons flour for each cup liquid). Continue heating a few more minutes to cook the starch in the flour.

CARAWAY DUMPLINGS

Makes 12 servings:

2 cups corn meal
2 cups sifted flour
6 teaspoons baking powder
2 teaspoons salt
6 tablespoons soft shortening
1¾ cups milk
2 eggs, beaten
2 tablespoons caraway seeds

Sift together dry ingredients. Add remaining ingredients. Beat with rotary beater 1 minute. Drop dumplings on hot stew. Cover; cook 12 minutes without removing cover.

VEAL BRUNSWICK STEW

Makes 8 generous servings:

2 pounds boneless veal, cubed
flour
½ cup salad oil
½ cup chopped onions
3 cups canned tomatoes
1 cup water
1½ tablespoons salt
1 tablespoon Worcestershire sauce
¼ teaspoon cayenne
2 teaspoons sugar
3 cups fresh or canned whole-kernel corn
3 cups fresh or canned lima beans

Cube veal. Put flour in paper bag. Place veal in bag and shake well to coat each piece. Heat salad oil in deep heavy kettle. Sauté veal until light brown. Add onions and cook, stirring occasionally until onions are clear. Add tomatoes, water, and seasonings. Cover and simmer until meat is almost tender. Add remaining vegetables. Continue cooking until vegetables are tender. Serve hot.

CURRIED BEAN SOUP

Makes 14 to 16 cups:

2 pounds dried beans
2 quarts water
2 teaspoons salt
2 pounds white onions
2 stalks celery
1 parsnip
1 green pepper, coarsely chopped
1 small red pepper, or ⅛ teaspoon cayenne
1 cup olive or salad oil
1 tablespoon curry powder

Clean the beans and cover with water; add salt and let stand overnight. Do not drain, but add all other ingredients except curry. Cover and simmer gently over low heat 2 to 3 hours, until beans are tender. Add more water if necessary as the beans cook. Add curry about 30 minutes before beans are done. Remove from heat and put the beans through a strainer. Place over low heat and stir to reheat thoroughly. Serve.

FOOD FOR 12 . . . . 3 COMMUNITY COOKS FEED 36

SPARERIBS AND BLACK-EYED PEAS

Makes 12 generous servings:

4 quarts boiling water
24 pieces spareribs
2 teaspoons salt
1 teaspoon pepper
1 cup coarsely chopped onion
2 bay leaves
6 sprigs parsley
2 pounds black-eyed peas
6 cups cooked rice

When the water is boiling in a large pot, add the spareribs and all other ingredients except peas and rice. Cover and reduce heat. Simmer for 2 hours. Remove ribs to a pan and cover.

• Put the peas to soak in water about 1 hour before ribs are done—or halfway through their cooking. When ribs are removed from the broth, drain peas and put them in the meat juice, cover and cook until tender, about 60 minutes. The peas should be bright-eyed as well as "black-eyed," not crushed or mushy.

• Serve this meal in big soup bowls or deep plates with a helping of rice, topped with the peas and some of the juice and an ample serving of spareribs. Best way is to return ribs to the pot when the peas are cooked, wrap the pot in a checkered tablecloth, and serve from it—a thing of beauty—marvelous smells—right on the table.

Corn-bread sticks are good with this . . . For dessert serve one of the colorful, tart Fruit Compotes to contrast with the rich meaty abundance of the dinner.

2 CASSEROLE DISHES . . . . BEST IN THE WORLD

Spain is one of the most delightful countries in the world to visit, but most of the people are very poor. It may appear strange indeed, after telling you that, to say that the poor people have on their tables several specialties of Spain anyone who has been there would travel miles to enjoy again.

One is Paella made of rice and the addition of various meats, fowl, or seafood. The contents vary, depending upon what the person cooking it can afford—for both the rich and the poor devour Paella—and according to whether or not it is being made inland or near the sea. This recipe is definitely Americanized to use frozen, canned, or fresh seafood, and it requires little time to make.

The second is the Cocido, which is the mainstay of families all over Spain. It, too, can be composed in harmony with the pocketbook. Its base is chick-peas. Paella and Cocido easily live up to the phrase so often heard in Spain when enthusiasm runs riot—"The best in the world." Well . . . we won't argue. These are! And they travel well or stay by the fireside for a satisfying supper. In case you wish to pronounce them as well as eat them, just think of Aunt Ella, only end it with *ya*—pa-el-ya. The Spanish lisp their words, as you probably know, so that if you pronounce Cocido as they do, it is *Cōtheedō*. In Mexico it would be called *Co-seed-o*. Take your choice, but don't fail to make these.

SEAFOOD PAELLA

Makes 12 servings:

3 tablespoons butter or margarine
2 cloves garlic, minced
3 tablespoons chopped onion
4 cups chicken broth, seasoned
2 cups white rice
2 cups brown rice
1 teaspoon saffron (optional)
2 pieces canned pimiento, sliced
1 12-ounce package frozen oysters, or 1½ cups fresh
4 cups fresh seafood, cooked (clams, crabmeat, lobster) or
1 can clams
1 can lobster meat broken into pieces
1 can crabmeat with cartilages carefully removed

Melt butter in 3-quart saucepan. Add garlic and onion and stir over low heat until blended and lightly browned. Add chicken broth and rice and saffron, and pimiento. Cook until rice is tender and has absorbed liquid. Meanwhile put oyster block in large skillet. Cover and place over medium heat until the block can be broken up. Add remaining seafood (if canned, include liquor). Cook uncovered until heated through, stirring constantly. Add to dry cooked rice; stir and serve steaming hot, garnished with parsley.

Add strips of canned pimiento, canned artichoke hearts, glistening black olives to make it a glamorous company dish.

For the finest effect, cook tiny clams in their shells or mussels in their black shells. Add scrubbed shells and all to the rice. Any way you make it, this is pretty and marvelously appetizing. If you want to carry this dish, make it in a Dutch oven, cover it tightly the minute it is finished. It can be reheated quickly or may not need reheating.

• Use shredded saffron by soaking in part of the liquid 2 hours. Strain and use liquid only.

SPANISH COCIDO A GOOD BOILED DINNER

Makes 8 servings:

1 pound (2 cups) chick-peas
4 cups water
2 tablespoons salt
4 quarts water
1 ham hock, or bone from baked ham with some meat on it
1 teaspoon pepper
6 medium onions, peeled
8 ¼-inch-thick slices smoked sausage
1½ cups cubed potatoes
1 cup cubed yellow turnips
1 cup cubed white turnips
1 large head cabbage cut into 8 wedges

Clean peas. Cover with water; add salt. Cover and let stand 6 hours or overnight. Drain and put peas in a large pot for cooking. Add 4 quarts water, ham, pepper, and onions. Cover and place over high heat until water begins to boil; reduce heat and simmer 1 hour. Add sausage slices and vegetables. Cover and continue cooking 30 minutes, or until peas are tender.

The vegetables are cut into 1½-inch cubes or simply quartered. Carrots in chunks or slices or small tender young whole carrots can be added with the vegetables. If you want to add chicken to this, it is very good. Put the cut-up chicken into the pot when it first comes to a boil.

If there has not been time to soak the peas, put them on to cook 4½ hours before you want to serve them, adding 2 teaspoons salt and the vegetables ½ hour before cooking is done.

FOR BIG DOIN'S . . CURRY FLAVOR FROM INDIA

INDIAN HOT POT

Makes 12 servings:

12 meaty pieces rabbit or chicken
¾ cup flour
2 teaspoons salt
1 teaspoon freshly ground black pepper
1 teaspoon mace
1½ tablespoons curry powder
½ cup butter or margarine
½ cup bacon drippings
1 cup chopped onion
12 cups chicken bouillon
2 cups apple slices, uncooked
⅔ cup moist coconut
2 teaspoons brown sugar
3 cups cooked rice

Rinse meat in cold water and drain on paper towel. Combine flour and seasonings in a paper bag; add few pieces of meat at a time, shake until meat is thoroughly coated. Melt butter and bacon fat in Dutch oven. Add meat and brown on all sides, removing each piece as browned. Add onion to the fat and cook until it begins to brown. Stir in flour from the bag and when lightly browned slowly add chicken bouillon. Add apple, brown sugar, coconut and return browned meat to the pot. Cover and allow to simmer over low heat until tender, about 2 hours. Serve in soup bowls with a piece of meat in each, surrounded by the thin soup and a spoonful of rice. If you want to serve 2 pieces of meat for each person, there is no harm in putting extra rabbit or chicken in the pot. If you abhor a thin soup, thicken the soup with flour, 1½ tablespoons per cup of thin broth.

ROSEMARY FLAVOR . . . . . FROM CONNECTICUT

LAMB HOT POT

• Serve hot crisp rolls with this, and a crisp vegetable salad made with lettuce, chicory, fresh spinach, or watercress and ripe tomato wedges—drenched at the last minute with French dressing.

• Fruit pie—any kind you like, really—is good with this.

Makes 12 servings:

3 pounds shoulder or breast of lamb, cubed
1 cup flour seasoned with 1½ teaspoons salt, 1 teaspoon pepper
¼ cup bacon drippings
2 cloves garlic
½ cup hot water
1 teaspoon rosemary
½ cup flour
3 tablespoons butter or margarine
4 cups water
6 cups cubed potatoes
1¼ cups chopped onion
2 cups sliced carrots
3 cups green beans

Combine meat and seasoned flour in paper bag. Shake until meat is coated. Melt bacon fat in large skillet and brown lamb cubes on all sides. Place in large casserole; add garlic and ½ cup water. Cover and bake in moderate oven (350 F.) 30 minutes. Remove garlic cloves and discard. Meanwhile combine rosemary with flour and stir into butter or margarine which has been melted in a skillet. Stir until browned. Add 4 cups of water slowly, stirring until gravy is thick. Salt to taste. Add potatoes, onions, and carrots to the meat in the casserole and cover with the gravy. Cover and continue baking another hour. Stir; add green beans. Cover and bake another 15 minutes.

BEEF STEW

Makes 12 servings:

½ pound bacon cut in pieces
3 pounds chuck beef cut in pieces
12 small onions, finely sliced
1 clove garlic
1 cup tomato juice
4 cups water
2 tablespoons meat extract
6 carrots, cut
8 medium-sized potatoes
½ cup diced celery (optional)
1 yellow turnip
2 tablespoons salt
¼ teaspoon pepper
¼ teaspoon rosemary
½ teaspoon basil
¼ teaspoon orange peel
½ cup flour
1 cup water
1 tablespoon flavored-for-salads wine vinegar (or wine vinegar)

Fry bacon pieces slowly in iron kettle. When slightly brown, remove and set aside. Add meat which has been rolled in flour; cook slowly until well browned. Add onions and garlic and cook over low heat 10 minutes. Add tomato juice and 4 cups water in which meat extract has been dissolved. Cover and simmer 2 hours. Add carrots, potatoes, celery, turnip, bacon pieces, salt, pepper, herbs, and orange peel. Cook 1 hour. Strain off juice—there should be 4 cups. If not, add tomato juice to make 4 cups. Combine flour with 1 cup cold water. Blend and stir into the juice. Cook over low heat until thick. Check gravy for seasoning; add wine vinegar. Pour over stew and cook 5 minutes longer.

COOK OR CARRY . . . . . IN PRESSURE COOKER

HUNGARIAN GOULASH

Makes 12 servings:

6 pounds beef (round) cut in 2-inch cubes
⅔ cup flour
⅓ cup bacon drippings
2 cups chopped onions
1 tablespoon salt
2 tablespoons sweet paprika
2 bay leaves
2 tablespoons caraway seeds
½ tablespoon marjoram
2 tablespoons chopped parsley
¼ cup cider
½ cup beef bouillon

Dredge meat in flour. Melt bacon fat in pressure cooker and add cubed meat, stirring constantly until browned on all sides. Add onions and seasonings and stir well. Add liquids; close the cooker and when 15 pounds pressure has been reached, reduce heat and cook at 15-pound pressure 25 minutes. Remove from heat but do not open until the pressure has been reduced. The meat provides the juice for Goulash, but if there is not enough gravy, make more in a skillet by melting 2 tablespoons butter or margarine, stirring in 3 tablespoons flour, and when blended and browned slowly stirring in 2 cups milk. Stir until thickened. Pour into the pot and seal for convenient carrying.

Hungarian Goulash, of course, holds a top place along with Steak and Kidney Pie as one of "the best meals in the world" and is good for company or for the family any day in the week. Don't save it for *totin'* fare alone. A pressure cooker is not necessary for Goulash.

It can also be cooked in a big iron pot or Dutch oven over very low heat until meat is tender, 2 to 3 hours, adding herbs and parsley the last ½ hour of cooking.

CHILE CON CARNE

Makes 24 cups:

1 cup butter or margarine
1½ cups finely chopped onions
7 large cloves garlic, chopped
8 cups (4 pounds) ground beef put through grinder twice
3 tablespoons chili powder
1 tablespoon salt
1 teaspoon red pepper
1 teaspoon black pepper
6 cans condensed tomato soup
1 can (No. 10) red kidney beans
2 cans beef bouillon

Melt butter or margarine in large pan (or make this in 2 pans and then pour it into a single large pot for carrying and serving). Add onion, garlic, and beef, stirring until meat is lightly browned. Add remaining ingredients. Cover and cook 30 minutes, stirring occasionally. Use chuck or round beef for this, but chuck has a fine flavor and is less expensive.

• Crusty buttered rolls, garlic-buttered French bread, or toasted corn bread squares are good with this.

BREAD FOR BIG DOIN'S . . . 4 SEASONED LOAVES

TOASTED FINGER LOAVES

Make fragrant toasted finger loaves by trimming crusts from white unsliced loaf *except bottom,* which remains. Slice down center to, but not through, the bottom crust. Slice across 6 or 8 times to form stubby "fingers." Brush these with seasoned, softened butter. Brown in hot oven (425 F.) 10 to 15 minutes, or until brown. Serve oven-hot.

GARLIC-MUSTARD FINGERS

Makes 8 to 12 Fingers:

3 cloves garlic, finely chopped
3 tablespoons rich prepared mustard
¼ cup melted butter or margarine
1 loaf unsliced bread

Combine garlic, mustard, and butter. Blend and spread on the fingers.

PAPRIKA LOAF

Makes 8 to 12 Fingers:

Add ½ teaspoon paprika to ¼ cup butter; mix well. Use a pastry brush to butter the fingers and press them together before browning in the oven.

PEANUT BUTTER LOAF

Makes 16 to 24 Fingers:

Add ⅓ cup peanut butter to ½ cup butter; blend. Spread on 2 loaves which have been cut into fingers. Brown.

CHEESE-TOPPED FRENCH BREAD

Have 1 6-ounce cheese roll, garlic-flavored or plain, at room temperature. Place in a bowl and blend in ¼ cup softened butter or margarine and ¼ cup vinegar, beating until smooth. Cut a loaf of French bread in half lengthwise, then slice crosswise, cutting down to the crust but not through it. Spread cut sides of bread with cheese mixture; sprinkle with paprika. Just before serving, toast under the broiler until delicately browned.

• Use any of the spreads for "Finger" Loaves on the French bread slices. Heat and serve hot.

RYE BREAD—FOR SANDWICHES

Makes 2 loaves:

3 packages active dry yeast
1 cup warm water (110 to 115 F.)
3 teaspoons salt
2 tablespoons ground *caraway seeds*
½ cup light molasses
½ cup hot water
2 tablespoons shortening
3½ cups sifted *all-purpose flour*
2¾ cups sifted *rye flour*

Dissolve yeast in warm water. Combine salt, caraway seeds, molasses, hot water, and shortening. Cool to lukewarm. Add yeast. Mix the all-purpose and rye flour; gradually stir into the yeast mixture. Rub a little flour onto the pastry board to prevent dough from sticking. Turn the dough onto the board; knead until smooth and satiny. Shape into a ball and place in a greased bowl; coat all sides with grease by turning it over in the bowl. Cover. Let rise in a warm place (80 to 85 F.) until double in size, 1½ to 2 hours. Punch down dough; form into a ball. Cover; let rest 10 minutes. Then shape into 2 loaves. Place in a greased 9 x 5 x 3-inch bread pan sprinkled with corn meal. Cover; let rise in a warm place until double in size, about 1 hour. Brush lightly with cold water. Bake 10 minutes in preheated hot oven (450 F.); reduce heat to moderate (350 F.). Bake 25 to 30 minutes. To prevent burning crust, cover with brown paper after baking 25 minutes.

BREAD STRIPS

Makes 24 sticks:

4 slices bread, ⅝-inch thick
1 teaspoon salt
paprika
2 tablespoons salad oil
¼ cup grated cheese
poppy seeds

Remove crusts from bread; cut each thick slice into 6 equal-size strips. Add salt and paprika to salad oil. Brush all sides of bread strips with salad oil; sprinkle with grated cheese, poppy or celery seeds. Place on ungreased baking sheet. Bake in hot oven (400 F.) 8 to 10 minutes, or until golden brown.

NOTE. Be sure to look at roll, biscuit, and bread recipes pp. 9–23.

SAVORY BREAD PUDDING

This casserole can replace bread and butter at a big gathering. It is a change and so easy to serve.

Makes 20 cups:

8 cups whole-wheat or protein bread, cubed and toasted
1 pound (2 cups) Cheddar cheese, grated
4 cups (1 quart) milk
1 cup chicken broth
4 eggs, beaten lightly
1 teaspoon salt
1 teaspoon dry mustard
2 teaspoons caraway seeds
1 teaspoon paprika
4 tablespoons chopped parsley

Grease a 6-quart casserole (or deep flat roasting pan, or use 2 3-quart casseroles) and arrange alternate layers of toasted bread cubes and grated cheese, ending with a layer of cheese. Place milk in a saucepan over low heat; add chicken broth, beaten eggs, salt, and spices, stirring until well blended. When warm but not boiling, pour over the bread and cheese mixture. Sprinkle with chopped parsley and bake in moderately hot oven (375 F.) about 50 minutes.

The bread cubes for this can be made very quickly by placing sliced bread, preferably 1 day old, on a chopping board and cutting through the whole loaf to form ½-inch cubes. Trim crusts if you must or leave them be.

CHAPTER 25

PLANNING FOOD FOR 50

It is a good idea to take for granted that everyone at a big gathering will be hungry, that the food will be good and the servings generous. On this theory, and using 1 measuring cup (not a teacup) for all measurements, as is done throughout this book, here is what you need to buy when its *Food for 50*.

TO SERVE	EACH PERSON	BUY
Bread		
Buttered rolls	1 roll with 1" cube butter in it	50 rolls 2 pounds butter
Toasted or Cheese Loaf Fingers	2–3 fingers	9 loaves 2 pounds butter 1 pound cheese
Plain half slices	3 pieces ½ ounce butter	4 loaves 1½ pounds butter
Coffee		
Regular	5–6 ounces (standard coffee cup)	1 pound, 2½ gallons water (2 pounds, 5 gallons water for 2 cups per person)
Instant	1 cup	2 2-ounce jars—10 quarts water
Cream (coffee)	2 tablespoons	1½ quarts
Cream (whipping)	1 tablespoon (heaping)	1 quart
Sugar (coffee)	1½ teaspoons	1 pound
Cubed sugar	1 large or 2 small	1 pound large cubes ½ pound small cubes

TO SERVE . .	.EACH PERSON .	BUY
Cake	1 slice	4 large cakes (12–14 slices each)
Desserts		
Cobblers, Fruit Floats, Puddings	¾-cup size	See recipes and increase by duplicate cooking
Ice cream, bulk	8 servings per quart	6½ quarts
Ice cream, brick	6 servings per brick	8½ quarts
Pies	1/6 of 9" pie	See quantity recipes
Meat		
Beef, pot roast, round	3–3½ ounces cooked	18–20 pounds
beef, standing rib	3–3½ ounces cooked	20–25 pounds
Chicken (for dishes containing cut-up cooked meat)	1½ ounces cooked clear meat	13–17 pounds drawn weight 17–20 pounds dressed weight
Chicken (roast)	2–3 ounces clear meat	25–35 pounds drawn weight 35–50 pounds dressed weight
Ground meat balls or loaf	1/5 pound	12 pounds
Roast leg of lamb	2½–3 ounces	20–35 pounds. Great variation in cooking and carving
Turkey (hen or tom)	2–3 ounces clear meat	20–25 pounds drawn weight 25–35 pounds dressed weight
Punch	1 punch cup	12½ quarts (50 cups). See quantity recipes
Salads	½-cup size	6½ quarts
Salad Dressing	1 tablespoon	4 cups
Soups	6–8 ounces	10–12 quarts See soup recipes
Vegetables		
Fresh	½ cup plus sauce or dressing	See Buying Guide List
Canned	½ cup	3 No. 10 cans
Frozen	½-cup serving	16 packages

HOW MUCH TO BUY . . . . FRESH VEGETABLES

Here is a chart to show you how many cups you can expect from a given amount of fresh vegetables. Only 13—considered the most aggravating and "hard to estimate"—are included. Since there is not space for the hundred or so that could be listed, these estimates will help you in figuring the others. No sauce, butter, liquid is included in the cup measurements. And by the way, ½ cup—measuring cup, that is—is considered a modest serving.

FRESH VEGETABLES	YOU BUY THIS MUCH	TO MAKE THIS NUMBER OF CUPS AFTER COOKING
Snap Beans	1 pound	3½ cups
Beets, topped	2 pounds	4 cups
Broccoli	1¾ pounds	6 servings (5 ounces each)
Brussels Sprouts	2 pounds	5 cups
Cabbage, cut in wedges	1¾ pounds	5 servings (4 ounces each)
Carrots, sliced	2 pounds	4½ cups
Cauliflower	1¼ pounds	4 cups
Celery, diced with tops	1-pound bunch	3 cups
Parsnips, cut in 2-inch strips	2 pounds	5 cups
Potatoes, mashed	2 pounds	4 cups
Spinach	2 pounds	4 cups
Sweet potatoes, mashed	2 pounds	3 cups
Turnips, diced	2 pounds	4 cups

HOW MUCH TO MAKE . . WHEN IT'S SOUP OR SALAD

OYSTER STEW QUICK TO MAKE—EASY TO INCREASE

Makes 12 cups:

2 12-ounce packages frozen oysters
milk
cream or evaporated milk, undiluted
¼ cup chopped onion
½ cup butter
1½ teaspoons salt
½ teaspoon pepper
¼ teaspoon marjoram (optional)
1¼ teaspoons thyme (optional)
2 tablespoons parsley

Place frozen oysters in 4-quart or larger saucepan. Cover; place over high heat until blocks can be broken apart with a fork or until edges of oysters begin to curl. Remove from heat, because oysters must be heated but not overcooked. Curling edges are a warning to quit the cooking. Drain oysters, reserving liquid. Measure oyster liquor; add milk and cream (or evaporated milk) in equal parts to make a total of 9 cups of liquid. Return oysters and liquid to the pot. Add butter, salt, pepper, and herbs. Place over low heat until liquid begins to simmer. Serve immediately, garnished with parsley.

For a richer stew, use all cream instead of milk.

POTATO SOUP FOR 50

Makes 56 cups:

16 cups mashed potatoes (frozen packages or freshly cooked)
7½ cups (3 No. 2 cans) onions
¼ cup salt
1½ cups melted butter or margarine
6 cans undiluted evaporated milk, heated
3 quarts boiling water
4 quarts seasoned chicken broth
1 teaspoon cayenne
⅓ cup Worcestershire sauce
2 cups chopped chives or parsley or
2 cups crushed, crisped bacon or French-fried onion slices

Combine mashed potatoes, onions, salt, and butter in 14-quart pot or in two 8-quart pots, making half recipe in each. Stir with potato masher until blended. Add warm milk slowly, beating until blended into mixture. Add water, chicken broth, and seasonings. Stir until blended and test seasoning, adding salt if necessary. Heat but do not boil; cover between servings.

CAESAR SALAD

Caesar Salad has attained fame in Southern California since Chef Caesar in Agua Caliente made that famous resort still more famous by originating this combination of greens which distinguishes itself by the use of raw egg and two types of cheese in the dressing. You may have encountered Caesar Salad already, but if not, here is how Chef Caesar made it:

TO PREPARE THE GARLIC-FLAVORED OIL: Cut 3 or 4 cloves of garlic into 1 cup olive oil. Let stand at room temperature for several hours before using. (Save any unused garlic oil for your next salad.)

Prepare about 2 cups crisp croutons by cutting bread into tiny cubes and toasting in a slow oven (300 F.) until thoroughly crisped and slightly browned.

P.S. It is a good idea to have croutons and garlic oil on hand all the time anyway.

LAST-MINUTE MIXING: Break iceberg lettuce into bite-size pieces—about 3 quarts. (Add any other odds and ends of greens you may have —romaine, watercress, etc.)

3 quarts iceberg lettuce, broken into small pieces
any greens you like
½ cup garlic-flavored oil
½ cup unseasoned salad oil—corn, cottonseed or peanut oil
1 tablespoon Worcestershire sauce
½ teaspoon dry mustard
salt and pepper
½ cup grated hard cheese
¼ cup Roquefort-type cheese
1 uncooked egg
½ cup lemon juice and pulp (2 to 3 lemons)
2 cups browned croutons

Put lettuce in a big salad bowl. Remove garlic from oil. Pour ¼ cup of the unseasoned oil over lettuce. Sprinkle lettuce with the Worcestershire sauce, mustard, salt, pepper, and grated cheese. Crumble the Roquefort cheese. Add. Break the unbeaten raw egg directly onto the greens. Pour on the lemon juice and pulp. Mix salad so thoroughly that every leaf is coated with the egg, seasonings, and cheese. Dip the crisp croutons into the remaining garlic oil and drain. Mix croutons into the salad just at the instant of serving.

CRANBERRY-GRAPEFRUIT SALAD

Makes 48 or 40 individual molds
Fills 1 pan, 18¼ x 12⅛ x 2 inches:

10½ envelopes unflavored gelatin
2 cups cold water
1 No. 10 can jellied cranberry sauce
8 cups (12 No. 80 cans) grapefruit sections, drained
3 cups (¾ pound) almonds, shredded

Soak gelatin in cold water 5 minutes. Dissolve over boiling water. Put cranberry sauce in saucepan over low heat. Beat with wire whip until smooth. Add dissolved gelatin and continue beating until well blended. Chill until slightly thickened. Pour half the thickened cranberry mixture into pan. Arrange grapefruit sections in a uniform layer over top of sauce; sprinkle nuts over fruits; cover fruit and nuts with remaining sauce. See that the gelatin mixture is evenly blended with fruit and nuts. Chill until firm.

CRANBERRY-APPLE SALAD

Makes 80 to 90 ½-cup servings
Fills 2 pans, 18¼ x 12⅛ x 2 inches:
Serve 2 x 2½-inch squares

9 envelopes unflavored gelatin
1½ cups cold water
1 can (No. 10) cranberry sauce
1½ cups (8 No. 300 cans) lemon juice
3 quarts ginger ale
2¼ quarts (10 to 12 medium) diced, unpeeled apples
2¼ quarts (2 pounds) diced celery
1 quart (1 pound) chopped nutmeats

Soak gelatin in cold water 5 minutes. Dissolve over boiling water. Heat jellied cranberry sauce over low heat, stirring with wire whip until smooth. Add dissolved gelatin and continue beating until smooth. Add lemon juice and ginger ale and stir until ingredients are thoroughly mixed. Chill until mixture starts to thicken. Fold in remaining ingredients. Chill until firm.

DESSERT FOR 50 . . . . 2 GUIDING RECIPES

PEACH-PLUM COBBLER

Makes 6¾ quarts fruit mixture; 50 biscuits; 1 sweet biscuit and ½ cup fruit each for 50:

INGREDIENTS	MEASURE OR WEIGHT	AMOUNT TO BUY
canned blue plums and juice	3 quarts	4 No. 2½ cans
canned sliced peaches and juice	3 quarts	4 No. 2½ cans
quick-cooking tapioca	¾ cup	1 8-ounce package

INGREDIENTS	MEASURE OR WEIGHT	AMOUNT TO BUY
sugar	2⅔ cups (1 pound 2 ounces)	2 pounds
flour	2 quarts, sifted (2 pounds)	2 pounds
double-acting baking powder	3 tablespoons	
salt	2 tablespoons	
sugar	⅓ cup	
shortening	2 cups	1 pound
eggs	4	4 eggs
milk	2 cups	1 pint

Drain fruits. Bring combined fruit juices to a boil. Combine quick-cooking tapioca and first amount of sugar; add to hot juice. Cook and stir until mixture thickens slightly; return to a boil. Remove from heat. Remove pits from drained plums. Add plums and peaches to hot tapioca mixture. Pour into shallow baking pans, distributing fruit evenly.

Sift together flour, baking powder, salt, and remaining sugar. Cut in shortening until mixture resembles coarse meal. Beat eggs and combine with milk. Add to dry ingredients, mixing until soft dough is formed. With a small scoop, drop dough on top of hot fruit mixture in pans. Bake in hot oven (400 F.) 20 to 25 minutes, or until biscuits are delicately browned. Serve hot.

Other Fruit Cobblers

Use other fruit combinations in similar quantities to make cobblers for 50, but always test the combinations you try. For sweetening, add more sugar for tart fruit.

PINEAPPLE CHIFFON PIE

Makes 48 servings:

1 can (No. 10) crushed pineapple (12 cups)
6 envelopes unflavored gelatin
2¾ cups syrup drained from crushed pineapple
24 egg yolks
2 cups sugar
2 cups syrup drained from crushed pineapple
⅔ cup lemon juice
½ cup grated lemon peel
24 egg whites
2 cups sugar
¼ teaspoon salt
8 baked 9-inch pie shells
chopped nuts
whipped cream

Drain pineapple thoroughly, reserving syrup. Soften gelatin in 2⅔ cups pineapple syrup. Beat egg yolks. Add 2 cups sugar and 2 cups pineapple syrup. Place in top of double boiler. Cook over hot water, stirring constantly until mixture thickens. Remove from hot water; add gelatin and stir until dissolved. Add lemon juice and peel and well-drained crushed pineapple. Let cool until mixture begins to congeal. Beat egg whites until stiff and carefully fold into mixture with remaining 2 cups sugar and salt. Pour into 8 baked and cooled 9-inch pie shells. Chill about 3 hours, or until set. Garnish top of pies with chopped nuts and whipped cream.

See Coffees and Punches for quantity recipes.

FOOD FOR THE BEREAVED . . SERVING IN A CRISIS

One of the impossible experiences in life is to know that a home must go on, its members being fed, when the loss of one of them has struck that home with grief. The blessings of friendship are never greater than at a time like this, when friends and neighbors take on the intolerable burden of preparing food for the family and for all those added to it who must also be fed during the emergency.

Unfortunately, fried chicken or ham, pies and cakes are apt to show up in abundance. These reveal generosity of time-consuming preparation by busy people. An attractive gift when it is placed on the table to help express the sympathy of the donor.

Less attractive to look at but easier on the strained and troubled family and relatives would be a nourishing soup. A good soup everybody will like. Most soups have the advantage of being improved as they are heated, or will stay unharmed and steaming hot for hours on end far into the night to fit into the irregular hours of the home where there is trouble.

A soup pot on a warmer, coffee on another or the makings for tea, bread and butter with cheese and a bowl of fruit offer delicious, sustaining, appetizing food as well as digestible fare for all those who would help themselves. These will be there, ready, adjustable, adequate, as delicious and attractive hours after the table was arranged as when the food first appeared.

A banana milk shake is delicious, but it also is almost the perfect food. Make one for the person who will eat nothing else. Serve Banana Milk Shake as dessert for everybody.

If cold meats, despite this suggestion, still are your choice, then serve a green salad with them and bread and butter. That should be enough for the filling part. For dessert have something simple, like berries in a bowl to spoon over ice cream, or a big bowl of soft custard, hot or cold, served with fresh nutmeg grated over it and cream on the side.

These require less time to prepare than the pastries or cakes, and they are kinder to those who need sustenance and are more easily assimilated than a heavier meal.

Here are recipes for the Banana Milk Shake, 2 quickly made soups, and the croutons so palatable with them. Sprinkle the croutons over the soup and serve no bread.

CREAMED CHICKEN SOUP

Makes 8 cups:

6 cups chicken broth
2 cups undiluted evaporated milk
¼ teaspoon nutmeg
onion salt to taste

Combine and heat in the top of a double boiler or in a saucepan over low heat, being careful not to let it boil.

This soup is quickly made and easy to increase either by doubling the recipe or by adding 2 or 3 cups chopped chicken for this amount of soup.

HERB CROUTONS

⅓ cup salad oil
¼ cup butter
1 tablespoon finely chopped onion
1 teaspoon salt
1 teaspoon paprika
½ teaspoon thyme
4 cups diced bread

Combine butter, salad oil, and minced onion; stir in salt, paprika, and thyme for a moment before adding the bread cubes, stirring them constantly until browned on all sides. Remove and serve with soups.

QUICK CRAB BISQUE

Makes about 12 cups:

¼ cup butter
½ cup chopped onion
2 cans tomato soup
2 cans undiluted cream of pea soup
1 can chicken broth
1 tablespoon chopped lemon peel
½ teaspoon allspice
2 teaspoons Worcestershire sauce
few grains cayenne
2½ cups crab flakes
2 cups undiluted evaporated milk, heated

Melt butter in 4-quart saucepan. Add onion and stir until it begins to brown. Add soups, diluting only tomato soup as instructed on the can. Stir until blended. Add lemon peel and seasonings and crab flakes. Stir until heated thoroughly (do not boil) and pour into serving pot or casserole. Add the hot milk, stirring constantly. Test for seasoning, adding salt to taste.

Serve immediately, or keep hot over a warmer, but do not allow it to boil at any time.

BANANA MILK SHAKE

Makes about 12 cups:

8 fully ripe bananas
2 quarts (8 cups) cold milk
1 cup crushed ice
1 pint vanilla ice cream

Select fully ripe bananas with peels flecked with brown. Remove peels; slice bananas into a bowl and beat with a rotary beater or electric mixer until smooth and creamy. Add milk; mix well. Add ice and vanilla ice cream and stir with a spoon to chill the contents of the bowl thoroughly. Serve in 2 large pitchers.

The banana and milk combination is a delicious, nourishing, almost perfect food and will agree with all ages.

part seven

NOVEMBER . . .
CHRISTMAS IS COMING

CHAPTER 26
THE SPIRIT OF CHRISTMAS

The pies were bubbling in the oven, mince with Christmas-bell pastry cutouts on top, cherry crisscross, and a cranberry meringue. These were for Nancy, a Christmas present she could bring out for thawing. The first snow was falling in time for Thanksgiving, which would be here in a few more days. Before it arrived, my pies would be done and in the freezer. Already baked pies, frozen, are not my preference. They are often better, fresher, in my opinion, when frozen unbaked, the baking being done when about ready to be eaten. But you don't have to do it that way.

Children of all ages were expected during the holidays at our house. Boys and girls should be talked with as well as fed when they are around the house, and holiday time is my big opportunity. No use spending a lot of time or more money than is in the kitchen purse for feeding the lot of them if I just get a head start now. That is what refrigerators are for, and oh, happy days these, with a freezing unit for holding my bundles. There is enough to do most of the feeding, with the minimum time spent in cooking, and with dallying in the kitchen rather than paying attention while I'm there, for the fun of it during the holidays is that I am rarely there alone. Good talk in the kitchen is the best there is, provided the cook doesn't have to think, "Two tablespoons flour . . . put in that butter before it burns, you idiot, it is already melted . . ." Things like that are upsetting and are to be avoided.

Christmas begins with the first present you make. Plan to make hard sauce in several different flavors, then save small baby-food jars for packaging your presents. Remove the tops of the jars with care, avoiding bending them, then paint the top of each one in a bright color or decorate with a Christmas sticker. Straighten a paper clip and use it dipped in colored enamel to make dots on the jar to reveal what kind of hard sauce it contains.

Make Ice Cream Sauces. Bottle them as you do the hard sauces.

If you have herbs growing in your garden, dry and bottle some for your friends in these same small containers, begged or borrowed from other households if you don't collect enough yourself. Save the wooden containers berries and fruit come in during the summer. Give them a bright coat of shocking pink or turquoise-blue paint and fill them with candies or homemade cookies wrapped in cellophane, and you have a fine present for someone for Christmas.

More time than money? Then give for Christmas: an envelope in which you offer your services, whatever your talents may be. To make a pair of curtains, to make a slip cover, to baby-sit a specified number of hours. This is a wonderful "time in the bank" for any young mother who receives it.

MAKE THE DECORATIONS . . . . FOR YOUR TREE

How long has it been since anyone in the family made ropes of popcorn or cranberries to string on the branches? If there are any children about, get them busy making yards and yards of these as well as colored paper chains which every child knows how to make. Wrap mints and hard candies in gay tissue-paper squares. Tie with a contrasting piece of yarn, make a bow, and let these dangle from the Christmas tree. Make yarn loops to secure between double paper stars or tiny Christmas stockings or hats cut out of the metallic paper pasted together, with the yarn loop caught inside when pasting; the loops dangle these little charmers from the Christmas tree. Cover boxes with wallpaper to hold some of the presents.

The food on a Christmas table is a decoration, but did you ever think of making a special cloth? Buy a few yards of theatrical gauze or tarletan. Get enough to cover the table and hang down ½ yard at each end. Two shades are better than one, since both colors show, and you could get a pure green and a bright red, putting one over the other. Cut the edges into scallops. Paste metallic-paper cutouts in each scallop.

Fill a tray with fruit or nuts or vegetables stacked in oblong rounds and push long candles down among them. On Christmas Day surround the vegetable center with either green leaves or with Christmas balls, or fill a glass bowl with nuts and mints and hard Christmas candies and candy canes poking out in various directions.

Have the children make many of the Christmas angels they learned to make in school. Make tiny ones, 2 or 3 dozen, to put on the Christmas tree. Make a big one for the center of the table, or make 2 medium ones to go on either side of the fruit bowl. If you are short of decorations for the Christmas tree, put some of the candy canes on the branches and dangle those foil-wrapped chocolate coins and lollipops on the tree. If you make crystallized ginger or candied orange peel, wrap pieces in cellophane and tie with colored yarn to hang from the tree.

Make a Christmas-tree salad to sit beside each plate for Christmas Day by slicing canned cranberry jelly ½ inch thick. Arrange can-sized rounds at the bottom and cut small ones for the second circle on top and a still smaller one on top of that until you have 4 graduated rounds of jelly. Add tiny little sugared gumdrops at intervals around the ledges to decorate the tree. And when you bake cookies, make cut outs which, when colorfully decorated, can be hung on the tree with yarn. Make ribbon bows to decorate a little tree. Fill the plastic bags usually used for storing food in the freezer with popcorn balls—don't fill them too full—and tie with red ribbon bows.

For center-of-the-table decorations use coarse wire mesh to make a cone, then build a little Christmas tree by sticking branches of spruce or pine into this and put a metallic star or elongated peak at the top, and either leave the rest of the tree undecorated or hang the tiniest of Christmas balls on the branches.

Another table decoration that can be made in a few minutes by using a three- or four-tiered china tea sandwich plate is to pile the tiers with cookie or popcorn balls.

Don't forget the sparkle any crystal you possess will add to the house. Clean it in ammonia water, bring out old vases you haven't used for years, and fill them with fragrant greens; these in cut glass, of course. Any crystal you have twinkles beautifully when filled with nuts or candles, greens or flowers or fruit or Christmas balls.

NOW IS A GOOD TIME . TO BAKE XMAS DECORATIONS

Mix the dough for the cookie trimmings now and freeze it. Or do the whole job as part of the Christmas excitement when the holidays arrive. Don't forget the biscuit Christmas tree and biscuit wreath described in Breads. Or bake a coffee ring and cover it with snowy frosting and candied cherries to resemble holly berries. Any of the three are a merry beginning on Christmas morning. However, let's stop anticipating and plan to bake these for Christmas. Nothing to stop you from decorating a whole tree with cookies, in the church or at home. Quite a sight, and they need not crowd off strings of cranberries or popcorn ropes.

CANDY TREE TRIMS

6 cups puffed rice
1 cup light corn syrup
½ teaspoon salt
1 teaspoon vinegar
2 tablespoons butter or margarine
1 teaspoon vanilla

Measure puffed rice into a shallow pan. Heat in a moderate oven (350 F.) 10 minutes. Pour puffed rice into a large greased bowl. Combine syrup, salt, and vinegar in a saucepan; cook until a few drops in cold water form a soft ball. Remove from heat. Add butter and vanilla; blend. Mixing quickly, gradually pour cooked syrup over the puffed rice. With greased hands shape into 1-inch balls. String on a thread with gumdrops between for Christmas garlands. Mixture may also be formed into other holiday shapes.

ORNAMENT COOKIES

Makes 3 dozen cookies:

1½ cups sifted enriched flour
1 teaspoon soda
½ teaspoon salt
⅔ cup shortening, soft
1 cup brown sugar
1 egg
¼ cup water
1 teaspoon vanilla
2 cups uncooked oats, quick or old-fashioned

Sift together flour, soda, and salt into a bowl. Add shortening, sugar, egg, water, and vanilla. Beat until smooth, about 2 minutes. Fold in rolled oats. Roll out on lightly floured board to ⅛-inch thickness; cut into Santas, angels, stars, and trees with floured cookie cutter. Bake on greased baking sheet in a moderate oven (350 F.) 12 to 15 minutes. When cool, spread the cookies with confectioners' sugar frosting. Decorate with sugar, candies, or coconut. Cut red ribbon in 12-inch lengths and fold in half. Spread back of each cookie with frosting; place center of ribbon in moist frosting on back of cookie; mount on 5-inch paper doily. When frosting is dry, tie on your Christmas tree.

CANDY SNOWMAN

15 cups puffed rice (about 1½ packages)
2½ cups light corn syrup
1 teaspoon salt
1 tablespoon vinegar
⅓ cup butter or margarine
2 teaspoons vanilla

Place puffed rice in large greased bowl. Combine corn syrup, salt, and vinegar. Cook until a few drops in water form a hard ball. Remove from heat; add butter and vanilla, stirring only enough to combine. Mixing quickly, gradually pour cooked syrup over puffed rice. Using about ⅔ of the mixture, shape the snowman's body over an empty coffee can turned upside down. Turn right side up and fill in additional candied puffed rice to curve over edge of can. Shape remaining candied puffed rice to form the head. Make face and buttons, using chocolate mints, cherries, and pecan halves.

Place paper lace doily on top the body to form collar, put round head on top.

Note: If candied puffed rice hardens before shaping is complete, put in moderate oven for a few minutes to soften.

A CHRISTMAS COOKIE TREE

For the tree base, use a sturdy piece of wood with a hole in the center. Firmly secure a 15-inch rod in the hole. Cut out and bake 1 large cookie to cover the base. Then make star-shaped cookies in graduated sizes from 8 inches to 1 inch. Bake 2 cookies of each star size (16 cookies). Bake 32 small round cookies to go between the star-shaped cookies. Make a hole in the center of all cookies before baking.

With all the cookies baked, it's time to assemble the tree. Frost each cookie with a thin coating of confectioners' sugar icing. Slip the cookie which fits the base over the rod first, then 2 round cookies, the largest star cookie, 2 more rounds, another large star, and so on, using the stars in graduating size with the smallest at the top. When all the cookies are assembled, put White Frosting Snow on each branch and drifts of snow on the base, using a cake decorator. On the point of each star put a little rosette of frosting and place in it a small red birthday candle. On the topmost star place a larger candle, and the cookie tree is complete.

CHRISTMAS TREE COOKIES

1 cup butter
2 cups sugar
2 eggs
2 teaspoons vanilla
4 cups sifted enriched flour
1 tablespoon baking powder
1 teaspoon salt
½ cup milk
3 cups rolled oats, uncooked

Cream butter and shortening. Gradually add sugar and cream well. Beat in eggs and vanilla. Sift together flour, baking powder, and salt; add to creamed mixture alternately with milk. Fold in rolled oats. Chill dough. Roll out on lightly floured board to ¼-inch thickness. Cut as directed above. Bake on greased baking sheet in moderate oven (350 F.) 12 to 15 minutes.

WHITE FROSTING SNOW: Add ¼ teaspoon cream of tartar to ½ cup egg whites. Beat until frothy. Gradually add 5 cups sifted confectioners' sugar, beating vigorously with electric mixer or rotary beater until icing is fluffy and thick.

CRANBERRY FLUFF

Cook 2 cups fresh cranberries with 1 cup sugar and 1 cup water until tender. Drain juice from berries (keeping both juice and berries).

Add enough boiling water to the hot cranberry juice to make 2 cups of liquid. Dissolve 1 package orange-flavored gelatin in the hot liquid. Chill until mixture is partially set. Beat until light and frothy. Fold in cooked cranberries. Whip 1 cup whipping cream and fold into cranberry-gelatin mixture. Chill until set. Fill Stars as directed below.

CANDY CAKE

15 cups puffed rice
1 cup coarsely chopped peanuts
1 cup crushed peppermint candy
1 cup sugar
1 cup light corn syrup
½ cup water
½ teaspoon salt
2 tablespoons butter

Heat puffed rice in a pan in moderate oven (350 F.) 10 minutes. Pour into large greased bowl; mix with peanuts and peppermint candy. Combine sugar, corn syrup, water, and salt in a saucepan; cover and bring to a boil; uncover and cook until a few drops in cold water form a firm ball (245 F.). Add butter, stirring until combined. Mixing quickly, gradually pour cooked syrup over the puffed rice. Pack into greased 10-inch tube pan. When cool, turn out on plate. Decorate with candied fruits and nuts. Slice and serve as a confection.

CANDY STARS

Makes 12 stars:

5 cups puffed rice
⅓ cup butter or margarine
½ cup peanut butter
½ pound fresh marshmallows (about 32)

Measure puffed rice into a shallow pan. Heat in moderate oven (350 F.) 10 minutes. Pour into a large greased bowl. Melt butter, peanut butter, and marshmallows in double boiler, stirring occasionally. Pour over puffed rice, stirring until evenly coated. Pack puffed rice mixture in bottom and on sides of greased star-shaped molds or custard cups, leaving centers hollow for filling. Cool thoroughly. Remove from molds. Fill centers with Cranberry Fluff which has set thoroughly.

MAKE CHRISTMAS LAST . . . WITH THESE SUPPERS

Everyone has his own idea about Christmas Dinner, but not everyone makes Christmas last a long time by celebrating it several times. That is what happens when you make some of the presents you give, when you have the children or your friends in to make the decorations for your tree, when you have them in again for a Tree-Trimming Supper. And if you leave your tree up until Twelfth-night, you could have another simple supper on the sixth of January for friends who would help you take it down.

CHRISTMAS EVE SUPPERS

Crab Bisque or Seafood Stew
Herb Croutons
Your Favorite Fruit Float

Cheese Rabbit à la Suisse
Tossed Green Salad with
French Dressing
Toast and Butter
Pumpkin Whip
Coffee

Potato Soup
Hot Brown 'n' Serve Rolls
Cranberry Angel Cake
Coffee

TREE TRIMMING REFRESHMENTS

Peanut Butter Soup
Toasted Finger Loaf
Popcorn Balls
Lemonade

Dorothy's Curried Lamb with Accessories
Rice Ring
Peppermint Parfait Pie
Hot Coffee or Cold Milk

Broiled Rock Lobster Tails with Melted Butter
Tomato and Watercress Salad
Cherry-Glazed Cheese Cake
Coffee

DESSERT AND NOG TREATS . WHILE TREE TRIMMING

Cookie Assortment Including
Black Walnut Cookies
Frosted Orange Drops
Unbaked Fruit Balls
Oatmeal Crispies
Ginger Scotch Shortbreads
Chocolate Calypso
Pitcher of Milk

Hot Mince Tarts
Apricot Egg Nog

Pumpkin Cake
Hot Chocolate

Biscuit Christmas Tree
Hot Coffee

Holly Berry Doughnuts
Fancy Christmas Cookies
Hot Chocolate

Pineapple Rolls—Cranberry Gems
Soft Butter Balls
Café au Lait

Maple Cream Roll
Mocha Java

Banana Milk Shakes
Crisp Sugar Cookies

Assortment of Appetizers
Crisp Crackers
Hot Loaf of French Bread
Fresh Fruit Bowl

Nesselrode Mold
Hot Spiced Cranberry Punch

Snappy Cranberry-Raisin Pie
Coffee Egg Nog

White Cake with Nesselrode Frosting
Hot Coffee

Biscuit Christmas Wreath
Hot Coffee

Peanut Butter Daisy Loaf
Hot Tea

Dark Chocolate Cake
Lemon Filling and Frosting
Cold Pitcher of Milk

Gingerbread Snowstorm
Hot Postum or Coffee

Brownies (four flavors or shapes)
Milk

Hot Open Apple Pie
Hard Sauce
Coffee

CHRISTMAS IN DENMARK . MEET A FOREIGN MENU

In Denmark Christmas is always celebrated Christmas Eve, and instead of our roast turkey their traditional bird is goose, roasted full of stuffing of prunes and apple slices. With it they would have red cabbage and little potato balls browned and glazed in sugar. Dessert is almost sure to be an apple cake, but the first course is almost as certain to be Rice Porridge with a lucky almond in it.

Every woman already knows what she likes to serve on Christmas, but in case you want a change from chicken or turkey, this Danish Christmas dinner would be good. Goose is the traditional feast in Germany too, and nothing could be better unless we could have reindeer for Christmas, as I expect they do in Iceland.

RICE PORRIDGE

Makes 8 cups:

9 cups milk
1 cup rice
¼ pound butter
1 cup raisins
1 almond

Heat the milk and stir in the rice. When the milk begins to boil, cover, reduce heat, and simmer over very low heat about 1½ hours. About 15 minutes before it is done, add the raisins and almond. As this is spooned out into the soup bowls a little cube of cold butter is put into the center of each dish, and of course the person who finds the almond in his bowl will know that his wish will come true.

ROAST GOOSE

Select a goose weighing between 8 and 10 pounds dressed. Wash and dry; rub inside and out first with lemon and then with salt, and sprinkle with pepper. If you like garlic, rub garlic on the inside of the bird as well. Fill the cavity loosely with Prune and Apple Stuffing. Sew or skewer the opening together and truss for roasting. Prick the skin with a sharp fork to let the fat run out, and roast about 18 to 20 minutes per pound, breast down in the roaster, in a slow to moderate over (325 to 350 F.). When half done, turn breast up and finish roasting. Baste frequently with drippings from the pan. In roasting goose, no additional fat will be needed. When brown and tender place on a hot platter; remove some of the plump prunes for garnish.

PRUNE AND APPLE STUFFING

Makes 4 cups:

2 cups seeded stewed prunes
1 cup peeled and cored sliced apple
½ cup chopped walnuts or pecans
1 cup soft bread crumbs
¼ cup melted butter
1 teaspoon salt

Combine all ingredients, mixing them lightly with a fork, and stuff the goosely loosely.

GIBLET GRAVY

Skim the fat from the roasting pan and begin the gravy by using the crusty drippings in the pan together with 1½ tablespoons flour for each cup of liquid. If you have cooked the giblets until tender, use this stock together with milk if you want cream gravy. Brown the flour by adding it to the drippings in the pan; stir in the giblet stock and giblets. Stir until thickened and serve.

RED CABBAGE

Makes 8 servings:

3 pounds red cabbage (about 6 cups)
4 tablespoons butter
2 tablespoons sugar
½ cup water
⅓ cup vinegar

Shred the cabbage. Combine butter and sugar in an iron saucepan. Stir until blended. Add the cabbage and allow it to steam about 5 minutes. Add the water and vinegar; cover again and simmer over low heat until quite tender, 2 to 3 hours, stirring occasionally.

You can make this even better by adding caraway seeds or a few slices of peeled apples while the cabbage is cooking.

For dessert try Applesauce Meringue Cake or Ginger Applesauce Refrigerator Cake.

MENUS . . . . . . 3 "NEW" CHRISTMAS DINNERS

Fine and fitting for Thanksgiving too, these meals are easy and delicious.

Hot Tomato Juice
Crabmeat Pie
Tossed Green Salad
Spiced Nectar Ice Cream
Coffee

Rice Porridge with Lucky Almond
Roast Goose
Prune Stuffing
Red Cabbage
Caramelized Potatoes
Applesauce Cake
Coffee

Barbecue Turkey or Chicken
Sausage Stuffing
Cranberry Sauce
Onion Soufflé Green Beans and Peppers
Fruit Cake with Hard Sauce
Frozen English Pudding
Coffee

4 FINE STUFFINGS . . . FOR CHICKEN OR TURKEY

Recipes for the goose dinner menu gave me the idea that perhaps you would like to try a new stuffing. If you would, here are 4 to choose from:

SOUTHERN CORN-BREAD STUFFING

Makes 12 cups:

CORN BREAD:

1 cup corn meal
2 teaspoons baking powder
1 teaspoon salt
1 egg
1 cup milk

Sift corn meal, baking powder, and salt. Add egg and milk. Pour into greased, floured pan. Bake.

DRESSING:

4 cups crumbled corn bread
½ cup chopped onion
1 cup chopped celery
¼ cup drippings or shortening
4 cups cubed stale bread
1 teaspoon salt
¼ teaspoon pepper
½ teaspoon poultry seasoning
1 egg
1 cup stock

Cool and crumble corn bread. Cook onion and celery in shortening until tender. Add corn bread and cubed bread; fry until lightly browned. Add salt, pepper, poultry seasoning. Beat egg slightly; add to stock; pour over dressing, stirring well. Excellent for stuffing poultry, veal, or flank steak. Half of recipe is ample for a chicken or a 1½-pound flank steak.

CORN AND SAUSAGE CHICKEN STUFFING

Makes 2 cups:

½ cup chopped onion
¼ cup butter
½ cup sausage
½ teaspoon thyme
1 cup fresh corn cut from the cob, or canned kernels

Sauté the onion in butter or bacon fat until it is lightly cooked but not brown. Add the sausage meat and cook for about 5 minutes over low heat. Mix with corn and stuff the bird for roasting.

PECAN STUFFING

Makes about 6 cups:

1 cup chopped onions
¼ cup melted butter
3½ cups prepared bread for stuffing
¾ cup chopped pecans
½ teaspoon nutmeg
2 tablespoons chopped parsley
2 teaspoons salt
1 teaspoon freshly ground pepper
⅔ cup chopped celery
½ cup chicken broth
chicken giblets, chopped (optional)

Cook the onions in the butter until limp. Combine all other ingredients, mix thoroughly, and allow to stand a little while before stuffing the chicken, being careful not to pack it too tightly.

OYSTER LEMON STUFFING

Makes about 6 cups:

1 cup chopped oysters
4 cups dry bread crumbs
4 tablespoons melted butter or margarine
1 teaspoon chopped capers
4 tablespoons canned or frozen lemon juice
2 tablespoons chopped pickle
2 teaspoons salt
dash of pepper
⅓ to ½ cup water

Mix ingredients, blending well. If dressing seems dry, moisten with oyster liquid or additional water. When stuffing turkey, allow about ¾ to 1 cup of dressing per pound of turkey. This amount is for small junior turkey.

CHRISTMAS AT MERCY HOSPITAL . . . CHILDREN'S DELIGHT

Aren't the Christmas holidays a nice way to end each year? Or are they? Are you happy or are you one of the lonely ones? It is easier not to be lonely during this gay feasting time if we keep Christmas in spirit, gathering others who are alone to spend an evening with us, to share our Christmas dinner, to help trim a tree. You might not want a tree except for them, and together your spirits will rise with the hope and pleasure given to others the birth of Christ should inspire.

Snow at Christmas makes it most delightful, and it would be nice to spend Christmas in Switzerland or in Denmark (where the goose Christmas dinner came from), for there the earth is blanketed in white, the air is laden with sparkle, and the sky is clearly filled with stars. But it is still nicer to spend Christmas at home, preferably with a family. If no family, then with friends or with lonely strangers or with children who can be made so happy but who have no family to think about filling their stockings.

The most memorable Christmas I ever spent was at Mercy Hospital in Kansas City, Missouri. It is a hospital for crippled children, and so far as I know no child has ever been a paying guest. Each small bed is occupied by a child who is without parents or whose parents are very poor, but as Christmas approaches, every little head is filled with wishes. "I wish Santa Claus would bring me . . ." Their hopes rise. Perhaps the miracle will happen. Santa Claus is very real to them. The heartbreaking thing was that they wanted so little.

The superintendent of the hospital had a heart that embraced each youngster in her great family. Long before affection was regarded as important as medication, rules at Mercy Hospital required children of different ages be grouped together for one nurse to care for. The children were loved, rocked, hugged, treasured as are the children in a fortunate home. Both children and nurses thrived on it. And as Christmas time approached it was unthinkable that the babies, the eight- and nine-year-olds, the bigger boys and girls who did not dare believe, should fail to find Christmas and Santa Claus their private miracle.

Gifts and money poured in each year for the purpose of buying presents. Great care was taken to list the things children told their nurses they hoped Santa would bring them. That one might want a rubber-tired tricycle and another a dollar watch made no difference. The wish and its fulfillment were what counted. If funds ran short, various well-heeled residents would receive a telephone call from the superintendent. "We need a tricycle with red wheels . . . We need a little teddy bear, the cuddly size . . . We need an Ingersol watch for Billy . . ." She always got them.

The night before Christmas, Santa Claus paid his Christmas Eve visit to be sure all was well. The children were in bed by this time, and at the foot of each bed the nurses had attached the child's first name. As Santa made his rounds, calling each child by his correct name, the astonishment and pleasure became unbelievable. Santa checked up on the present they wanted most, just to make sure. After such divine excitement the exhausted children belatedly went to sleep.

On Christmas Day no nurse was allowed to have leave. Her job was at the hospital, for each boy and girl, except the few who could not be moved, were transported to the large room to assemble around the gigantic tree that had been trimmed, its base heaped high with packages. There in their braces, in wheel chairs, some on cots, they admired the tree and breathlessly awaited Santa Claus. He was not long in appearing. Each child received the identical presents all children can use. Colored pads of paper, pencils, crayons, useful childish accessories were handed out. Then came the *Big Present,* the thing they had wanted most. They always got it.

Disbelief, delight, joy, never before seen on the faces of these children, were bright lights in the big room that day. Santa Claus had been appearing here for years, but he had never been able to stay quite to the end of the celebration, for his voice would finally break, and when the sight of those sweet radiant faces moved him beyond endurance he would run before the children discovered he was a mere mortal—a man who could no longer keep back his tears. That, believe me, was Christmas.

CHAPTER 27

NEW YEAR'S EVE

New Year's Eve or the new year's first day finds most of us hung-over with holiday sentiments. Although a well-spent orgy of love, affection, laughter, and giving, we may be thoroughly fatigued from the pleasant ordeal. Let us hope Christ's birthday celebration leaves one and all with a renewed spirit for the new year, good resolutions which will be kept, and close friends to invite for New Year's Eve Supper or an Open House for families at dusk on New Year's Day.

Remember the notion that black-eyed peas must be "eaten for luck" on New Year's. Serve a dish of them for fun or food along with these.

Remember the Christmas Eve and Tree-Trimming menus, and serve one of them or one of these easily managed menus for suppers or one of the Open House menus. Each menu is for all ages—from the tots to the tottering—beloved all.

HAUOLI MAKAHIKI HOU!

This is Happy New Year in Hawaiian, and a happy day it would be if you were there. In the event you are not able to walk in the gentle Hawaiian sun, surrounded with beauty in every direction, eating some of the food as it is served there could be a pleasant thing. In Hawaii *luau* is the word for feast. Any fish or seafood feast would be appropirate, but chicken is a favorite luau dish too.

Hawaiian Fruit Punch
Chicken Luau
Sliced Tomatoes—Yams
Red and White Cole Slaw
Pineapple-Coconut Ice Cream or Mango Fruit Float
Coffee

Chicken South Seas
Green Beans—Sweet Potatoes
Tossed Green Salad
Lani Laiki or Nesselrode or Cranberry Angel Cake
Coffee

NEW YEAR'S . . . . OPEN HOUSE REFRESHMENTS

5 Pie Suppers
(Serve small wedges from several pies to each guest)

Assorted Angel Pies and Hot Tea or Hot Chocolate

Party Pies and Café au Lait

Parfait Pies and Hot Black Coffee or Cold Milk

Mincemeat Tarts and Coffee

Pumpkin Tarts and Cold Milk

Easy Filling Suppers

Hot Mulled Cider
Tuna Tamale Pie
Orange and Grapefruit Cake Cobbler
Demitasse

Broiled Rock Lobster tails
Tossed Green Salad
Lemon Refrigerator Cake

Nog Parties

Coffee Egg Nog
Salad Dreams
Strawberry Festival Punch
Cheese Balls
Christmas Fruit Cake Slices or Crisp Cookies

Apricot Egg Nog
Hot Cheese Fritters—Oatmeal Crispies

INDEX